SCANDAL AND REFORM

DISCARD

Lawrence W. Sherman

SCANDAL AND REFORM

Controlling Police Corruption

UNIVERSITY OF CALIFORNIA PRESS

Berkeley • Los Angeles • London

364.13
She

Prepared in part under grant number 75-NI-
99-00-24 from the National Institute of Law
Enforcement and Criminal Justice, Law Enforcement Assistance Administration, U.S. Department of Justice. Points of view or opinions
stated in this document are those of the author
and do not necessarily represent the official position or policies of the U.S. Department of Justice.

University of California Press
Berkeley and Los Angeles, California
University of California Press, Ltd.
London, England
Copyright © 1978 by
The Regents of the University of California
ISBN 0-520-03523-2
Library of Congress Catalog Card Number: 77-79236
Printed in the United States of America

1 2 3 4 5 6 7 8 9

For
Catherine, Tom, and
the reform chief
in Central City

Contents

Figures and Tables

Foreword

Some authors may promise more in the title than is justified by the content of their publication. But this book by Lawrence Sherman, although modestly presented as a study in controlling police corruption by examining organizational scandal and reform in police departments, is much more than that. What is said about police and their departments is often true for many public organizations as a simple substitution of any other public official for that of the police makes abundantly clear. Moreover, this volume by drawing upon organizational theory challenges traditional notions about the intractability of corruption and the limited possibilities for organizational change. Weaving the woof of political and occupational cultures with the warp of organizational structure and leadership in administration, Sherman clarifies their connections. The strategic focus on scandal and its role in organizational reform sheds new light upon the connections between organizations and their environment. All of this is done in a convincing way that should make sense to those who make public policy or administer organizations.

Unlike much work on deviant behavior, the focus of this study is on deviant organizations rather than their deviant actors, not on corrupt police officers, but on corrupt police organizations. The symbolic nature of police corruption and the organizational control of corrupt behavior are central threads in the analysis.

Something more is involved in the corruption of public organizations than employee crime and failing to abide by organizational rules. That something more comes about when behavior violates a fiduciary relationship, when it violates a public trust and corrupts public virtue. This is evident in the symbolic nature of corruption.

Defining criminal conduct by public officials as corrupt behavior rather than as criminal conduct is in itself symbolic. Investigation into "police corruption" rather than into "criminal police officers" symbolizes a public unwillingness to regard criminal and other forms of misconduct by public officials simply as criminal matters that require criminal sanctions. It is not the misdeeds of officials that are corrupt but that such behavior by persons in their public role is a misuse of power and authority that is a matter of public trust in public organizations.

Scandal is a symbolic public reaction to an organizational breach of trust. Sherman's trenchant analysis of how breaches of public trust are transformed into organizational scandal increases our understanding of how violations of public trust become transformed into a collective response of public moral outrage, one that defines a public organization as responsible for violation of trust.

There is a delicate balance between police misconduct and the symbolic labeling of a department as corrupt. The dilemmas and risks police administrators face in exposing and cloaking employee subversion of the organization's goals are sympathetically and systematically explored by Sherman. Both the role of leadership in administration and organization strategies and tactics to control corruption are examined.

Scandal does not necessarily lead to the control of police misconduct. While scandal ordinarily realigns the structure of power in an organization by replacements and shifts in the top echelon of administration and by their reform strategies, the new structure may be no more stable than one it replaces since the causes of instability are endemic to an organization and its environment. Much depends, therefore, on what policies are selected to control misconduct.

Sherman enhances our understanding of both the power of such strategies to bring about control of official misconduct and their limits. He systematically explores two major types of strategies. Premonitory strategies restrict opportunities for misconduct while proactive strategies of investigation detect and apprehend officers whose behavior subverts the organization's goals. Particularly illuminating is the analysis of how such strategies are limited in controlling different kinds of misconduct. What is clear is that the more organized the subversion within an organization, the more amenable it is to both types of strategies. Since unorganized strategies are least amenable to control by administrative policies, strategies, and tactics, an organization is always vulnerable to the least organized forms of misconduct. Fortunately for police administrators, an organization is most vulnerable to scandal when organized forms of misconduct are exposed.

The central role of leadership in reform administration exposes yet another source of organizational control of misconduct, that of normative control. Selznick has emphasized that the central role of leadership in administration is to infuse an organization with value. What seems clear in Sherman's analysis of reform chiefs who appear to transform their organization is that they infuse their organization with moral values, often ones that go far beyond the simple bounds of an organization's domain. Reform chiefs characteristically adopt a stance of moral virtue and outrage but more to the point perhaps they are aware that public officials, like Caesar's wife, must be beyond reproach. Breaches of the moral order are mended and public trust restored by visible normative control.

The visibility of official behavior is a critical element in both organizational control of officials and public trust in the organization. The less visible official behavior to both organizational and public scrutiny, exaggerated as it is in police departments by the necessity of official secrets, the more considerable the capacity of officials and their organizations to thwart control in the public interest. Sherman's book makes a substantial contribution to our understanding of the amenability of official behavior to organizational control. At the same time it lays the groundwork to explore broader questions of how trust relationships are built and maintained as well as of how they are violated and can be controlled.

The price of scandal as a public response to the violation of public trust comes high and may often outweigh the gains of reform. The infusion of public office with official trust lies at the heart of public trust. Our understanding of the violation of public trust and its control will be greatly enhanced when we better understand how trust relationships are built and maintained. The capacity of guardians to control, while considerable, is limited and no one guards the guardians well on a routine basis. Paradoxically, trust has always been regarded as a solution to the problem that not one of us can always be watched.   ALBERT J. REISS, JR.

Yale University
December, 1977

Preface

Scandal is a mighty weapon. It can topple governments and destroy careers. It can tarnish the reputation of an entire profession. It can cause misery and suffering among the families of its subjects. Like any punishment, it may harm the innocent as well as the guilty. But it can also be an agent of change.

The central purpose of this study is to explore the role of scandal in controlling police corruption. A study of this nature is necessarily grounded in the unique characteristics of the American police, and more particularly in the characteristics of the four police departments in which the field research was done. Yet all of the questions and many of the answers can be applied more generally to other kinds of organizations subjected to scandal. What are the origins of the scandalous behavior? How does that behavior become subjected to scandal, and why does scandal happen when it does? How does the organization respond to scandal, both internally and externally? Does the scandalous behavior change after a scandal occurs? If it does, is the change in the behavior due to scandal itself, or more directly to changes produced by scandal in the structure and policies of the organization?

The importance of these questions increases almost daily in the present aftermath of the biggest scandal in the nation's history. Now that criminality has been detected in the highest office in the land, no institution or person seems immune to scandal. Our largest corporations, our military academies, the Congress, and countless other respected institutions at the center of American society have been tarnished by scandal in the years since Watergate. From 1970 to 1976, the number of public officials indicted annually on federal corruption charges increased more than five times, from 63 to 337.[1] These developments raise what may be a central question of our era. Does scandal merely demoralize these institutions and render them ineffective, as many have claimed? Or does scandal reform its subjects, producing a permanent improvement in their level of integrity?

The police institution affords an excellent opportunity for the study of scandal. Unlike some of the newer subjects of scandal, the police in the United States have been regularly subjected to scandal throughout their history. Police departments provide numerous examples of scandals producing no reform. But they also provide a few examples of scandals producing a substantial change in the scandalous behavior. The great frequency of police scandals may limit the extent to which conclusions derived from studying the police can be generalized to other institutions subjected to scandal less frequently. The long history of scandal over police corruption, however, offers a broad time perspective for assessing the consequences of scandal.

Another reason for a study of scandal to focus on the police is that scholars tend to be pessimistic about the potential for changing the police.[2] Indeed, repeated scandals over police corruption are often cited as evidence of the failure of reformers to improve police conduct. Most scandals may fail to produce successful police reform, but it does not follow that police reform is impossible, nor that scandal can never be an agent of posi-

1. "337 Indicted for Corruption in Public Office," *LEAA Newsletter*, Vol. 6 (April 1977), pp. 1, 14. [Law Enforcement Assistance Administration.]
2. For a critique of this viewpoint, see Lawrence W. Sherman, "Police Corruption Control: Environmental Context versus Organizational Policy," in *Police and Society*, ed. David H. Bayley (Beverly Hills, Calif.: Sage Publications, 1978).

tive change.[3] This book presents plausible evidence that, under certain conditions, substantial police reform can follow a corruption scandal.

A central thesis of this study is that scandal over the conduct of an organization stems from conflict over the basic goals or identity of the organization, over what Selznick calls the organizational "character": i.e., what the organization is about and what its purpose is for existing.[4] Conflict over organizational goals is not confined to the members of an organization; it can encompass all those interests, groups, and other organizations that have a stake in the conduct of the organization in question. Organizations vary in the extent to which the diverse interest groups constituting their working environments agree with their goals. Since their creation in the 1840s, American police departments have been subjected to widespread disagreement in their working environments over the purposes and conduct of policing.[5] Compromises and accommodations over police goals permit periods in which the police are paid little attention, but public crises such as scandal signal a breakdown in what Ohlin calls the "structure of accommodation."[6] Given the unstable structure of accommodations in the police environment, it is not surprising that police scandals seem to occur more frequently than scandals over other kinds of organizations.

3. For a pessimistic view of scandal's impact on the police, see David H. Bayley, *Forces of Order: Police Behavior in Japan and the United States* (Berkeley: University of California Press, 1976), p. 82.

4. Philip Selznick, *Leadership in Administration* (New York: Row, Peterson & Co., 1957), p. 55.

5. See, e.g., James F. Richardson, *The New York Police: Colonial Times to 1901* (New York: Oxford University Press, 1970).

6. Lloyd Ohlin, "Organizational Reform in Correctional Agencies," in *Handbook of Criminology*, ed. Daniel Glaser (Chicago: Rand McNally, 1974), pp. 995–1020. See also Alden Miller, Lloyd W. Ohlin, and Robert B. Coates, *A Theory of Social Reform: Correctional Change Processes in Two States* (Cambridge, Mass.: Ballinger Publishing Co., 1977), pp. 34–46 and Chapter 9.

   Scandal does not seem to resolve the conflict over
police behavior. Rather, scandal realigns the structure
of power over a police department, and the new structure may be no more stable than the one it replaces. The
continued instability of the police department's environment has important implications for the selection
and implementation of policies for controlling police
corruption in the wake of a scandal. These policies fall
into two categories: administrative policies for blocking
corruption opportunities, and investigative policies for
detecting and apprehending corrupt officers. In order
to work properly, both strategies require extensive information about what police officers are doing. Such
information is exceedingly difficult to obtain in an organization that disperses its employees across an entire
city to work alone or in pairs. The difficulty of monitoring police behavior directly leaves the police executive
ignorant of the true extent of police corruption unless
he adopts indirect means of gathering information.
These indirect means are usually surreptitious, generally distasteful in a society valuing privacy, and always
opposed by the officers subjected to them. Police executives appointed to reform a corrupt department are
forced to walk a treacherous path between doing too
much and doing too little.

   These are the major themes of the book. Scandal is
both a sanction punishing deviant organizations and an
agent of change. Change in corrupt police departments
is indeed possible, particularly after a scandal occurs.
Scandal results from conflict over organizational goals,
and it realigns the power structure of the police environment to support the goal of an honest police department. The success or failure of reform depends
upon the nature of organizational strategies for controlling corruption. These strategies can only succeed by
gathering information about corrupt police behavior, a
task made difficult and ethically questionable by the dispersed manner in which police departments are organized.

The book begins with a brief description of the scandal and reform process in the four police departments studied. Part I then provides a theoretical framework for studying the social control of deviant organizations and a substantive analysis of corrupt police departments as deviant organizations. Part II describes the social control of corrupt police departments, including both external control by scandal and internal control by administrative policy. Part III measures the effects of social control upon police corruption by describing changes over time in the organization of corrupt police behavior. The conclusion makes some generalizations about the process of scandal and reform in corrupt police departments.

The idea for this study was born in 1971 while I was employed as a research analyst in the New York City Police Department. During that period of scandal generated by the Knapp Commission, and reforms introduced by Police Commissioner Patrick V. Murphy, my major concern was to understand the role of the reform police executive as the principal agent of change in corrupt police departments. Caught in a crossfire of external demands to clean up corruption and internal demands to defend the reputation and morale of the organization, the reform police executive is an important and fascinating subject of study. The original purpose of this research was to provide policy guidance for reform police executives by discovering the administrative policies most clearly associated with a decline in police corruption. Even though the purpose of the study became broader during the course of the research, I still attempt to fulfill that initial purpose.

Support from the Ford Foundation in 1972–73 allowed me to review the literature on police and corruption with this question in mind: Why are some police departments more corrupt than others? More precisely, what accounts for the wide variation in the nature and scope of police corruption? While some hunches could be developed from secondary evidence,[7] the enormous difficulty in measuring police corruption cross-sectionally necessarily limits an empirical approach to such an inquiry. Support from the National Institute of Law Enforcement and Criminal Justice in 1974–76 made it possible to measure changes over time in police corruption in four American police departments. The departments were selected on the basis of three criteria: research access to official police reports on investigations of corruption; a reputation for having successfully controlled corruption under a reform police executive; and differences in geographic region and department size.

Using a wide variety of information sources, I attempted to measure the extent to which police corruption was organized before, during, and in some cases, after the period that a reform police executive was in office. Corruption is by nature secretive, and it would have been futile to try to count the number of either corrupt police officers or corrupt police acts. Instead of measuring the quantity of corruption, I tried to measure the quantity of *organization* present in whatever acts of corruption were alleged, disclosed, or discovered by any source. Scouring the newspapers, official files, and the memories of participants and observers, I literally mapped out the known corruption activities occurring over the time period studied. The time-maps became visually unclear, but they suggested ways of analyzing various dimensions of the organization of police corruption in quantitative terms.

Police administrators have often pointed out that many of my "data" are based on evidence too weak to obtain even an indictment, let alone a criminal conviction. True enough. But my concern is not with proving that corruption existed; that is taken as an assumption. Nor am I concerned with what Officer X truly did or did not do on a certain day; I am neither a detective nor an

7. See Lawrence W. Sherman, "Towards a Sociological Theory of Police Corruption," in *Police Corruption: A Sociological Perspective*, ed. Lawrence W. Sherman (New York: Anchor Books, 1974), p. 1–39.

investigative reporter. Rather, my concern is with patterns of human behavior and how they change over time. Even if several of the instances of corruption in my analysis—many of which did produce criminal convictions—are false allegations, the analysis can still be valid as a description of patterns. It seems reasonable to assume that smoke is only found near fire, and that a pattern of activity (e.g., prostitution payoffs) would not be alleged about any individuals in a city unless it were true of at least some individuals in the city.

This study was made possible by the willingness of many officials to open their files and their minds to a highly sensitive inquiry. In keeping with their trust, their names cannot be mentioned, but their contributions to the study must be. Where the conclusions here differ from their own, I ask only that they appreciate the more distant perspective of the social researcher.

Officials who can be thanked by name include Police Commissioner Michael J. Codd, First Deputy Commissioner James Taylor, Inspector Patrick Murphy, Inspector Frank Smith, and especially Assistant Chief John Guido, all of the New York City Police Department. Chief George T. Hart and former City Manager Wayne Thompson of Oakland, as well as City Manager James Taylor and Police Commissioner John McClellan of Newburgh, were generous with their assistance.

Former New York City Police Commissioner Patrick V. Murphy, now President of the Police Foundation, deserves special thanks for letting me join his team in the hectic days of scandal and organizational reform in New York. Gerald Caplan and John Gardiner deserve thanks for their efforts in funding the research. David Farmer and William Saulsbury were the most helpful of project overseers.

Suzanne Weaver, Burton Clark, John Gardiner, Eva Sherman, Richard Hall, William Trigg, and Donald J. Black all made valuable criticisms of the manuscript. Master typist Harriet Spector deserves special thanks for many long hours of overtime.

My greatest debt is to Professor Albert J. Reiss, Jr., whose encouragement and intellectual contribution gave shape to the study. No one has contributed more than he to the systematic empirical study of police behavior and to the theory of organizational deviance. His tolerance for my use of indirect evidence was matched only by his insistence on my conducting the field research in as systematic a fashion as possible. In supervising the research as a doctoral dissertation, he prevented or removed a goodly number of flaws in design and analysis. Those that remain must be attributed only to me.   L.W.S.

Albany, New York
September, 1977

Introduction:

FOUR SCANDALS, THREE REFORMS

Virtually every urban police department in the United States has experienced both organized corruption and a major scandal over that corruption.[1] While a complete census of corrupt urban police departments has never been taken, the published evidence is extensive enough to justify this assertion.[2] The assertion may even be true for just the period since World War II. There is almost no evidence, however, regarding the *consequences* of corruption scandals in urban police departments. Given the frequent repetition of corruption scandals in a number of police departments, it seems reasonable to assume that most corruption scandals are not followed by permanent reform. Yet some police departments have experienced successful reforms. The problem this study

1. William J. Chambliss, "Vice, Corruption, Bureaucracy and Power," *The University of Wisconsin Law Review*, Vol. 1971, pp. 1150–1170. See also Antony Simpson, *The Literature of Police Corruption: Volume 1. A Guide to Bibliography and Theory* (New York: The John Jay Press, 1977); Ralph Lee Smith, *The Tarnished Badge* (New York: Thomas Y. Crowell and Co., 1965); and Robert H. Williams, *Vice Squad* (New York: Thomas Y. Crowell, 1973). Even the Metropolitan London Police (Scotland Yard) have experienced corruption, scandal, and reform in recent years. See Barry Cox, John Shirley, and Martin Short, *The Fall of Scotland Yard* (London: Penguin Books, 1977).

2. The police departments subjected to scandal over organized corruption include, for example, Los Angeles, Denver, Seattle, San Francisco, Kansas City, East St. Louis, Chicago, Indianapolis, Louisville, Buffalo, Philadelphia, Miami, and Boston. A survey of corruption scandals collected by a national clipping service in the summer of 1973 also showed scandals in small towns and rural sheriff's departments. (Internal memorandum, the Police Foundation.)

only begins to address is why some and not other scandals are followed by successful reform.

As a first step in distinguishing the conditions of successful and unsuccessful post-scandal reform, three police departments were selected for study on the basis of their reputations for successful reform: New York City; Oakland, California; and Newburgh, New York. A fourth case, pseudonymous "Central City," was selected just after a scandal occurred, because it could be studied in the process of post-scandal reform rather than historically.[3] As it happened, Central City was apparently a case of unsuccessful reform, but its failure is very useful in illuminating the conditions of success in the other three departments.

All four of the police departments had experienced corruption for many years before the major scandal occurred that is studied here. Two of them, New York and Central City, had also suffered earlier major scandals in relatively recent years. But only one, New York, had been previously subjected to repeated and unsuccessful attempts at reform. What follows is a summary of the history of corruption and scandal in each of the four police departments studied.

3. The use of a pseudonym to identify Central City was a condition of the grant of access to confidential sources there. The salient differences between Central City and the other case studies are as follows:

DIFFERENCES AMONG THE FOUR CASE STUDIES

Differences	New York City	Central City	Oakland, Calif.	Newburgh, N.Y.
Population*	8,000,000	750,000	376,000	26,200
Police Dept. Size*	30,000	1,100	700	70
Years under Study	1970–75	1963–75	1952–60	1970–75
Form of Government	Strong Mayor	Strong Mayor	Council-Manager	Council-Manager
Geographic Region	Northeast	Midwest	West Coast	Northeast

*Approximate

NEW YORK

The continuing corruption of law enforcement in New York City from colonial times to 1971 has been well documented.[4] Although New York police have used their official powers to protect or commit every crime from burglary to election fraud and murder, the main source of police corruption there has always been the purveyors of illegal pleasures: prostitution, alcohol, gambling, and, in recent years, narcotics. The first major scandal over police protection of vice activities occurred in 1894, when the Lexow Committee of the New York State Senate conducted hearings on police corruption at the request of a crusading investigative clergyman, Charles Parkhurst. The testimony of an endless procession of gamblers, prostitutes, madams, and policemen painted a picture of a police department thoroughly corrupted, existing solely for the personal profit of its members. The hearings assured the election of a reform mayor who appointed Theodore Roosevelt head of the police department.[5] Roosevelt instituted some reform policies, but corruption persisted in a more sophisticated, less visible manner.[6] Roosevelt went on to other offices, and corruption eventually returned to "normal."

Similar scandals and attempts at reform have occurred in New York in almost regular twenty-year cycles. The Curran Committee in 1911, the Seabury Report in 1932, the investigation of gambling "czar" Harry Gross in 1951, and the Knapp Commission hearings in 1971 all exposed widespread and highly organized police corruption.[7] Every one of these scandals was apparently associated with the appointment of a new police

4. See James F. Richardson, *The New York Police: Colonial Times to 1901* (New York: Oxford University Press, 1970); and Gerald Astor, *The New York Cops: An Informal History* (New York: Scribner's, 1971).

5. Lincoln Steffens, *Autobiography* (New York: Harcourt Brace and Company, 1931), Chapters X–XI.

6. Lincoln Steffens, *The Shame of the Cities* (New York: McClure, Phillips and Co., 1904; Hill and Wang, 1957), p. 206.

7. City of New York, Commission to Investigate Allegations of

commissioner who was expected to reform the department. But however successful their reforms may have
been in the short run, none of the earlier reform executives succeeded in reforming the New York City Police
Department on a lasting basis.

Perhaps the most intensive unsuccessful effort at reform was the most recent one, in the aftermath of the
scandal over gambler Harry Gross' payoffs to hundreds
of police officers.[8] A succession of reform commissioners tried to control corruption by tightening the central
control over the department. Rigid bureaucratic procedures were established for almost every phase of police
activity, with a heavy emphasis on maintaining written
records of every official action. Procedures were particularly strict in the enforcement of vice and gambling
laws. But the paper work failed to prevent corruption,
and was twisted to serve as a mechanism of defense in
case of corruption investigations. Moreover, it was un-
derstood that while the top officials would punish officers foolish enough to be caught at corruption, "the
brass" did not really want to know about any corruption
that may have been going on.[9] In fact, the reluctance to
initiate investigations helped to precipitate the most recent scandal.

In 1966, an officer named Frank Serpico was invited
to join a gambling "pad": a group of officers in a
plainclothes gambling squad who were paid off by a
gambler. Serpico refused to join, as he had refused similar offers in the past. At the suggestion of a fellow
officer who was assigned to the Department of Investigation (the city's anti-corruption unit), Serpico told the

---

Police Corruption and the City's Anti-Corruption Procedures, *Commission Report* (New York: George Braziller, 1973), pp. 61–64.

8. See Norton Mockridge and Robert H. Prall, *The Big Fix* (New
York: Henry Holt, 1954).

9. Allan N. Kornblum, "The Moral Hazards: Strategies for
Honesty and Ethical Behavior in the New York City Police Department" (Ph.D. dissertation, Princeton University, 1973); interview
with William P. McCarthy, former First Deputy Commissioner of the
New York City Police Department, January, 1975.

captain in charge of that department's police detail about the existence of the "pad." The captain, according to Serpico, warned that such accusations could result in his being found in the East River. Serpico then tried, successively, to interest the commander of the police area in which he worked, the First Deputy Police Commissioner, the mayor's assistant for police matters, and the Commissioner of Investigation. None of these officials took any action in response to Serpico's allegations. Finally, in late 1967, the area commander initiated an investigation of the pad identified by Serpico. Dissatisfied at the failure of high officials to undertake more general efforts against police corruption, Serpico and several other police officers supplied information to the *New York Times* that was published in April of 1970.[10]

In response to the *Times* stories, the mayor appointed a committee to investigate the allegations. The committee included the district attorney of Manhattan and the police commissioner, both of whom had responsibility for controlling police corruption. After the police commissioner publicly attacked the *Times* stories for using unreliable sources, the committee recommended that an "independent" body be created to investigate the allegations. The mayor then appointed a "blue ribbon" Commission to Investigate Allegations of Police Corruption and the City's Anti-Corruption Procedures, chaired by former Assistant District Attorney Whitman Knapp.[11] The police commissioner resigned before the Knapp Commission launched its investigation, and a new commissioner, Patrick V. Murphy, was quickly appointed.

10. David Burnham, "Graft Paid to Police Here Said to Run into Millions." *New York Times*, April 25, 1970, p. 1. See also Peter Maas, *Serpico* (New York: Viking, 1973); City of New York, *Commission Report* (n. 7 above), pp. 196–204; and David Burnham, *The Role of the Media in Controlling Corruption* (New York: The John Jay Press, 1976).

11. It is interesting to note that one of the Commission members, Cyrus Vance, later became Secretary of State, while another, Joseph Monserrat, was later convicted on corruption charges himself in connection with the New York City Board of Education.

Murphy had been a New York City police commander for almost twenty years, serving most of that time in such corruption-free units as the police academy. He had served as the reform chief of the Syracuse (New York) Police Department after a gambling corruption scandal there, and he had also headed the Washington, D.C. and the Detroit police departments. When he returned to New York in October of 1970, the Knapp Commission investigation was just getting under way. Thus, Murphy was put in the rather awkward position of being a reformer before the corruption scandal had fully unfolded. Not until October of 1971, when the Knapp Commission held its public hearings, was the full extent of police corruption publicly disclosed. In the year between his appointment and the commission hearings, Murphy struck a difficult balance between demonstrating strong policies against corruption and not antagonizing the rank and file and their public supporters who claimed that police corruption was minor and isolated.

The Knapp Commission hearings destroyed the police union's argument that police corruption was confined to a few "rotten apples" in an otherwise healthy barrel.[12] While the union president labeled the Knapp Commission evidence "a tale concocted in a whorehouse," the testimony of corrupt police officers and the tape-recorded evidence they had gathered after being "turned" to work as undercover agents for the commission provided overwhelming documentation of highly organized corruption in almost every area of the department. Chairman Knapp called upon Murphy to "bite the bullet" and acknowledge the existence of pervasive corruption—which, in effect, Murphy did. And while Murphy had already punished a number of commanders for being too lax with corruption, the most severe anti-corruption policies were not adopted until a new deputy commissioner for vice enforcement was ap-

12. City of New York, *Commission Report* (n. 7 above), pp. 5–6. See also Lawrence W. Sherman, ed., *Police Corruption* (Garden City, N.Y.: Anchor Books, 1974), pp. 6–12.

pointed just before the Knapp hearings. The hearings provided the external pressure necessary to justify, both internally and externally, draconian measures against corruption.

In August of 1972, the Knapp Commission recommended that the governor appoint a Special Deputy State Attorney General to supersede the five New York City district attorneys in all investigations of corruption in New York's criminal justice system. The special prosecutor took office in September of 1972. The Knapp Commission had operated on a minuscule budget with a few borrowed federal investigators, but the special prosecutor's office was well funded and well staffed. Nonetheless, most of the police corruption cases ultimately prosecuted by that office were developed either by the Knapp Commission or by police department anticorruption squads. This point is important for the comparability of the four police departments studied here, since only New York had a special anti-corruption prosecutor during the reform period and beyond. While the existence of a special prosecutor may have had some deterrent effect on corruption, the only difference it made in the investigation and prosecution of police corruption was that the police department corruption investigators were able to obtain subpoenas and access to a grand jury more easily than with the district attorneys.[13]

After two and a half years of drastic reforms and almost daily headlines, Murphy resigned in April of 1973. His handpicked successor, Donald Cawley, served only nine months, resigning when a new mayor was elected. Another high official of Murphy's administration, Michael Codd, was appointed commissioner in January of 1974. Both Cawley and Codd continued Murphy's anti-corruption policies apparently without major changes.

From all indications, the most recent episode of scandal and reform in the New York City Police Department has reduced police corruption to a very minimal level.

13. Interview with John Guido, Commander of the Internal Affairs Division, New York City Police Department, 1975.

"Pads" and other highly organized forms of corruption seem to be virtually extinct. Six years after the Knapp Commission hearings, corruption no longer appears to be widespread. Evidence presented in subsequent chapters covers only the years up to 1975, but other indicators of a high level of integrity could still be found in 1977. A film producer, for example, observes that it is no longer necessary to pay off the police when filming location shots on the streets of New York.[14] While skeptics may find it difficult to believe that law enforcement in New York is organizationally honest, all of the available evidence points to that conclusion.

OAKLAND

California police departments have long enjoyed a reputation for honesty far superior to that of their eastern counterparts. While that reputation may be deserved today, it was certainly not valid thirty years ago. In the years just after World War II, California policing was no less subject to control by corrupt political influences and racketeers than policing elsewhere in the nation.[15] The Oakland Police Department in 1954 was no exception to that rule.

A port city and a terminus of major railroads, Oakland has always had a large population of unattached males providing a prime market for vice services. The vice services, in turn, once provided a prime market for police extortion. One Oakland officer recalled his father's tales of police shaking down prostitutes early in the century. Another described the systematic robbery

14. "TV Producers Are Nibbling at the Big Apple," *New York Times,* July 31, 1977, p. D21. See also "After Knapp, the Police Seem Less Corruptible," *New York Times,* July 4, 1976, Section 4, 4.

15. State of California, Special Crime Study Commission on Organized Crime, *Combined Reports* (Sacramento: California State Board of Corrections, 1950), and *Final Report* (Sacramento: California State Board of Corrections, 1953); Joseph Gerald Woods, "The Progressives and the Police: Urban Reform and the Professionalization of the Los Angeles Police" (Ph.D. dissertation, University of California at Los Angeles, 1973).

by police of black shipyard workers every Friday night after the workers had been paid and had cashed their checks in the local bars.

While police corruption was not as diverse in Oakland as it was in New York or other larger cities, it was apparently as pervasive and well organized. Fewer types of corruption may have been practiced, but the vice corruption that did exist seems to have been tightly controlled at the precinct level.

A major police corruption scandal occurred just after the turn of the century, but the police escaped intensive public scrutiny for the next fifty years. Earl Warren built a career on his prosecutions of official corruption in Alameda County in the 1920s and '30s, but he left the Oakland Police Department largely unscathed. His convictions of Oakland officials did lead to the adoption of a city manager form of government in 1931, which insulated the police somewhat from corrupt political control. But despite this reform, a city council member was allegedly arranging for paid police protection of gambling operations as late as 1953.[16]

The year 1953 was a difficult one for the Oakland Police Department. Two officers were accused of committing a burglary, another was charged with sexually harassing a woman, and a third was named as a bagman for gambling payoffs.[17] Yet all of this produced what we shall later define as a "little scandal": a brief, shallow reaction of public disapproval. After reporting the corruption stories as they occurred, the major newspaper probed no further. The events were serious enough to have been the subject of a "big" scandal, but no big scandal occurred.

A new city manager, Wayne Thompson, was appointed in late 1954. His predecessor had run a "caretaker" style of administration for twenty years, generally deferring to local business interests in providing minimal city services and minimal property taxes. Thompson

16. *Oakland Tribune*, April 7, 1953.
17. *Oakland Tribune*, January 16, January 28, and April 17, 1953.

had grown up in Oakland, and had been city manager of nearby Richmond since the end of World War II. He had ambitious plans for Oakland, one of which was reforming the police department. But in order to take the drastic action necessary for fighting police corruption, Thompson felt that a public justification was needed. That is, he decided that his solution could only be imposed after the problem of police corruption had been impressed upon the public.[18]

After only a few months in office, Thompson found an opportunity to dramatize the weaknesses of the police. A police sergeant tried to extort a payment from a hardware store owner who had been drinking prior to a minor traffic accident. When the extortion victim refused to pay, he was abducted at night and taken into the Oakland hills by two police officers who beat and robbed him. When he tried to file a complaint at the local precinct station, the extortion victim was subjected to further harassment. The chief's office eventually investigated the case, but little came out of the investigation for several months. In early 1955, a reporter caught wind of the story and called Thompson before publishing it. Thompson called a press conference, publicly rebuked the police chief, and ordered that all future complaints of police misconduct be relayed immediately to the city manager's office.[19]

The district attorney soon called several police officers before a grand jury to testify in the extortion and cover-up case. Meanwhile, another corruption case was disclosed in the newspapers, this one alleging that detectives had taken gifts from burglars in jail awaiting trial.[20] The prosecutor seized on this case as well, and a "big" scandal was underway. Thompson asked the publisher of the *Oakland Tribune* to keep police corruption in the headlines.[21] For over two weeks, the police were front-

18. Interview with Wayne Thompson, May 9, 1975.
19. *Oakland Tribune*, January 4, 1955.
20. *Oakland Tribune*, January 15, 1955.
21. Interview with Wayne Thompson, May 9, 1975.

page news. When there was no new development in the corruption cases to report, a "background" story on management problems in the police department appeared. The police chief went on sick leave shortly after the scandal began, and resigned a few weeks later.[22]

Thompson immediately appointed Captain Wyman Vernon as the reform chief. A University of California graduate who had joined the Oakland Police Department during the Depression, Vernon had served under Thompson previously as chief of the Richmond Police Department on a one-year leave from Oakland. Vernon had also been a reformer in Richmond, reshaping an old-fashioned police operation into a modern bureaucracy. As head of the Traffic Division in Oakland, Vernon had been largely isolated from the primary forms of police corruption. Yet he knew that corruption was extensive, and he moved quickly to control it. His first act was to appoint an "inspector general" responsible for investigating all police misconduct. The department was given notice that the old rules of the game were gone, and that all misconduct would be punished rather than covered up.

Within a year, most forms of police corruption had disappeared. A few organized forms of corruption persisted up to 1959, Vernon's final year in office. But the gambling and prostitution payoffs—which had never been disclosed publicly during the scandal—apparently ceased during Vernon's first year in office. Many old officers retired, and a "new breed" of Oakland officer was recruited from across the nation. The police code of silence was broken by a few officers who turned in other officers for misconduct. Thompson and Vernon took such a strong stance against corruption that reform spread beyond the police department into the general political culture of the community.[23] Some city officials

22. *Oakland Tribune*, January 22–February 8, 1955.
23. Lawrence W. Sherman, "Corruption Scandals and Political Change: Police and Civic Culture" (paper presented to the 1977 Annual Meeting of the American Political Science Association,

were reportedly scared out of their own corrupt activities by fear of Vernon's spies. Enforcement of gambling laws became so rigid that even church bingo games
were forced to close.

All of Vernon's successors have continued his policies
for controlling corruption. The character of the Oakland Police Department today remains basically that
which Vernon shaped in 1955. The Oakland police have
been studied by major scholars of the police and subjected to intense public criticism regarding their relations with blacks and radicals.[24] But there have been
almost no allegations of widespread, organized corruption in the Oakland Police Department since 1955.[25]
The reform of the Oakland police is one of the most
lasting of any American police agency.

NEWBURGH

Unlike New York and Oakland, Newburgh had always had close ties between the dominant political party
and police corruption. Such ties seemed to disappear in
New York after the Harry Gross scandal nearly led to
the indictment of a mayor, and in Oakland the nonpartisan system of government kept corrupt ties of police to
politicians on a personal rather than a party level. While
Newburgh has long had a city manager form of government, political parties have never been banned from
local politics. Years of control over the city and county
by the same party (Republican) once meant that every
police official in Newburgh owed his job to—or had
purchased it from—the party. The civil service rules for
appointment and promotion notwithstanding, patron-
age was the real police personnel system.[26]

Washington, D.C.).

24. James Q. Wilson, *Varieties of Police Behavior* (Cambridge,
Mass.: Harvard University Press, 1968), pp. 263–266.

25. Only one former Oakland officer interviewed claimed that
organized vice corruption persisted after mid-1955.

26. Wilson, *Varieties of Police Behavior*, p. 244.

Ever since its heyday as a transport center, Newburgh had been the center of vice activities in Orange County. Prostitution was centered in a locally famous brothel patronized by judges and other politicians. The brothel and the several gambling operations in town paid the party for protection from the police. They also made small courtesy payments directly to the police. In the late 1960s, the local economy seriously deteriorated, and the vice industry changed as well. The brothel was closed down by a state police raid and razed by urban renewal bulldozers. Narcotics dealing mushroomed in the large black community, with no tribute from the dealers paid to the party. The police took advantage of the national narcotics scare to "crack down" on dealers—stealing their drugs and cash while making arrests. Police burglary of businesses, the form of corruption that precipitated the scandal, also appears to have begun only in the early 1970s after the appointment of a new chief.[27]

Allegations of police thefts from narcotics dealers were first made public in late 1970. Like the disclosures of police corruption in Oakland in 1953, however, the allegations of corruption in Newburgh in 1970 only produced a little scandal. One citizen group demanded an investigation, but most of the public seemed disinterested. The little scandal may have been a green light for more police burglary and thefts from narcotics dealers, for the frequency of such crimes (as was later discovered) increased substantially.

The Newburgh police stepped over the limits of safe corruption when they burglarized the local outlet of a large national corporation, Sears, Roebuck and Company. A Sears employee happened to observe police officers taking merchandise out of the store late at night, and reported the theft to the Sears security staff. The regional security director for Sears demanded that

27. Interview with Deputy Police Commissioner Thomas Wohlrab, February, 1976; but see *Newburgh Evening News*, January 16, 1973, reporting burglaries as early as 1965.

the chief arrest the officers responsible for the theft. The chief, who had been the ringleader of the burglary, reported that the charge was unfounded; all his officers, he said, had been elsewhere at the time.[28] The Sears official then asked the state police to investigate. One officer "cracked" under interrogation, and others quickly joined in giving evidence in exchange for leniency. The investigation quickly spread beyond the Sears burglary to encompass several other burglaries and thefts from narcotics dealers. The district attorney, though tied to the Party, had no choice but to prosecute fifteen of the department's sixty-four officers (23 percent); he resigned midway through the prosecution, and was later rumored to be under federal investigation himself. All fifteen officers were convicted, and the chief was sentenced to eleven years in "Sing Sing" (Ossining Correctional Facility).[29]

The indictments of the police were handed down in early 1972, and the trials were not completed until later that year. The department was left in a state of uncertainty, not knowing if further indictments or a more wide-ranging investigation would be forthcoming. The deputy chief served as acting chief, playing a caretaker role. In November of 1972, a reform slate of Democrats gained control of the city council and decided to change the managerial structure of the police department. Instead of having a civil service chief appointed from the ranks (at about $12,000 per year), the new council created an untenured position of police commissioner (at $25,000 per year) to be appointed at the pleasure of the city manager. Two deputy police commissioners (at $18,000 per year) were to be appointed at the pleasure of the police commissioner. This structural change allowed "outsiders" to be appointed to run the police department.

The first police commissioner was appointed in early 1973. A former assistant district attorney of Orange

28. Interview with Thomas Wohlrab, February, 1976.
29. *Newburgh Evening News*, March 2, 1973.

County, he was only an "outsider" in the sense that he was not a career police officer. In keeping with his background, he devoted most of his time to investigating past corruption in the department. After a year of "mopping up," he charged a few officers with violations of administrative rules, and then he resigned. He did not introduce new policies and he did not try to "reform" the department in the sense in which the word is used in this study.[30]

Not until the spring of 1974, a full two years after the scandal began, was a reform police executive appointed. James Taylor, the second police commissioner, was a true outsider. A graduate of the Michigan State University School of Police Administration, Taylor had been a police official in several midwestern departments, most recently in a small city outside Minneapolis. He had had little contact with police corruption in his previous jobs, but he had a plan for controlling corruption in Newburgh. After hiring two former colleagues (also from the midwest) as deputy police commissioners, Taylor established a close surveillance over the department. At the same time, he brought the department into the twentieth century, implementing for the first time in the department's history such basic procedures as compiling full crime statistics. Taylor felt so confident about his control of the department that, unlike the other reform police executives in this study, he requested that his department be included.

Using the same approach and types of sources as in the other cities, I could not find reports of police corruption in Newburgh subsequent to the 1972 scandal. Many sources described the department as still being "shell-shocked" from the scandal as late as 1975. Whatever the reason, corruption appeared to be nonexistent at the time Taylor was appointed. And from all indications, there was still no corruption five years after the scandal. Taylor was promoted to city manager in late

30. Interview with former Police Commissioner James Taylor, October 8, 1975.

1975, but he continued to keep tight control over the police department through a former deputy commissioner who replaced him as commissioner. Indeed, some critics complained that Taylor's control was too tight, and the department was ready to move on to a more participatory, less authoritarian style of management. The premise of that critique was that the Newburgh Police Department was a basically honest organization that could be trusted not to abuse its authority—a far cry from the corrupt organization of the early 1970s.

An important aspect of the long-term reform of the Newburgh police was the removal of the department from control by the Republican Party. The voters helped speed this development by electing Democrats to the city council. But Taylor insured against a return of "machine" control by eliminating the leadership of the party through federal investigations. At Taylor's urging, the (Republican) U.S. Attorney launched a broad investigation of (Republican) political corruption in Orange County. Two top political leaders died just before they were to be indicted, it was rumored, one of them reportedly by suicide. The county Republican Party chairman was indicted, and he was convicted in 1976 on charges of fixing a criminal case.

CENTRAL CITY

Central City has a long history of police corruption and scandal. Since the turn of the century, over one hundred police officers have been accused by name of corrupt activities. However, only five have ever been convicted on criminal charges. Prosecutors, judges, and juries have shown repeated tolerance of police corruption. Mayors and political leaders have fostered police corruption as a means of insuring substantial "contributions" to the party from vice operations. Politicians have even run vice operations themselves; one former mayor was alleged to have financed a brothel. While one party was never in control long enough to develop a "machine," the relationship of police corruption to political control changed little from administration to administration; only the cast of characters changed. As a former mayor reportedly said: "The purpose of the police is to give the graft to the Republicans when the Republicans are in power and to the Democrats when the Democrats are in power."

Since World War II, Central City has had a number of little scandals over police corruption. The first big corruption scandal occurred in 1963, while the Democrats were in power. A federal gambling raid uncovered a list of names of police officers whom the gambling operation paid for immunity from arrest. After a year of jurisdictional disputes by the federal and local prosecutors, the evidence finally resulted in the local indictment of twenty-two active or retired police officers. The indictments produced a big scandal, but the community was hardly united in disapproval of the defendants. A citizens' group was formed to collect charitable donations for the defendants' families, and several defendants were given jobs in the public school system. One defendant was convicted, but charges against the others were dropped when the key witness refused to testify. The cleared defendants were reinstated as police officers with back pay. Corruption had apparently ceased while the charges were pending, but it gradually returned to its pre-scandal scope after the charges were dropped.

The Republicans gained power in 1968 and reportedly took control of the vice payoffs. Little of the vice money went to police officers, but all officers were pressured to ignore the crimes of those who had paid the party for protection. In return, the party tolerated minor "free-lance" forms of corruption by the police: payoffs to allow illegal parking, kickbacks from tow-truck drivers called to accident scenes, shakedowns of street prostitutes and tavern owners violating liquor laws, thefts from arrested suspects, and bribes for changing testimony at criminal trials to "fix" the outcome. In the early 1970s, the police reportedly began

selling protection to the rapidly expanding narcotics industry, but it is unclear whether these arrangements
were "free-lance" or coordinated through party officials.

An interesting feature of the linkage between police
corruption and politics in Central City is that the mayor
was not a participant in any aspect of that linkage and
was apparently ignorant of its existence. Diverse sources
agree on this point, and the mayor's own actions prior to
the big scandal support it. In 1972, the mayor heard
hints of corruption among high police officials, and he
created a little scandal by publicly asking those officials
to submit statements of their net worth. The police
union aroused public sentiment against this move, and
the mayor withdrew his order. He then asked the chief
to establish a new system of internal corruption controls,
but the chief ignored the request. A rumored federal
investigation of police corruption was also reported to
have been dropped at that time.

The local newspaper, however, began to look into
police corruption. By mid-1973, a team of investigative
reporters had found a number of sources within the
police department who provided detailed information
about corruption activities. Friction between the county
police and the city police encouraged the former to
"pump" city police prisoners in the county jail for information about corruption in the city police. By early
1974, the reporters had gathered enough allegations
confirmed by independent sources to publish a series of
front-page stories on police corruption. The result was a
major scandal.

The mayor, who was running for statewide office that
year, quickly asked the chief of police, the deputy chief,
and the public safety director to resign. The deputy
retired from the department, but the chief reverted to
his civil service rank of major because he had not served
enough years to be eligible for a pension. The mayor
appointed a special police investigating unit to follow up
on the newspaper's allegations and report directly to

him. This unit was dubbed the "Truth Squad," since it defined its mission as determining the truth of the newspaper stories. For the most part, the unit found that the stories were untrue, or at least lacking in evidence sufficient for criminal prosecution. A few minor indictments were obtained against low-ranking officers, but none of the allegedly corrupt top police officials were ever indicted.

The mayor decided to appoint an outsider as police chief, but was restricted by the city charter to candidates with a bachelor's degree in police administration and ten years of supervisory experience in law enforcement. Only one local candidate fit the requirements, and there was no time for undertaking a national search. The mayor appointed a retired federal police official who was teaching criminal justice at a local college. The new chief was greeted by the press with enthusiasm, but the "honeymoon" did not last for long. The press never challenged the reform chief's integrity or vigor in investigating corruption, but it did attack him for failing to embrace the rebellious police officers who had provided information to the press. The chief's view is that he made reasonable overtures to the rebellious officers, but they refused to provide the specific information required for taking corruption cases to a grand jury.

The scandal continued for almost a year. The district attorney, a crony of the party leaders, indicted two reporters for allegedly attempting to bribe a police officer in the course of their investigation. The voters turned the district attorney out of office in the fall election, and the new district attorney dropped the charges against the reporters. The mayor lost his home county in his unsuccessful bid for statewide office, even though the newspaper responsible for creating the scandal endorsed his candidacy. Both the mayor and the reform chief remained in office for one more year, until the mayor retired and a Democratic mayor was elected.

Corruption declined substantially in Central City during the first year of the reform administration. Whether this change is attributable to the scandal or to the re-form policies is an issue we shall examine in detail later on. The important point here is that the policies adopted by the reform chief to control corruption dif-fered substantially from those policies adopted by the other three reform chiefs studied. Although the evi-dence is far from conclusive, it is plausible to argue that the Central City experience in 1974–75 was a case of unsuccessful reform. The funding for our research project came to an end before enough time could elapse to see if corruption would expand as the effects of scan-dal wore off. Based on the analysis of corruption control policies offered here, a prediction can be made that or-ganized corruption will soon flourish again in the Cen-tral City Police Department. The former mayor agrees with this assessment, citing the resilience of the corrupt relationships among police and criminals. The main rea-son for the predicted failure of reform in Central City is that adequate systems for collecting *information* about police corruption were not established. Without such information, police corruption probably cannot be con-trolled.

Part I

The Problem

1. Deviant Organizations

It is often said that we live in an organizational society. What is not often said is that organizations, like individuals, frequently deviate from social norms and are subject to social control. There are many crimes in a modern society that an individual cannot commit alone, or even in concert with other individuals *qua* individuals. The resources, technology, and even the incentive for committing many crimes are only to be found in formal organizations. Industrial air pollution, discriminatory employment practices, price-fixing, and fraudulent corporate financial reporting are examples of crimes that only formal organizations are capable of committing. The decisions to commit these criminal acts are made by individuals, but they are collectively made for the benefit of formal organizations by individuals in control of those organizations. If these crimes are defined as organizational actions, then the organizations committing them can be defined as deviant organizations.[1]

1. The concept of organizations as deviant actors is a subject of a long debate in sociology and at law. For a review of the legal history of corporate responsibility for criminal acts, see Christopher D. Stone, *Where the Law Ends: Social Control of Corporate Behavior* (New York: Harper and Row, 1975). The first sociological discussion of deviant organizations was apparently Edwin Sutherland's *White Collar Crime* (New York: Dryden Press, 1949), although the conception of organizations as deviant actors was somewhat confused. One critic of Sutherland described his approach as "economic anthropomorphism," and called for inquiry on the behavior of humans, not organizations (Gilbert Geis, "Toward a Delineation of White Collar Offenses," *Sociological Inquiry*, Vol. 32 (Spring 1962), pp. 160–171). But students of organizations have found the conception of organizations as actors to have considerable utility. See, e.g., Richard Hall,

Police departments in which corruption is so systematic that criminals can purchase immunity from arrest are deviant organizations, as distinct from organizations in which deviance occurs. Most police departments have some members who commit corrupt acts from time to time, but the so-called "rotten apple" in a clean barrel cannot sell immunity from arrest by any officer but himself. Police enforcement powers are generally the same for every officer in a department, and criminals cannot achieve total immunity from arrest unless every officer agrees not to invoke his arrest authority. Where such extensive cooperation among officers occurs, scandals often label the police department itself, and not just its officers, as corrupt: a deviant organization.

It is important to distinguish deviance committed *by* organizations from deviance committed *in* organizations. Deviance committed by an organization is collective rule-breaking action that helps achieve organizational goals. Deviance committed in an organization is individual or collective rule-breaking action that does not help to achieve organizational goals, or that is harm-

Organizations: Structure and Process (Englewood Cliffs, N.J.: Prentice Hall, 1977); and James S. Coleman, *Power and the Structure of Society* (New York: W. W. Norton and Company, 1974). Recent work in this area has attempted to fuse the theory of organizations with the theory of deviance. See Albert J. Reiss, Jr., "The Study of Deviant Behavior: Where the Action Is," *The Ohio Valley Sociologist*, Vol. 32 (1966), pp. 1–12; M. David Ermann and Richard J. Lundman, "Deviant Acts by Complex Organizations: Deviance and Social Control at the Organizational Level of Analysis" (paper presented at the Annual Meeting of the American Sociological Association, San Francisco, 1975); James Frey, "Some General Observations on Deviant Behavior by Organizations" (paper presented at the Annual Meeting of the American Sociological Association, Chicago, 1977); and Richard J. Lundman, "Police Misconduct as Organizational Deviance" (paper presented at the Annual Meeting of the American Sociological Association, Chicago, 1977). See also Laura Shill Schrager and James F. Short, Jr., "Toward a Definition of Organizational Crime" (paper presented at the Annual Meeting of the American Sociological Association, Chicago, 1977).

ful to those goals. Sexual exploitation of secretaries, for example, is a deviant action committed in the context of organizational power hierarchies, but it neither benefits nor directly harms the goals of most organizations. Embezzlement and employee theft of materials owned by an organization are examples of deviant actions that directly harm the attainment of an organizational goal of making a profit.[2] Price-fixing and fraudulent advertising, however, are rule-breaking actions that help to achieve the profit goals of the organizations that decide to commit those actions. The distinction between deviance by and in organizations depends upon the currently operative goals of an organization, which can be defined for analytic purposes as the goals imposed by those who run the organization.[3] The goal imposed by those who run a corrupt police department may be the attainment of personal wealth by its members.

The social control of organizations, like the social control of individuals, is both external and internal.[4] Society's norms for organizational conduct are "internalized" by organizations in varying degrees, just as they are in individuals. Certain factions and individuals within an organization may try to make the organization

---

2. Susan Shapiro has attacked the "who benefits" criterion for distinguishing among types of crime in organizations ["A Background Paper on White Collar Crimes" (unpublished manuscript, Yale University, 1976)]. Her argument rests on the difficulty of assessing the intent of the individuals engaging in criminal behavior. However, if consequences are examined without regard to intent, this problem may be avoided. See, e.g., Schrager and Short, "Toward a Definition of Organizational Crime." Nonetheless, even consequences may be difficult to assess objectively. One scholar, for example, has argued that employee theft is functional for maintaining the harmony needed to achieve organizational goals. See Melville Dalton, *Men Who Manage* (New York: John Wiley and Sons, 1959), Chapter 7.

3. James D. Thompson, *Organizations in Action* (New York: McGraw-Hill, 1967), p. 127.

4. The concept of social control has been defined in many different ways. One definition includes virtually every social process that tends to induce conformity to social norms. See, e.g., August B.

behave in conformity to social norms, just as the con-
science is said to influence the behavior of individuals.
When internal social control fails to keep organizational
behavior in conformity to social norms, the social environment of an organization, like that of an individual,
may punish it. External punishment, in turn, can have
important consequences for the internal social control
of organizations, just as it can for individuals.

The analogy between individuals and organizations as
deviant actors cannot be pressed too far. While both can
be defined as units of analysis, they differ in important
ways. Organizations do not have a "mind," they are not
"motivated," and they cannot experience emotions.
Moreover, they cannot be put in prison—although they
can be fined and stigmatized. The dynamics of organizational behavior are fundamentally different from the
dynamics of individual behavior. It is precisely for this
reason that the study of deviance and social control
of organizations requires a different theoretical framework from the study of deviance and social control of
individuals.

The purpose of this chapter is to explore the theoretical issues concerning the social control of deviant
organizations—issues central to scandal over, and reform of, corrupt police departments. Drawing on key
concepts from organizational theory,[5] the chapter ad-
dresses three questions that can be asked about any de-

Hollingshead, "The Concept of Social Control," *American Sociological
Review*, Vol. 6 (1941), pp. 217–224. A somewhat narrower conception,
defines social control as social definitions of and responses to deviant
behavior. See Donald Black, *The Behavior of Law* (New York:
Academic Press, 1976), p. 107. This study generally employs the
narrower conception of social control, but the allusion to individuals
"internalizing" social norms admittedly draws on the broader conception. See, e.g., John Finley Scott, *Internalization of Norms: A
Sociological Theory of Moral Commitment* (Englewood Cliffs, N.J.: Prentice Hall, 1971).

  5. As suggested by Reiss, "The Study of Deviant Behavior,"
p. 12.

viant actor, individual or organization. First, what are the general conditions leading to the actor's becoming deviant? Second, what are the conditions under which external social control is mobilized against the deviant actor? Finally—the question to which the bulk of this book is addressed—what are the consequences of the mobilization of external social control? This chapter shows the distinctive nature of these questions when applied to organizations rather than to individuals, and applies the questions to the process of scandal and reform. Corrupt police departments are used in this chapter as the major examples of the issues applying to all deviant organizations, but the particular characteristics of corrupt police departments are discussed in Chapter Two.

· SOURCES OF ORGANIZATIONAL DEVIANCE

· Organizations become deviant in two ways. One way is the adoption of organizational goals that are deviant from societal norms or laws. The other way is the organizationally approved use of means that deviate from societal norms or laws in order to achieve societally legitimate organizational goals. Both ways of becoming deviant produce organizational conduct that violates societal norms or laws, but each way of becoming deviant has separate sources.

Deviant Goals

Formal organizations are distinguished from all other forms of social organization by their deliberate creation for the purpose of achieving a set of goals.[6] It has long been observed, however, that the formal or original goals that organizations are manifestly created to achieve are often "displaced" by other goals.[7] These informal or "real" goals may displace the formal goals

6. Peter M. Blau and W. Richard Scott, *Formal Organizations* (San Francisco: Chandler Publishing Co., 1962), p. 5.
7. Philip Selznick, *TVA and the Grass Roots* (Berkeley and Los Angeles: University of California Press, 1949).

because they are more conducive to the growth and survival of the organization; indeed, self-perpetuation of the organization is the most commonly cited informal goal.[8] But there are other kinds of informal goals that can entail grave risks to organizational survival. Adopting informal goals that are directly contrary to the formal goals of an organization entails the risk that the organization's environment will act to punish or even destroy the organization. Why, then, do some organizations adopt informal goals directly opposed to their formal goals? Why do police departments, created to arrest criminals and deter crime, fall into league with criminals and commit crime? How is it that such deviant goals are adopted by organizations?

The answer lies in the general process by which the "real" goals of an organization are determined, in the continuing interaction between organizations and their environments. Different sectors of an organization's environment, as well as different groups within an organization, have different interests in the conduct of the organization. These differences often yield conflicting sets of goals that the various external and internal groups would like to see the organization adopt as its "real" goals. The survival and growth of an organization, and the formal goals the organization was created to achieve, are only two sets of many possibly conflicting goals.

Police departments are particularly subject to internal and external conflict about the goals they should adopt. The legal system defines the purpose of police organization as enforcement of all the laws. The client systems of police organizations define the police purpose as intervening in some social situations and not others, the definitions of which categories may vary from one client or group of clients to the next. The political system may define the purpose of police organizations as preserving the present character of community politics, particularly

8. Robert K. Merton, *Social Theory and Social Structure*, enlarged edition (New York: The Free Press, 1968), p. 253.

the influence of local elites. The police administrators may define their goals as the department's "survival" in its present character and membership. Factions within police organizations may wish to destroy the present character of the organization and substitute new goals, perhaps the formal goals set by the legal system.

Given ongoing conflict about what the real goals of the organization should be, who determines what the real goals are, to the extent that they can be determined at all? That is, of all the competing sets of goals offered *for* the organization, how are the real working goals *of* the organization arrived at? Thompson suggests that the real goals of an organization are set by those actors powerful enough to participate in the "dominant coalition" of an organization: "Almost inevitably this includes organizational members, but it may also incorporate significant outsiders. . . . In this view, organizational goals are established by individuals—but interdependent individuals who collectively have sufficient control of organizational resources to commit them in certain directions and withhold them from others."[9] Put another way, a dominant coalition consists of a few people acting in concert who can marshal the most power for running the show and are best able to force the members of the organization into compliance with the goals set by these few. Where this dominant coalition is weak, however, *or* if it lacks the necessary resources or technology, it might be unable to force the organization into compliance with its goals.[10]

It is important to stress that the dominant coalition is "a process, not an entity."[11] Conflicts and realignments may occur within the coalition over time and from issue to issue. The rapidity and constancy of the rate of change within the coalition varies among organizations,

9. Thompson, *Organizations in Action*, p. 128.
10. For a review of recent research on compliance in organizations, see Amitai Etzioni, *A Comparative Analysis of Complex Organizations*, revised edition (New York: Free Press, 1975).
11. Thompson, *Organizations in Action*, p. 138.

but all organizations experience some change over time in dominant coalitions. Dominant coalitions in corrupt police departments seem to be replete with intrigue and power struggles, and such conflict seems to make deviant organizations more vulnerable to external social control. The most significant change in corrupt police departments, however, seems to be one in which the coalition setting goals deviant from societal norms is replaced by a new coalition setting goals in conformity with societal norms: the process of reform that can follow scandal.

The question remains of why dominant coalitions in some organizations adopt deviant goals. The specific causes of deviant goals may be as universal as human greed or as particular as the structure and setting of each formal organization. Two general sources of deviant goals, however, can be identified, or at least located. One source is the organization's environment. While the general environment of an organization may expect the organization to adopt its formal goals as its real goals, certain sectors of the environment have more power than others in shaping the real goals of the organization. Examples of these powerful sectors include holders of large blocks of corporate stock, Parent-Teacher's Association activists, organized consumer groups, and corrupt politicians who influence police departments' hiring and promotion decisions. Organizations vary in the extent to which they are vulnerable to these powerful sectors of the environment. Government agencies headed by executives holding civil service tenure, for example, are generally said to be less vulnerable to environmental influences than agencies headed by political appointees whose tenure depends upon the pleasure of their superiors. Powerful sectors of the environment of an organization vulnerable to such influence can impose deviant goals upon the organization, just as they can force compliance with formal goals. Regardless of the content of the goals imposed, organizations dominated by such powerful environmental groups are often called "captive" organizations.[12] And some organizations, of course, are more captive than others.

A second source of deviant goals for organizations is that which makes them worth capturing: their resources. An organization's resources structure its opportunities for achieving deviant goals. A police department does not have the resources required for investing in fraudulent businesses, but a Teamster's Union pension fund does.[13] Conversely, a pension fund does not have the resources to sell criminals immunity from arrest, but a police department does. Both kinds of organizations have resources that make them attractive to would-be captors in their environments. By the same token, these resources can also be put to use for the personal gain of the members of an organization, rather than of its captors. Differences in the propensity of different kinds of organizations to adopt deviant goals may well be due to the differences among organizations in the extent to which their resources can be exploited for the personal gain of either organizational captors or members. Schools or monasteries, for instance, do not have much in the way of resources exploitable for personal gain, except perhaps in their limited purchasing activities that may be vulnerable to kickbacks from suppliers. The primary resource of any regulatory or law enforcement agency is its tremendous authority to invoke or withhold its enforcement powers—which may explain why regulatory agencies seem more prone to corruption, and particularly to corruption by capture, than other kinds of organizations.

Deviant Means

The adoption of deviant organizational goals is distinct from the use of deviant means to attain legitimate goals. Price-fixing and commercial bribery, for example, are violations of law, but they are employed in pursuit of

12. Ibid., pp. 30, 37.
13. John Hutchinson, *The Imperfect Union: A History of Corruption in American Trade Unions* (New York: E. P. Dutton, 1972), p. 257.

the socially legitimate, formal goal of business organizations of making profits. Similarly, police failure to observe due process requirements in arresting suspects is an illegal practice, but such practices are usually viewed as supportive of the formal goal of police organizations of fighting crime; even police brutality is often perceived by police officers in this light. The sources of deviant practices for achieving legitimate goals may lie in the extent of the disjunction between prescribed goals and required means.[14] That is, the more difficult it is to achieve legitimate goals through legitimate means, the more likely it may be that organizations adopt illegitimate means in order to achieve their goals. Many American corporations, for example, explain their use of commercial bribery in foreign countries by claiming that prevailing local custom in those countries makes it impossible to do business (a legitimate goal) without bribery (a deviant means).

The extent of the disjunction between goals and means varies from one organization to another, and within organizations from one task to another. Businesses may be more likely than churches to adopt deviant means; sales departments may be more likely than production departments to adopt deviant means. In police departments, the investigation of crimes with victims is more feasible to accomplish legitimately than is the investigation of crimes without victims. Victims provide testimony serving as evidence sufficient for making arrests. In crimes without victims, police officers must supply their own testimony about their observations of a suspect's criminal acts; such observations are very difficult to make, and the frequency of police perjury in non-victim crime cases is accordingly greater than it is in cases of crimes with victims.[15]

The present study is not concerned with organiza-

14. Merton, *Social Theory and Social Structure*, Chapter VI, "Social Structure and Anomie."

15. See, e.g., Jonathan Rubinstein, *City Police* (New York: Farrar, Straus and Giroux, 1973), pp. 375–401.

tions that adopt deviant means for attaining legitimate goals. They are noted here merely as part of a general framework for viewing deviant organizations. Organizations become deviant by adopting either deviant goals or deviant means, but the vulnerability of an organization to social control may not depend on the sources of its deviance. The central question is whether deviance remains at an individual level within an organization, or becomes a characteristic of the organization itself.[16]

The boundary between individual and organizational deviance is marked by the dominant coalition's stance towards the deviant practices in question. Where deviant acts occur in the face of active opposition by the dominant coalition, the deviance can be characterized as individual, no matter how widespread it is within the organization. Where deviant acts by organizational members are condoned and even expected by the dominant coalition, the deviance is organizational; the organization is deviant.[17] This distinction becomes crucial when an organization is subjected to external social control, for such control can often be avoided if the dominant coalition can demonstrate its ignorance of the

16. Theoretical approaches to deviance include both an "objective" definition of deviants as actors who break rules, regardless of whether their rule-breaking is ever detected or labeled as deviant, and an "interactionist" definition of deviants as actors who are socially labeled as deviant. Compare Howard S. Becker, *Outsiders* (New York: Free Press, 1963), and Jack P. Gibbs, "Conceptions of Deviant Behavior: The Old and the New," *Pacific Sociological Review*, Vol. 9 (Spring 1966), pp. 9–14. These differences in approach can also be found at the organizational level of analysis; compare Reiss, "The Study of Deviant Behavior," with the "objective" definition of organizational deviance implicit in Lundman, "Police Misconduct as Organizational Deviance." The present work adopts the "objective" definition of deviance as rule-breaking.

17. Lundman ("Police Misconduct as Organizational Deviance") adds two additional criteria to the definition of organizational deviance: organizational socialization of new members to gain their approval of deviant practices, and peer group support of deviant practices. Since socialization and peer group support are common attributes of individual deviance as well as of organizational deviance, those additional characteristics do not seem to be useful in

deviant practices.[18] But by the time the practices are exposed to public view, it may be too late. The organization may be labeled deviant regardless of the true stance of the dominant coalition. The more effective way for deviant organizations to avoid external social control is to prevent any attempts to mobilize social control against them.

MOBILIZING SOCIAL CONTROL

In order for deviants to be punished, a network of actors and institutional processes must be set into motion, or mobilized.[19] A burglar cannot be sent to prison unless the police, prosecutor, and judge all take action to put him behind bars. It may be necessary to mobilize other actors as well, such as informants and witnesses. The failure or refusal to mobilize at any one point in the network of social control may result in the deviant escaping punishment.[20] Punishment depends upon the mobilization of the entire network of social control, and the chances of that occurring are greater for some categories of deviant acts and actors than for others. For a number of reasons, it seems that, in general, social control is more likely to be mobilized against deviant individuals than against deviant organizations.

Four obstacles hinder the mobilization of social control against organizations. First, this society does not routinely allocate resources to the control of deviant organizations, concentrating its resources instead upon the control of deviant individuals. Second, organiza-

---

distinguishing organizational deviance from individual deviance in organizations.

18. Reiss, "The Study of Deviant Behavior," p. 9.

19. Donald J. Black, "The Mobilization of Law," *The Journal of Legal Studies*, Vol. 2 (1973), pp. 125–149; and Matthew Silberman, "Law as Process: A Value-Added Model of the Mobilization of Law" (paper presented at the Annual Meeting of the American Sociological Association, Chicago, 1977).

20. Albert J. Reiss, Jr., "Discretionary Justice," in *Handbook of Criminology*, ed. Daniel Glaser (Chicago: Rand-McNally, 1974), pp. 679–699.

tions often develop the capacity to keep information about their deviant activities from reaching any potential control systems that do exist. Third, organizations are often able to prevent other organizations from exercising control over them. Finally, even when a social control network is mobilized against a deviant organization, there are few effective means available for punishing the organization, since the nature of punishment is necessarily different for organizations than for individuals. Nonetheless, each of these obstacles can be overcome, and social control is often successfully mobilized against organizations. The seeds of mobilization can be found in the breakdown of these obstacles that protect organizations from social control.

Resources for Control

The American legal system is basically organized for the control of individuals, not organizations.[21] Some exceptions to this rule can be found for certain types of organizations and certain types of organizational activity. Organizations engaged in interstate transport of goods, for example, are subject to control by the Federal Interstate Commerce Commission. Similarly, corporate financial reporting is controlled by the Securities and Exchange Commission. Such special-purpose regulatory agencies notwithstanding, there are vast areas of organizational activity for which no routinely mobilized network of social control exists. The absence of such networks is due to the failure of this society to allocate social resources to the external social control of organizations.

The failure to allocate resources to the social control of organizations has at least two sources. One is a problem of definition: much of what is defined sociologically as deviance committed by organizations is defined legally as deviance committed by individuals. Police departments cannot be criminally prosecuted for selling gamblers immunity from arrest. The legal system can

21. Donald R. Cressey, *Criminal Organization: Its Elementary Forms* (London: Heinemann, 1972); and Stone, *Where the Law Ends.*

only respond to such behavior by prosecuting individual police officers for bribery, or, at most, by prosecuting a group of police officers for conspiracy to commit bribery. Except for the narrowly defined special-purpose regulatory offenses, organizations cannot be held legally culpable for organizational deviance. Individuals may be incarcerated for their roles in organizational deviance, but the roles are quickly filled by other individuals, and the deviant activity continues. The law does not define most deviant behavior in organizational terms, so it does not allocate legal resources to the goal of incapacitating deviant organizations.

A second source of the failure to allocate resources to the social control of organizations is the social expectation that organizations will control themselves. That is, organizations are often assumed to be capable of exercising internal control over the behavior of their members. School administrators are assumed to be able to detect and to punish teachers who molest their students, auditors hired by businesses are assumed to be able to detect embezzlement, and police supervisors are assumed to be able to detect police corruption. The problem with this kind of assumption, however valid it may be in a particular case, is that it equates the behavior of an organization's members with the behavior of the organization. It makes no allowance for the organization itself becoming deviant; that is, it makes no allowance for deviant acts by individual members of an organization conforming to a set of socially deviant organizational goals (or means) directed by the dominant coalition of the organization. As long as an organization is successful in keeping its deviant behavior hidden from public view, the public assumption that the organization is adequately controlling the behavior of its members will continue to appear valid.

Nonetheless, organizational deviance is carried out by individuals, and social control resources are often allocated against individuals who carry out organizational deviance. While the punishment of such individuals does not incapacitate a deviant organization, it can contribute to a labeling process by which the organization is socially defined as deviant. The prosecution of large numbers of organizational members, and particularly of members near or at the top of the organization's hierarchy, provides evidence that the deviance is something more than individual aberration. If the deviance is defined as organizational in character, and the character of the organization is labeled deviant, then the organization is in effect punished, as we shall see later. The concentration of social control resources on individuals may hinder the mobilization of social control against organizations, but it cannot prevent it entirely.

Information for Control

No matter how great the resources allocated to establish social control networks, the networks cannot be mobilized without information about deviant acts.[22] That is, unless the occurrence of a deviant act is made known to agents of social control, they can take no action against it. The police do not arrest a burglar, for example, unless they know (1) that a burglary has occurred, and (2) the identity and whereabouts of a burglary suspect. Information about deviant acts and actors is not a sufficient condition for the mobilization of social control, but it is a necessary one. Consequently, deviants who wish to avoid social control will try to conceal their actions, or at least their identities, from as many people as possible. Deviant organizations are particularly adept at concealing their deviant acts, since they can marshal more resources for maintaining secrecy than can many deviant individuals. By controlling information about their deviance, deviant organizations prevent the use of that information for control.

22. See, e.g., Albert J. Reiss, Jr. and David J. Bordua, "Environment and Organization: A Perspective on the Police," and Jerome H. Skolnick and J. Richard Woodworth, "Bureaucracy, Information, and Social Control: A Study of a Morals Detail," both in *The Police:*

The flow of information about deviant acts is channeled by two kinds of social organization: the social organization of deviant behavior and the social organization of society. How many people learn of deviant acts is a joint function of the way in which the acts themselves are organized, and the way in which society is organized in relation to those acts. Consider first the organization of society. The residential organization of a high-rise public housing project, for example, is different from the organization of a low-rise tenement in ways that make information about a burglary in the latter more likely to circulate.[23] Similarly, drunken and disorderly conduct in public is likely to become known to more people, and particularly to the police, than the same behavior in private.[24] Deviant actors often anticipate these differences in the organization of society, and organize their deviant activities in ways that offer the least possible exposure to other people. Burglars seek out points of entry least exposed to public view, and corrupt police accept payoffs in private locations.

When more than one person participates in the commission of a deviant act, the possibility of a participant passing information about the act to other people is increased. The more participants, the greater the possibility of "leakage" of information. The information may not be leaked directly to agents of social control. A trusted friend or a relative may be told of the act by one of the participants, and they may pass the information on to others; eventually the information may reach agents of social control. In order to foreclose this possibility, codes of secrecy, punishment for leakage of information, and "need-to-know" restrictions on access to

---

Six Sociological Essays, ed. David J. Bordua (New York: John Wiley and Sons, 1967), pp. 25–55 and 99–136, respectively.

23. Reiss and Bordua, "Environment and Organization," p. 44.

24. Arthur L. Stinchcombe, "Institutions of Privacy in the Determination of Police Administrative Practice," *American Journal of Sociology*, Vol. 69 (1963), p. 158.

information often develop in deviant groups.[25] These procedures for information control are less sophisticated in "project" crimes—in which a particular group of individuals assembles to commit only one crime and then disperses—than in those criminal organizations in which the same members engage in criminal activity on a continuing basis.[26] Indeed, one of the major characteristics of what is generally referred to as "organized crime" is that it is organized to control and restrict the flow of information about its crimes.[27]

Control systems acquire information about deviant acts in two basic ways.[28] First, information may be brought to the attention of the control system at the initiative of people external to that system. If the system responds to that information, the system may be called "reactive." Or, second, information may be sought out at the initiation of the control system. When it responds to information gathered in this manner, the system may be called "proactive." When control systems organize reactively to control a category of deviance, the mobilization of control can only occur when information about such events is made *available* to the control system by external actors. When control systems organize proactively to control a category of deviance, the mobilization of control can only occur when information about such events is *accessible* to the intelligence technology of the control system, i.e., can be located by control agents who go out to look for it.

Deviant organizations adopt strategies for keeping information about their deviance unavailable to reactive

25. Philip Selznick, *The Organizational Weapon* (New York: McGraw-Hill, 1960); and Albert K. Cohen, "The Concept of Criminal Organisation," *The British Journal of Criminology*, Vol. 17 (1977), pp. 105–106.

26. Compare Peter Letkemann's discussion of project crime in *Crime as Work* (Englewood Cliffs, N.J.: Prentice-Hall, 1973) with Francis A. J. Ianni's discussion of a criminal organization in *A Family Business* (New York: Russell Sage Foundation, 1972).

27. Reiss and Bordua, "Environment and Organization," p. 46.

28. Reiss and Bordua, "Environment and Organization."

control systems and inaccessible to proactive control systems. Codes of secrecy, for example, keep information from falling into the hands of those who, for whatever reasons, might make the information available to social control systems. "Need-to-know" restrictions on the circulation of knowledge, such as the cell structure of the American Communist Party,[29] are an example of strategies for making information inaccessible to such proactive control methods as informers and double agents. Even if the organization is penetrated by control systems, these strategies for keeping information inaccessible insure that the information gathered will be insufficient for successful criminal prosecution.

Another factor affecting the chances of detection and prosecution of deviance is the timing of social control. Social control agents may acquire information about deviant acts before, during, or after their occurrence.[30] When social control systems acquire information about deviant acts before or during their occurrence, the systems may be called "premonitory." When social control systems acquire information about deviant acts after they have already occurred, the systems may be called "postmonitory." Just as premonitory health-care systems often use early warnings to take preventive action against disease, premonitory social control systems often use early warnings to take preventive action against deviance. Premonitory evidence of criminal acts, especially interception of criminal behavior as it occurs, is usually more convincing in criminal trials than postmonitory evidence. Premonitory systems of social control seem to be more effective at both preventing and punishing deviance. Yet premonitory control is only possible to the extent that information about deviance is both available and accessible to control systems.

Despite the general effectiveness of organizational strategies for keeping information about deviance un-

29. Selznick, *The Organizational Weapon.*
30. Albert J. Reiss, Jr., Lectures, Yale University, 1973. See also Ermann and Lundman, "Deviant Acts by Complex Organizations."

available and inaccessible to control systems, the strategies cannot always be pursued successfully. Mistakes, oversights, accidents, and inaccurate predictions about how many people will learn of a particular deviant act can allow information to become available or accessible to control. Information seems particularly likely to be made available to reactive control systems when conflict occurs within a deviant organization, in which case the mobilization of external control can be used as a weapon in the internal struggle over power and organizational goals. By the same token, internal conflict in deviant organizations makes information more accessible to control systems trying to penetrate the organization: informers within the organization are more easily recruited when organizational members are disgruntled rather than loyal, or when they are split into factions rather than tightly controlled. As Simmel observes, "Secret societies which, for whatever reasons, fail to develop a tightly solidifying authority are, therefore, typically exposed to very grave dangers."[31] The grave danger to which conflict-ridden deviant organizations are exposed is leakage of information that is essential, although not sufficient, for the mobilization of control.[32]

Discretion to Control

Information alone cannot mobilize a social control network against deviance. An affirmative decision to respond to information about deviance is required, regardless of whether the information was acquired proactively or reactively. All participants in a network or potential network of social control, including both citizens and officials, exercise discretion over their decisions to mobilize against a deviant act or actor. Often this discretion is guided by a proper concern for putting

31. Georg Simmel, *The Sociology of Georg Simmel*, ed. and trans. Kurt Wolff (New York: Free Press, 1950), p. 371.
32. Not all deviant organizations, of course, attempt to keep their deviance a secret. Homosexual rights organizations, for example,

scarce resources to most effective use. But discretion not to act can also be influenced by less legitimate concerns. Deviant organizations often "contract" with other organizations and actors who *could* mobilize social control if information about the organizational deviance ever reached them. "Contracting," the negotiation of an agreement for the exchange of performances in the future,[33] need not be formal or even explicit. But its clear effect is to compel potential control actors not to mobilize against a deviant organization in exchange for certain performances by that organization.

Minor criminals often contract with police officials for immunity from arrest for their own crimes in exchange for a supply of information about more serious crimes committed by other criminals. Similarly, police departments often contract with prosecutors to forego prosecution of police misconduct in exchange for a supply of police investigative resources to be used at the discretion of the prosecutor.[34] The Federal Bureau of Investigation has appeared reluctant to investigate misconduct by local police because of its dependence upon police for vital information regarding federal offenses.[35] Agreements not to prosecute can also be explicitly purchased, as organized crime and vice operations have done with local police departments.[36] In the event of public disclosure of decisions not to mobilize control,

publicize their deviance in order to openly challenge the norm from which they deviate. See Cohen, "The Concept of Criminal Organization," p. 109.

33. Thompson, *Organizations in Action,* p. 35. See also Howard Aldrich, "Resource Dependence and Interorganizational Relations: Local Employment Service Offices and Social Services Sector Organizations," *Administration and Society* 7 (1976), pp. 419–454.

34. City of New York, Commission to Investigate Allegations of Police Corruption and the City's Anti-Corruption Procedures, *Commission Report*, 1972 (hereinafter cited as Knapp Commission Report), p. 256.

35. Herbert Beigel and Allan Beigel, *Beneath the Badge: A Story of Police Corruption* (New York: Harper and Row, 1977), p. 12.

36. Cressey, *Criminal Organization.*

implicit contracts entail less risk than such explicit contracts as bribery because implicit contracts can be more easily explained as a legitimate exercise of discretion.

Two legitimate grounds are often cited by control agents to account for their failure to mobilize control in response to information about deviance. One is that the information in question is false, or that the source of the information is not reliable. The other is that the information is insufficient for meeting the standards of proof required for a criminal conviction. Neither ground is easily subjected to empirical testing; the actual fate of any prosecution cannot be known for certain until it has run its full course. But official agents of social control invoke their expertise to back up their assessment that the information is either false or will not yield a verdict of guilty.

Deviant organizations are often able to employ their resources to contract successfully for decisions not to mobilize control. This obstacle to mobilization, however, can be overcome by public exposure of information that appears to the public to justify mobilizing social control. The legitimate grounds for decisions not to mobilize may protect official social control agents from punishment, but they do not protect the deviant organizations. Public exposure of information about organizational deviance may produce public demands for mobilization of control, regardless of the "expert" judgments of official control agents. If control agents fail to respond to public demands for mobilization, they may be removed through the electoral process. Prosecutors who fail to indict police officers in the wake of police corruption scandals, for example, are often defeated when they run for reelection.[37] Even if one actor in a social control network refuses to mobilize, other actors can do so independently. Federal and state prosecutors often step in where local prosecutors fear to tread. No matter how

---

37. John J. McGlennon, "Bureaucratic Crisis and Executive Leadership: Corruption in Police Departments" (Ph.D. dissertation, The Johns Hopkins University, 1977), p. 143.

many contracts a deviant organization negotiates for discretion not to mobilize, public exposure of information about deviance can lead to mobilization. Only one obstacle to punishment of deviant organizations will then remain: the difficulty of imposing punitive sanctions against the organization itself, rather than against the individual members of the organization.

Sanctions for Control

Punitive sanctions for deviant behavior are both material and symbolic. The legal system relies upon material sanctions, such as incarceration and fines. Extralegal systems of social control may also rely on material sanctions, such as the execution of members of criminal gangs who leak information. In most aspects of everyday life, however, extralegal systems of social control employ sanctions directed at the symbolic aspects of deviant actors: their reputations, status, trustworthiness, and the essence of their characters. For example, lying at cocktail parties may be punished by the person being branded a liar; while he may only be guilty of lying at cocktail parties, the label of "liar" can be applied to his character in general, such that any of his statements in any context may be distrusted. Relatively few material sanctions can be applied to organizations, and then with questionable impact.[38] But symbolic sanctions can be applied to organizations as well as to individuals. Both individuals and organizations have public identities, and public identities are always vulnerable to redefinition and stigmatization.

When social control is mobilized against a deviant organization, a battle of definition ensues. The organization generally tries to define the deviance against which control is mobilized as individual deviance by its members and not as deviance which is characteristic of the

38. On the difficulty of punishing organizations, see Alan Dershowitz, "Increasing Community Control over Corporate Crimes—A Problem in the Law of Sanctions," *Yale Law Journal*, Vol. 71 (1961), pp. 280–306; Robert W. Ogren, "The Ineffectiveness of the Crimi-

entire organization. At the same time, actors in the control network may try to label the deviance as organizational, and the character of the organization as deviant. If the organization loses the battle of definition of its identity, then it is, in effect, punished by the only sanction that can harm the organization as a whole: disgrace and degradation of status.[39] The success in imposing this symbolic sanction may be independent of any legal or administrative material sanctions imposed against individual members of the organization. Rather, the imposition of a symbolic sanction against the organization is a matter of manipulation of appearances.

Organizations can be publicly labeled as deviant even if they do not satisfy the "objective" definition of a deviant organization suggested earlier. Regardless of the real stance taken by the dominant coalition towards the deviant practices of organizational members, the appearance of high-level support for the deviance can provide adequate grounds for a social definition of the organization's character as deviant. The dominant coalition may attempt to avoid the appearance of support for the deviant practices by claiming to have been ignorant of their existence, by claiming that the practices were less widespread than is alleged, or by claiming to have taken aggressive but unsuccessful action to control the deviant practices. To the extent that social control actors can counter any of these claims with strong evidence, the chances for successful application of the deviant label are increased. The dominant coalition's failure to take steps to control the deviance is perhaps the most

---

nal Sanction in Fraud and Corruption Cases: Losing the Battle against White-Collar Crime," *American Criminal Law Review*, Vol. 11 (Summer 1973), pp. 959–988; and Stone, *Where the Law Ends*, Chapter 11.

39. For a contrary view, see Schrager and Short, "Toward a Definition of Organizational Crime," p. 5; compare Frey, "Some General Observations on Deviant Behavior by Organizations." For evidence on the punitive aspects of scandal as labeling, see Chapter 3.

damaging kind of fact, because it raises the critical question of resources for control: if the organization does not control the conduct of its members, who will?

Deviant organizations often succeed in escaping a deviant label. Moral responsibility in our society is still generally attributed to individuals rather than to social systems, and the bias of the public audiences of any attempts to label deviant organizations may be in the direction of attributing blame to individuals. But when social control agents concentrate on the application of the symbolic sanction of labeling the entire organization, rather than just on material sanctions against its members, then it is possible to punish the organization as a whole by stigmatizing or spoiling its identity.[40]

The destruction of an organization's reputation for being trustworthy of conforming to social norms can have two severe consequences for the organization. One is the replacement of the incumbent dominant coalition with a new set of actors and interests, a realignment of the structure of power over the organization. The other is the allocation of resources for routine external social control of the organization, for surveillance of its conduct on a continuing basis. The crash of the stock market in 1929, for example, resulted in both extensive changes in the leadership of many corporations and the creation of the Securities and Exchange Commission to regulate corporate financial reporting practices.[41] Similarly, the Knapp Commission scandal over police corruption in New York resulted in new leadership in the police department and the appointment of a special prosecutor to monitor police corruption from outside the department. The question remains, however, of what consequences these changes and the destruction of organizational reputation that caused them will have upon the deviant conduct of an organization.

40. Erving Goffman, *Stigma: Notes on the Management of Spoiled Identity* (Englewood Cliffs, N.J.: Prentice-Hall, 1963).
41. Robert Chatov, *Corporate Financial Reporting: Public or Private Control?* (New York: Free Press, 1975).

CONSEQUENCES OF CONTROL

The consequences of external social control on individual subjects have long been debated by scholars. Put very crudely, one school of thought holds that punishment of individuals makes them less likely to repeat their offenses, while another school holds that punishment makes repeated offenses more likely.[42] Deterrence theorists have assembled considerable evidence to support the notion of *general* deterrence (scaring most people in a population from doing something by punishing most of the few who do it), but the evidence is much less clear for the notion of *specific* deterrence (scaring the specific individuals punished for deviant acts from repeating the behavior that led to their punishment).[43] Neither is there clear evidence for the competing hypothesis of secondary deviation, that regardless of the initial causes of an individual's deviance, the labeling of that individual as a deviant may become a cause in itself, sustaining the continued or future performance of the deviant behavior.[44] While this controversy remains unresolved at the level of individual behavior, the issues have never been raised at the level of organizational behavior.

The secondary deviation hypothesis can be transposed from the individual to the organizational level, and has already found support at the level of nonorganized groups. For example, the labeling of English "mods and rockers"[45] and of "hippie" marijuana users[46] by a "moral panic" over their deviance, quite apart from any material legal sanctions, seemed to

42. Bernard A. Thorsell and Lloyd M. Klemke, "The Labelling Process: Reinforcement and Deterrence," *Law and Society Review*, Vol. 6 (1972), pp. 393–403.

43. See, e.g., Jack P. Gibbs, *Crime, Punishment, and Deterrence* (New York: Elsevier, 1975).

44. See, e.g., Edwin Lemert, *Human Deviance, Social Problems, and Social Control* (Englewood Cliffs, N.J.: Prentice-Hall, 1967).

45. Stanley Cohen, *Folk Devils and Moral Panics* (London: Paladin, 1973).

46. Jock Young, "The Role of the Police as Amplifiers of De-

amplify rather than reduce the deviance of those groups. No evidence exists for secondary deviation by formal organizations, but the logic of the hypothesis is readily adaptable to organizations as deviant actors.

That is not the case with the deterrence hypothesis, which distinguishes between specific and general effects of punishment. The theoretical problem is which form of deterrence, specific or general, applies to deviant organizations punished symbolically by labeling at the same time that some of its individual members are punished by material legal sanctions. If the organization is defined as the deviant actor, then the specific deterrence hypothesis would apply; if the individual members of the organization are defined as a population of deviant or potentially deviant actors, then the general deterrence hypothesis would apply. The specific deterrence hypothesis predicts that the organizational deviance is less likely to occur after punishment; the general deterrence hypothesis predicts that the frequency of deviance among organizational members is likely to be lower after a few members are punished. The two deterrence hypotheses are not inconsistent, but they do demonstrate the importance of the choice of the level of analysis to be employed in studying deviant organizations.

One possible consequence of external social control of deviant organizations is an increase in internal organizational control of deviant behavior among the organization's members. If such a change occurs, it is appropriate to shift the level of analysis from the organizational to the individual level. If the labeling of the organization causes a replacement of the dominant coalition, and the new leadership adopts a strong stance against the organizational deviance, then by definition the organization is no longer deviant. The focus of social control necessarily shifts to controlling deviance in organiza-

---

viancy, Negotiators of Reality, and Translators of Fantasy," in *Images of Deviance*, ed. Stanley Cohen (London: Penguin, 1971), pp. 27–61.

tions. The change in the dominant coalition does not necessarily mean that the deviance supported by the previous coalition will cease immediately; far from it. Instead, an important question of compliance in organizations is raised: how can the leadership of an externally punished deviant organization reform the organization? In this context, internal reform of the organization by its leadership is a problem of changing the behavior of its individual members. All of this, of course, presumes that external control of the organization produces a change in the membership of the dominant coalition. That was in fact the case in the four police departments presently under study, but it is by no means clear that labeling always produces changes in the membership and goals of organizational leadership.

The analytic value of the conception of deviant organizations presented here is limited mainly to studying the sources of the deviance and the mobilization of external control. The consequences of external control, insofar as they change the nature of internal control, are best examined by employing individual organizational members as the units of analysis. External punishment is apparently a rare event in the lives of most organizations, as it is in the lives of most individuals. The more important determinant of day-to-day behavior may be the nature of internal control. While the application of external control can have important effects upon internal control, it is internal control that may be the strongest influence on the organization's future conduct. The chances of a deviant organization, once punished, becoming recidivist seem to depend heavily on the extent to which internal control can curb the deviant behavior of the organization's individual members. External punishment may well have an immediate and direct effect on the behavior of the organization's members. But the long-term effects of external punishment on organizational deviance may depend on what effect external control of the organization has upon internal control of its members.

2. Corrupt Police Departments

This chapter analyzes corrupt police departments from the perspective of the social control of deviant organizations. Drawing mainly on the four case studies, the chapter explores the major questions considered in the last chapter in terms of their specific application to police departments. First, it describes the ways in which police departments become corrupt. Second, it examines the vulnerability of both corrupt police departments and police corruption activities to the mobilization of social control. Third, some predictions are offered about the effects of social control on both corrupt police departments and police corruption activities. The purpose of the chapter is to provide a basis for the later discussion of how social control was actually mobilized against and in the four police departments, and what the consequences of control were. Before considering the three major issues, it is necessary to define and clarify the distinction between police corruption activities and corrupt police departments.

Police corruption is an illegal use of organizational power for personal gain.[1] The personal nature of the gain distinguishes corruption from brutality, perjury, illegal search, or other law violations committed in the pursuit of such legitimate organizational goals as fighting crime. The organizational nature of the power used

1. This is a simplified version of an earlier definition. See Lawrence W. Sherman, ed., *Police Corruption: A Sociological Perspective* (New York: Anchor Books, 1974), pp. 5–6. For a discussion of both the conceptual and administrative problems in defining police corruption, see Herman Goldstein, *Police Corruption: A Perspective on Its Nature and Control* (Washington, D.C.: Police Foundation, 1975), pp. 3–5.

illegally excludes many crimes committed by policemen, such as burglary committed by a city police officer in his suburban town of residence in which he has no contact with the local police. That particular burglary would merely be a crime. A burglary committed by the same officer in his own police jurisdiction, under the protection of his colleagues or aided by his organizational knowledge of his colleagues' practices, would be both a crime and an act of police corruption.[2]

Other definitions of corruption are certainly possible, but this one is the most useful for studying police corruption as a form of deviance that can be both individual and organizational. Police corruption inverts the formal goals of the police organization. It is a use of organizational power to encourage and create crime rather than to deter it. But as long as the illegal use of police power for personal gain is not fostered by the dominant coalition of a police department, police corruption is only a form of individual deviance in organizations, one that is harmful to organizational goals. Even though many officers are engaged in police corruption activities, the police department is not corrupt unless the dominant coalition adopts as an organizational goal the personal financial gain of the organization's membership. Conversely, even though many officers do not engage in police corruption activities, the department is corrupt if the dominant coalition does foster police corruption as an organizational goal. Police corruption activities can exist without a corrupt police department, but a corrupt police department obviously has police corruption activities. A corrupt police department is an organization that adopts corruption as an organizational goal.

2. A distinction between police corruption and police criminality (e.g., vice protection payoffs to police versus burglaries committed by police) is suggested by James Q. Wilson, "The Police and Their Problems: A Theory," *Public Policy*, Vol. 12 (1963), pp. 190–216. While that distinction may be useful for some purposes, it is not necessary from the standpoint of considering police corruption as organizational deviance.

BECOMING A CORRUPT POLICE DEPARTMENT

Most police departments have members who commit corrupt acts from time to time.[3] Only some police departments, however, become corrupt police departments. The four departments studied here became corrupt in two different ways. Three of them (Oakland, Newburgh, and Central City) adopted corrupt goals as a result of capture by the political environment. One of them (New York) adopted corrupt goals solely for the benefit of the members of the department, exploiting the tremendous organizational resources available for that purpose. While the other three departments incidentally exploited organizational resources for the personal gain of their members, only in New York was that the primary consequence of adopting deviant goals.

Capture by the Political Environment

Capture by the political environment is probably the leading explanation of why police departments become corrupt, perhaps because police corruption has often been studied in conjunction with corrupt political machines.[4] But the politicians and officials who try to influence the police directly are not the only element of the political environment that constrains police departments into becoming corrupt. The wider community and the electorate are also important actors in the capture of police departments for the purpose of imposing corrupt goals.

Community tolerance, or even support, for police corruption can facilitate a department's becoming corrupt. Community attitudes favorable toward corrup-

3. Antony Simpson, *The Literature of Police Corruption: Volume 1. A Guide to Bibliography and Theory*, (New York: The John Jay Press, 1977).

4. John Landesco, *Organized Crime in Chicago* (Chicago: University of Chicago Press, 1929, 1968); V. O. Key, Jr., "The Techniques of Political Graft in the United States" (Ph.D. dissertation, University of Chicago, 1936); William F. Whyte, *Street Corner Society* (Chicago: University of Chicago Press, 1943), pp. 111–146; and John A. Gardiner, *The Politics of Corruption* (New York: Russell Sage Foundation, 1970).

tion, and toward the vice activities corruption often makes possible, tend to deny the legal norms from which police corruption is deviant. Such attitudes imply that corruption is consistent with the formal police goal of fighting crime, and that a corrupt police department is merely accommodating the tastes of the community it serves. Since American police agencies are locally controlled, community attitudes favorable to corruption supplant state laws against bribery and make a corrupt police department conform to local norms.

Community attitudes toward corruption are difficult to measure. Public opinion polls[5] mask the possibility that the respondents are concealing their true feelings in order to answer in accordance with state law. Different sectors of the public may have very different attitudes towards both vice and the police corruption that protects it.[6] The modal community attitude, whatever it may be, can also change very quickly, catching even the police departments themselves by surprise. Public reactions to revelations of police corruption are perhaps the best indicator of public attitudes. Passive reactions to such revelations may help police departments to become corrupt.

All four police departments suffered a "little scandal" two years prior to the big scandal that mobilized external social control. Only in New York did the little scandal demonstrate substantial public disapproval of police corruption. In the other three cities, public passivity toward the corruption issue could be interpreted as a tacit sign of approval. Remarkably, the corruption disclosed in the little scandal was in one instance (Oakland) more serious than that later disclosed in the big scandal. Such graphic displays of community tolerance of police corruption may have encouraged the police department's definition of its behavior as proper rather than deviant.

5. For reports of survey research on public attitudes towards police corruption, see David H. Bayley, *The Police and Political Development in India* (Princeton: Princeton University Press, 1969), Chapter 11; and Gardiner, *The Politics of Corruption*.
6. Whyte, *Street Corner Society*, p. 136.

In Central City, the general lack of public concern with the revelations suggesting systematic police corruption in 1972 was consistent with almost a century of public tolerance of police corruption. Despite frequent allegations of corruption and even prosecutions of police officers, Central City juries almost never convicted police officers for corruption. The sympathetic public response to the 1964 indictments of police officers for gambling corruption—providing jobs and charity for the indicted officers—seemed to be a clear indication of community denial of legal norms against corruption. In effect, Central City seemed to have exempted the police from the laws against bribery, at least until the big scandal of 1974.

Similar public reactions occurred in response to disclosures of police corruption in Oakland and Newburgh. The Oakland police were accused of committing burglary and protecting gambling establishments two years prior to the big scandal, but the politicians linked to the gambling protection were supported by the electorate in the next election.[7] The Newburgh police were publicly accused of stealing from arrested suspects two years prior to their big scandal, but only one small public group reacted with any demands for an investigation of the charges.[8] Only in New York did the "little scandal" revelations produce any apparent public disapproval; they also resulted in the creation of the Knapp Commission, which in turn created the big scandal a year and a half later. The New York City Police Department, however, was not a captive of its political environment, so the negative public reaction could not be expected to have any impact upon corruption.[9]

Public tolerance of police corruption not only encourages police departments to become corrupt, it also supports the control of police departments by corrupt politicians. Corrupt political control does not require the existence of a political "machine," which was absent

7. *Oakland Tribune*, April 22, 1953.
8. *Newburgh Evening News*, November 6, 1970.
9. See p. 41.

from all of the cities except Newburgh. Nor does it seem
to be prevented by the city-manager or the nonpartisan
forms of municipal government, as the Newburgh and
Oakland cases demonstrate. Rather, corrupt political
control seems to be made possible by informal systems
that allow politicians to influence personnel decisions
within the police department. The most important decision of this nature is the selection of the chief police
executive, but promotional decisions at all ranks were
subject to political influence in Oakland, Newburgh,
and Central City prior to their big scandals.[10] By determining who will occupy key positions of power within a
police department, and by making as many members of
the police department as possible obligated to the politicians, political leaders can impose their own goals on the
department—including protection of vice for the
financial benefit of the political party in power or of the
party leaders themselves.

Just as corporate contributions have been the lifeblood of national politics, vice protection payoffs have
been the lifeblood of local politics.[11] As one Los Angeles
politician put it, "the purpose of any political organization is to get the money away from the gamblers."[12] The
only way politicians can extract money from gamblers is
through the sale of immunity from police interference
in gambling operations. The only way that immunity
can be sold is through corrupt political control of the
police department.

In the extreme form of politically dominated corrupt

10. Interview with Wayne Thompson, former Oakland City Manager, May 9, 1975; James Q. Wilson, *Varieties of Police Behavior* (Cambridge, Mass.: Harvard University Press, 1968), p. 244; and newspaper articles and interviews in Central City, 1974.

11. Joseph Gerald Woods, "The Progressives and the Police:
Urban Reform and Professionalization of the Los Angeles Police"
(Ph.D. dissertation, University of California at Los Angeles, 1973);
David R. Johnson, "A Sinful Business: Origins of Gambling Syndi-
cates in the United States, 1840–1887," in *Police and Society*, ed. David
H. Bayley (Beverly Hills, Calif.: Sage Publications, 1977).

12. Woods, "The Progressives and the Police," p. 315, quoting
Wilbur Legette.

police departments, the officers whose exercise of discretion protects vice operations receive none of the protection money, although they may have to collect it on behalf of the party.[13] Police managers may receive some of the money, or they may receive safe tenure in their jobs as their only "payoff." Of the four police departments studied here, this extreme form was present only in Newburgh, which also had stronger political control than the other three departments. In Newburgh, safe tenure included the right to make free-lance money from non-vice sources, as well as a small share of the gambling payoffs for the chief and his commanders. In Oakland and Central City, vice operators made direct payoffs to police officials. The greater control of corruption by police in Oakland and Central City corresponded to their relatively lesser degree of political capture.

Oakland in the early 1950s had a very weak political structure, dominated entirely by the economic interests in that community. The city-manager/nonpartisan-council form of government had been in effect since Earl Warren's investigations of corruption led to the charter reform of 1931. Following that reform era, the downtown business interests reportedly picked candidates for the city council who would keep the taxes low on downtown business properties. In return, the business elites allegedly tolerated whatever payoffs the councilmen could extract from the small-scale gambling and prostitution operations in town. The long-term (twenty years) city manager ran a passive caretaker administration, and the councilmen allegedly dealt directly with the police. The commanders of the three patrol precincts were particularly powerful and allegedly were able to provide complete immunity from vice enforcement. The rank and file reportedly followed their orders regarding vice enforcement, and some of them en-

13. Gardiner, *The Politics of Corruption*; and William Chambliss, "Vice, Corruption, Bureaucracy, and Power," *The University of Wisconsin Law Review*, Vol. 1971, pp. 1150–1170.

gaged in free-lance extortion from non-vice-related criminals.

Central City had a similar structure of corruption within the department, but a very different form of political domination. No public official in the executive branch of this strong mayor form of government seemed to be directing police enforcement policy at all. Rather, the county chairman of the party in power dealt directly with the police commanders, in the name of the mayor but without the mayor's knowledge. While the mayor admitted to having had what Lazarsfeld calls "half-knowledge" that there was some corruption going on, the mayor was unsuccessful in his attempts to gain more knowledge. As Lazarsfeld points out, the half-knowledge position lets an executive off the hook at both ends: it is a defense from charges of both culpability in corruption and inadequate management.[14]

The fact that complete immunity from police interference could be purchased by criminals in Oakland, Newburgh, and Central City indicates that those police departments were corrupt at the organizational level. While some police officers personally profited from the corruption of the organization, the prime beneficiary of the organizational deviance was the political environment that had captured the police department. The character of the community—such as the availability of vice activities and the possibility of "fixing" minor cases through political influence—as well as the character of the police department were both dependent upon the political environment's capture of the police department in those three cities. In New York, however, the primary source of the police department's corruption was the extensive resources of the organization, resources that were exploited for the personal gain of the department's membership and not for the personal gain of any actors in the political environment.

14. Lecture by Paul A. Lazarsfeld, Department of Sociology, Yale University, 1974. See also Christopher Stone, *Where the Law Ends* (New York: Harper and Row, 1975), pp. 60–62.

Abuse of Resources

The legal authority of police departments and the nature of law violations in their jurisdictions provide organizational resources that can be exploited for personal gain. The nature of these resources varies greatly among and within police departments according to the nature of police tasks performed and the social characteristics of the police task environment. Some police departments have greater resources for exploitation than others, just as some police units within the same department have greater resources than others. These resources are what make a police department worth capturing. By the same token, a police department that is not a captive organization can exploit the resources for internal profit. In all cases, however, exploitation of these resources for personal gain is an inversion of the formal goals of the organization.

Differences in the extent of organizational resources suitable for corrupt exploitation help to explain why some police departments and not others become corrupt. Federal drug enforcement agents, for example, are constantly confronted with opportunities to make illicit money: bribes or thefts from drug pushers, for instance, and inaccurate accounting for the large sums of money advanced to agents for narcotics "buys." U.S. Secret Service agents, on the other hand, are rarely confronted with any opportunities for illicit gain from any sources. The tasks of the two federal agencies provide very different levels of resources for corruption. It is no surprise, then, that the two agencies with the same political environment should have very different histories of corruption—the former frequently corrupt,[15] the latter apparently uncorrupted.

Within law enforcement agencies, functional divisions of labor affect corruption opportunities. The Traffic Division is mainly limited to bribes from motorists, detectives tend to develop corrupt relations with professional

15. Interview with John Ingersoll, former Director, U.S. Bureau of Narcotics and Dangerous Drugs, November 8, 1975.

thieves, and patrol division corruption can be as diversified as the patrol task itself; even the records section may sell information to private detectives, or the crime reporting section may sell burglary location data to burglar alarm salesmen.

Geographic differences also affect organizational resources for corruption opportunities. A New York congressman once reported that some patrol officers working in midtown Manhattan asked him to have them transferred up to Harlem, where they could make more money—presumably from the higher density of vice operations Harlem offers as opportunities for police payoffs.

Community demands for police corruption are also a varying organizational resource for corruption. Merchants may encourage police to accept free meals and Christmas gifts; big banks and hotels may make regular payments for police presence at robbery-prone times (e.g., when the bank opens in the morning); and prominent citizens may patronize illegal establishments protected by police payoffs. Perhaps the ultimate expression of citizen desire for a corrupt police is the Denver businessman who burglarized his own premises as an insurance fraud, and then allowed the patrolmen who responded to the burglary call to steal anything they wanted from his store.[16]

Police corruption may change over time in relation to changes in law-violating behavior. Traffic-related corruption was unknown before the mass production of the automobile. Similarly, heroin-related corruption was informally forbidden, if not unheard of, in local police agencies until the phenomenal growth of the heroin industry in the late 1960s.[17] The time lag between New York and Central City in reports of extensive corruption in heroin enforcement is identical to the reported

16. Ralph Lee Smith, *The Tarnished Badge* (New York: Thomas Y. Crowell, 1965), pp. 221–223.

17. Jerome Skolnick, *Justice Without Trial* (New York: John Wiley, 1966), p. 208; and Peter Maas, *Serpico* (New York: Viking, 1973), p. 93.

lag between the coastal and interior cities in the spread
of heroin addiction: about five years, from 1968 in New
York to 1973 in Central City.[18] In both places, the old
police corruption morality of taking "clean" money
from gamblers but not "dirty" money from drug
pushers seemed to break down in the face of the far
greater sums the boom industry of heroin could offer to
corrupt police officers.

But the opportunities for corruption can contract just
as easily as they can expand. The assimilation of the
Chinese community in Oakland produced a declining
demand for organized ethnic gambling in the mid-
1950s, which in turn made gambling corruption that
much easier for the reform chief to control.[19] A decline
in one source of corruption may lead to an increased
reliance on another source; the Newburgh police
seemed to compensate for the loss of payoffs from a
local brothel (closed by the state police) by stealing
money from narcotics pushers more often. (These
examples cite "natural" changes in the police task environment. Planned changes in the task environment are
also possible. Chapter Five will review the use of
planned change in the task environment as an internal
organizational corruption control strategy.)

The New York City Police Department in 1970 probably had greater resources for corrupt exploitation
than any of the other three departments studied. The
scope of police authority encompassed more aspects of
city life than in the other cities, ranging from enforcement of a complex public health code to extensive
power over the construction industry. In addition, the
vice industry in New York was probably larger on a per
capita basis than in the other cities. The widespread
community practice of "tipping" in order to obtain special treatment in so many phases of business and gov-

18. James Q. Wilson, "The Return of Heroin," *Commentary*, April,
1975, pp. 46–50.
19. Interview with former Oakland Police Captain John Giudici,
May 1, 1975.

ernment regulation naturally extended to public practices of "tipping" the police.

At the same time, the New York City Police Department was relatively insulated from political control. A strong police union had defeated the mayor's attempt to establish a civilian-dominated board for reviewing public complaints about police misconduct, thus perpetuating the long tradition of New York City mayors having little control over the police. Even in the nineteenth-century heyday of "machine" rule from Tammany Hall, the New York police had managed to prevent politicians from capturing the department and its illicit revenues.[20] While the other three police departments studied also profited internally from corruption, only in New York was police corruption completely divorced from political control.

The concept of resources for corruption should not imply that all police officers will seize every opportunity for corruption that they confront. Individual officers vary greatly in the degree to which they seek out such opportunities, from the totally honest to the passive "grass-eaters" to the extortionist "meat-eaters."[21] Similarly, police departments vary greatly in the extent and nature of the corrupt practices in which their members engage. Much of that variation is accounted for by differences in the organizational resources for corruption opportunities, as well as by differences in political environment. Differences in corruption between two law enforcement agencies with similar exploitable resources and similar political environments can perhaps be accounted for by the central variable for this study: social control, both from outside and inside the agency. Police departments that do not become corrupt may be under tighter control than those that do. Police departments that do become corrupt may stay that way because they

20. Lincoln Steffens, *Autobiography* (New York: Harcourt, Brace, 1931), p. 248.
21. Knapp Commission Report (New York: George Braziller, 1972), p. 4.

are successful in preventing attempts to mobilize external control. Success in preventing control is highly dependent on the way in which corruption in corrupt police departments is socially organized.

Two kinds of social organization affect the vulnerability of corrupt police departments to social control. First, the social organization of police corruption *activities* in corrupt police departments (as well as in "honest" police departments) varies in ways that affect the accessibility of information about corruption to *internal* systems of control. Second, the social organization of corrupt police *departments* varies in ways that affect the availability of information about corruption to *external* systems of control. This section shows how the social organization of police corruption activities and of corrupt police departments affects the mobilization of social control. The next section shows how social control affects the social organization of police corruption.

The Social Organization of Police Corruption

Police corruption activities are socially organized in two basic forms, each of which has very different implications for the accessibility of information to proactive control. The two forms are *arrangements* and *events*. All corrupt acts are events, in the sense that something discrete happens: Citizen X gives money to Officer Y to avoid a speeding ticket. But some corrupt acts are more than discrete events, in that they are exact duplicates of previous and future interactions between the same individuals. Officer Y may take money from speeding motorists every day of his career, but it is unlikely in a large police department that he will take money from the same motorist twice. Captain Z of the vice squad, on the other hand, may take bribes from only ten people during his entire career, but those bribes will be paid to him by the same persons month after month. Officer Y's corruption is repetitive. Captain Z's corruption is duplicative.

Duplicative corruption events, taken as a whole, may be described as arrangements. Arrangements may be organized among several officers (e.g., a "pad"), or they may be solo ventures of one officer relating to one or more citizens. Other kinds of corrupt acts will be referred to here simply as events. Some corruption events may be repeated more often than others, but all events share the quality of being unique combinations of individuals. The acts which comprise a corruption arrangement are not unique, one-time combinations of individuals, and that is the major difference between events and arrangements in their vulnerability to detection by proactive social control systems.

The more predictable the occurrence of a deviant act, the more *vulnerable* it is to detection—if anyone should ever try to detect it.[22] Corruption arrangements are more predictable than corruption events, because the same people duplicate their interaction on a regular basis. Organized arrangements with many people participating are even more predictable than arrangements involving fewer people, because more people are involved in the duplicative routine, any one of whom can be subjected to surveillance or subversion. Either outside surveillance or an inside informer can predict when and where the next episode in an arrangement will take place. Predictions of this nature allow control agents to gather strong evidence by apprehending the participants in the act. Such predictions are not possible for corruption events, which occur whenever and wherever the opportunity arises. Arrangements are more vulnerable to control than events.[23]

Repetitive corruption events are more vulnerable to

22. Albert J. Reiss, Jr., "Discretionary Justice," in *Handbook of Criminology*, ed. Daniel Glaser (Chicago: Rand McNally, 1974), p. 683.

23. The upper echelons of a hierarchically organized arrangement, however, may be less vulnerable to detection than even those merely engaging in events. Hierarchical structures insulate those at the top from direct association with incriminating evidence. See, e.g., Stone, *Where the Law Ends*.

control than nonrepetitive events, again for reasons of predictability. Theft of money from arrested drunks occurred repetitively in the Oakland Police Department jail in 1959. The drunks were all different, but the location and the officers were always the same. Thus it was easy for the chief to have undercover actors arrested as drunks to see if their money would be taken (it was). Moreover, the fewer the duplicative aspects of events, the less vulnerable they are to detection. Thefts of money and heroin from drug pushers take place at different locations as well as with different pushers. With only one duplicative link—the corrupt officer—to the repeated but unique events, the predictability of narcotics "scores" and therefore their vulnerability to control is much less than that for rolling drunks at the jail, in which both the location and the officers are duplicated.

Arrangements and events differ only in their vulnerability to *premonitory* control: detection methods which intercept the deviance as it occurs.[24] They are both equally susceptible to *postmonitory* control: the gathering of evidence after the fact in order to prove that the violation occurred and to connect the violation with the violator. Participants in either arrangements or events may be equally likely to testify about the past crimes of others in exchange for a reduced sentence when they themselves are caught. If anything, an event is more likely to be reported than an arrangement, because arrangements are more often consensual and events more often create a victim role; victims seem more likely to complain than consensual participants. Corrupt police officers are generally shrewd in their choice of victims, however, seeking those with social stigma (drunks, pushers, prostitutes) whose credibility in any formal accusation is limited.[25] The probability that victims of police corruption events will be unable to mobilize social control compensates for their greater

24. See p. 20.
25. Nicholas Pileggi and Mike Pearl, "What Happens When Cops Get Caught," *New York Magazine*, July 23, 1973, pp. 23–29.

likelihood to try to do so. Thus arrangements and events are roughly equal in their vulnerability to post-monitory control.

A corrupt police department does not generally employ premonitory control methods to detect police corruption. By definition, such departments approve of corruption and do not seek to punish it, except in excessive instances that threaten to draw public attention to police corruption in general. Outside agencies, such as federal and local prosecutors, do not usually employ premonitory methods to detect police corruption either. In the absence of either external or internal premonitory control, corruption arrangements are free to flourish regardless of their greater vulnerability to premonitory control. Unless an outside agency initiates an investigation of a corrupt police department, the social organization of police corruption makes no difference in the probability of external control being mobilized. The social organization of police corruption does have important implications for the success of internal control strategies adopted after a scandal by an honest dominant coalition. But it is the social organization of the corrupt police department itself that determines the vulnerability of the department to the mobilization of external control. Because external control is in most cases reactive to information about police corruption, the safety of a corrupt police department from external control depends upon its organization for internal control of information.

The Social Organization of Corrupt Police Departments
Corrupt police departments are socially organized in relation to a number of informal rules regarding police corruption. The purpose of the rules is to minimize the chances of external control being mobilized against the department. Rules about dividing the money gathered by corruption minimize friction and the threat of a disgruntled participant mobilizing external control. Rules about how to obtain the money reduce the threat of

outside observation of corrupt activity. Most important for the public interest are rules about the limits of corruption. The intention of such rules is to keep corruption at a "reasonable" level in order to avoid attracting attention. Similar "limits" have been found among longshoremen, waiters, and other occupations in which employees regularly steal from their employers.[26] A consequence of the rules is that there may be less dollar-volume of corruption than there would be without the rules.

One weakness in the rules governing organized corruption is that it is often unclear to whom the rules apply. It is very rare that an entire police department will actively participate in the same, or any, corruption arrangements. Even politically directed police corruption relies primarily on the legitimate, formal police department hierarchy to implement its corrupt nonenforcement policies, rather than relying on payoffs to all officers whose discretion must be controlled. Those officers who do not participate financially in the corruption generally commit no crime, so the financial participants in the arrangements have no strong hold over them. In order to create complicity, the corruption participants will often try to entangle the nonparticipants in some kind of formal rule-violation which can be used against the nonparticipants if they should ever threaten to invoke control against corruption. Sex on duty with a prostitute was a method commonly used in Central City, but Christmas "gifts" from protected businesses can serve this purpose equally well.

In most police departments, but especially in corrupt police departments, the cardinal rule for all members is silence.[27] Many or most of the officers may have no direct knowledge of how corruption arrangements

26. Gerald Mars, "Dock Pilferage: A Case Study in Occupational Theft," in *Deviance and Social Control*, ed. Paul Rock and Mary McIntosh (London: Tavistock, 1974).

27. See, e.g., William A. Westley, *Violence and the Police* (Cambridge, Mass.: M.I.T. Press, 1970), pp. 111–118.

work, or who gets paid what, where, or why. But their general knowledge of police enforcement policy and incidents to which they have access as officers is potentially threatening and must be controlled. Officers are socialized into never cooperating with investigations of their colleagues. Whether or not he participates financially in corruption activities, an officer's adherence to the "blue curtain of secrecy" rule puts him squarely within the corruption "system": the members of the organization who comply with the deviant goal.

At the fringes of the system are two classes of deviants from the (societally deviant) norms of the "system," as depicted in Figure 1. Both classes consist of loners who are outside the system. One is an honest, zealot fringe. The other is an unusually corrupt, evil fringe. Both pose grave threats to a corruption system, but it is the evil fringe to which the system reacts most aggressively. The evil fringe consists of officers who commit free-lance acts of corruption beyond the system's approved limits, thereby threatening to draw attention to corruption throughout the department. The zealot fringe merely insists on adhering to the legal norms for the department, but in pursuing impartial enforcement of all the laws the zealots may become martyrs, punished by their superiors. It is the zealot fringe which often does the most to mobilize external control, as they did in Central City and New York.[28]

Central City, with all its history of politically organized corruption arrangements, was always quite hard

28. Mobilization of external social control is becoming such a frequent phenomenon in the federal government that steps are being taken to protect the mobilizers with U.S. Civil Service Commission safeguards from reprisal. See *New York Times*, June 26, 1977, p. 38. See also Charles Peters and Taylor Branch, *Blowing the Whistle* (New York: Praeger, 1972); Helen Dudar, "The Price of Blowing the Whistle," *New York Times Magazine*, Oct. 30, 1977, pp. 41–54; "Federal Waste Tied to Aides' Fear of Speaking Out," *New York Times*, Dec. 6, 1977, p. 13; Lawrence W. Sherman, "The Breakdown of the Police Code of Silence," *Criminal Law Bulletin*, Mar.–Apr. 1978, pp. 149–153.

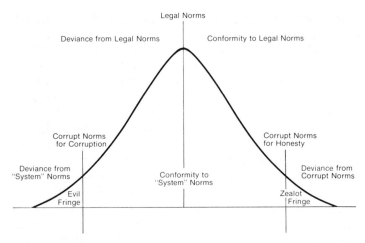

Figure 1 Deviance and Conformity in Corrupt Police Departments*

on the evil fringe. As far back as 1967, when the other
political party was in power, a special internal investigating team was formed to investigate a police officer who
was running a stolen-car ring. The leader of that successful investigation went on to become chief when
party control shifted in 1968. As chief he did not create
an Internal Affairs Division to investigate public complaints against police officers, but he did use his intelligence unit to investigate tips he received about the evil
fringe. The crimes committed by that fringe were not
necessarily more serious than any approved by the system. For example, it is rumored that narcotics dealing
by police officers was approved by the system. But the
fringe crimes did tend to attract more attention, particularly that of federal investigators. By controlling these
more visible crimes, the pre-scandal chief thwarted sustained public attention on the issue of police corruption.
    The zealots in Central City offer a different story.
Primarily younger officers, all had suspicions of sys-
temic corruption, though none had direct knowledge.
The traditional role for honest officers in such depart-

*This figure is adapted from Leslie Wilkins, *Social Deviance* (London: Tavistock, 1965), p. 46.

ments had been to suffer in silence on a lonely beat or to seek out a position in a corruption-free unit such as the police academy. But the new breed of zealots in Central City chose to confront the system by arresting criminals who had paid the system for immunity from arrest. When one officer, for example, could get no approval for his arrest of a bootlegger, he went to federal Treasury agents for help (and in the process, tape-recorded the bootlegger claiming that he paid the chief and his deputies on a regular basis). When the bootlegger was arrested by the Treasury agents, the chief immediately had the young officer interrogated, held incommunicado for twenty-four hours, and transferred to another job.

In an accelerating spiral of deviancy amplification,[29] this zealot and others like him only caused more trouble, not less. They were punished by the system with harassment from supervisors and charges of petty infractions. These punishments for a righteous cause transformed the self-definition of the zealots into martyrs. The claims of the police department on their loyalty were weakened by the extent to which they defined the department as a deviant organization. Once these claims were neutralized, once it became clear that social control of police corruption could not be mobilized within the police department, it was almost inevitable that they should try to mobilize other forms of social control. For as one form of social control breaks down or becomes ineffective, it is generally true that substitutes will be sought out.[30]

Police zealots do not usually seek to mobilize *legal* control systems. In New York in 1970, in Central City in 1972, in Cincinnati in 1975, and in many other cities,

29. Leslie Wilkins, *Social Deviance* (London: Tavistock, 1965), pp. 88–95.
30. This is a more general formulation of the proposition that law is invoked as other systems of social control become ineffective. See Donald J. Black, "The Boundaries of Legal Sociology," *Yale Law Journal*, Vol. 81 (May 1972), pp. 1086–1100.

zealots have mobilized the news media against police corruption. Much of the power of the media lies in its ability to mobilize legal action, but its power to label organizations as deviant is almost independent of legal responses to news reports. The decision of the news media to disseminate information provided by zealots is a crucial part of the process of making a scandal, and will be considered in the next chapter.

The foregoing discussion recites the failures of two different kinds of social control. One is the long-standing failure of social control *over* corrupt police departments, the failure that led the zealots to take action. The other is the breakdown of social control *within* corrupt departments—that is, the corrupt dominant co-alition's control of the loners. Control over the evil fringe is relatively easy, because such externally legiti-mate forms of social control as arrest and dismissal can be used. But there are no externally legitimate means for excising the zealot fringe. If corrupt police depart-ments cannot maintain internal cohesion and com-pliance with their deviant goals, or if they cannot at least "cool out" the complaints of their zealots,[31] then they are vulnerable to the mobilization of external social con-trol.

The mobilization of scandal against the New York and Central City police departments resulted from internal failure to control the zealots. Police officers in both those cities provided the information about cor-ruption that led to the mobilization of external control. In Oakland and Newburgh, the mobilization of scandal resulted from internal failure to control the evil fringe, whose excessive corruption attracted outside attention. Indeed, in Newburgh the evil fringe was led by the chief of police himself. Obviously, the distribution depicted in Figure 1 varies widely from one department to another, and within departments over time. The greater the proportion of organizational members found in either

31. Erving Goffman, "On Cooling the Mark Out: Some Aspects of Adaption to Failure," *Psychiatry*, November 1952, pp. 45–63.

fringe of the distribution, the greater the probability may be of external control being mobilized.

In all four cases studied here, the mobilization of external control was fueled by conflict over organizational goals. In the cases of New York and Central City, the conflict was initially internal, and organizational members employed external social control as a weapon in their struggle to have the organization comply with its own legal goals. In the cases of Oakland and Newburgh, the conflict over goals was external; outside actors interested in the character of the police department employed social control to compel the department to conform to legal norms. And in all four cases, the conflict was won by those supporting legal goals. A new dominant coalition attempted in each instance to have the department comply with legal norms. The methods of seeking compliance included changing the nature of internal social control. In order to predict the consequences of both external and internal control of corrupt police departments, the effects of social control on the social organization of police corruption must be considered.

EFFECTS OF SOCIAL CONTROL ON THE ORGANIZATION OF POLICE CORRUPTION

The impact of social control upon deviant behavior can be analyzed in at least three different ways. One approach is to count the number of deviant acts occurring before and after the mobilization of social control. If the deterrence hypothesis is correct, then deviant acts will become less frequent after punishment occurs. If the secondary deviation hypothesis is correct, then deviant acts will become more frequent after punishment occurs. A similar approach is to examine the seriousness of deviant behavior before and after punishment. However measured, seriousness would be predicted to decrease or increase after punishment, according to the deterrence and secondary deviation hypotheses respectively.

A third approach to analyzing the consequences of social control is to measure the organization of deviant behavior.[32] Like the frequency and seriousness of deviant behavior, the social organization of deviance is a quantitative variable, something that there is more or less of at different times and in different places. Under the deterrence hypothesis, the quantity of organization in deviant behavior would decline after punishment. Under the secondary deviance hypothesis, the quantity of organization would increase after punishment. Because indicators of organization are the most accessible to research on highly secretive deviance, it is this approach to analyzing the consequences of social control that is most feasible to employ in research on corrupt police departments.

Organization is defined as cooperation among individuals, or the capacity for collective action.[33] It is measured by the quantity of collective action present in any group of people. Some groups act more collectively than others, and are therefore more organized. Similarly, some groups act more collectively at certain times than at others, and their quantity of organization therefore changes over time.[34] Corrupt police officers and the citizens participating in police corruption are more organized in some police departments than in others. The quantity of organization in police corruption also changes within police departments over time.

The quantity of organization in police corruption can be measured by several indicators of cooperation in police corruption behavior. Police corruption that occurs voluntarily between both police and citizens, for

32. I am indebted to Albert J. Reiss, Jr., for this suggestion.

33. Donald Black, *The Behavior of Law* (New York: Academic Press, 1976), p. 85. See also the earlier work in this vein cited by Black.

34. North American Indian tribes, for example, become more organized during wars and hunts. See, e.g., Robert H. Lowie, "Some Aspects of Political Organization among the American Aborigines," *Journal of the Royal Anthropological Institute of Great Britain and Ireland*, Vol. 78 (1948), pp. 11–24, cited in Black, *The Behavior of Law*, p. 88.

example, is more cooperative than police corruption in which citizens are coerced into participation or victimized. Police corruption in which two or more officers act jointly is more cooperative than police corruption in which a single police officer acts alone. Police corruption arrangements are more cooperative than police corruption events, because arrangements are cooperative undertakings extending over longer periods of time than events. The relative frequency in a given period of time of voluntary versus coerced corruption, joint versus lone corruption, or arrangements versus events is an indication of the overall quantity of organization in police corruption during that period of time.

The quantity of organization present in police corruption activities has two important consequences. One consequence is the relative profitability of corrupt activities. The other consequence is the relative vulnerability of corruption to detection by premonitory control methods. Organization is a weapon for the accomplishment of any goal.[35] The more organization, the more it is generally possible to accomplish. A regular, dependable income from corruption is not possible for either police officers or corrupt politicians controlling police departments without a substantial amount of organization. Cooperative action among police and citizens participating in corruption makes possible, for example, the operation of a gambling "joint" in a specific location without the financially disruptive interference of police raids and arrests.[36] If there is not enough cooperation within the police department to guarantee that a gambling location will be free from police interference, then the gambling operators will be less likely to pay any money or as much money to any police officers. And if

35. Philip Selznick, *The Organizational Weapon* (New York: McGraw-Hill, 1960).
36. Jonathan Rubinstein, "Gambling Enforcement and Police Corruption" (paper prepared for the Commission on the Review of the National Policy Toward Gambling).

there is not enough voluntary cooperation on the part of the gambling operators to make regular payments even for total immunity from arrest, then the gambling operators may try to elude police harassment by frequently changing their locations; and such changes will probably reduce the gambling operators' revenues. A high level of cooperation in police corruption by all participants often makes possible the most profitable situation for all concerned.

At the same time, the more organized police corruption is, the more vulnerable it is to premonitory control. Organization makes police corruption more predictable, and predictable actions are more easily observed and intercepted as they occur. Evidence obtained by control agents while a crime is occurring is generally more likely to lead to a criminal conviction than evidence obtained after the crime has occurred. Police officers investigating corruption are more credible witnesses than the kind of citizens who are usually in a position to testify about police corruption. A police officer's testimony that he observed a prostitute give money to another police officer is usually more convincing to a jury than a prostitute's testimony that she gave money to a police officer. If the payment was a one-time event, then it would have been difficult for police corruption investigators to have been present at the scene of the payment. But if the payment was part of an organized arrangement, then it was predictable enough for corruption investigators to have planned to be present at the scene.

The quantity of organization present in police corruption is thus a two-edged sword. On the one hand, more organization makes possible more profitable kinds of corruption. On the other hand, more organization creates more vulnerability to premonitory control. Presumably, the costs and benefits of organization are evident to the participants in police corruption, and their assessment of both factors determines the quantity of organization present in corruption activities. The deterrence hypothesis predicts that a calculation that the risks of corruption outweigh its potential gains will produce a lower level of organization in corruption activities. The secondary deviation hypothesis predicts that such calculations are irrelevant, and that the quantity of organization present in corruption will increase if the police department is labeled deviant. Since the dominant coalition of all four police departments studied was changed by the scandal, however, the secondary deviation hypothesis would seem to be inappropriate for predicting the level of organization in police corruption after the scandal. Once an honest dominant coalition takes over a police department, the deviant actor in question is no longer the police organization, but rather the individual police officers and citizens participating in corruption. The level of analysis shifts from a single organization to a large population of individuals, and the general deterrence hypothesis is therefore more appropriate.

The general deterrence hypothesis predicts the consequences of both external and internal control. The central element of both forms of social control is threat: the threat implied to all by the punishment of a few, or by the implied capacity to detect and punish all. Scandal punishes the police department as an organization and removes its deviant leadership. But scandal also implies the possibility of premonitory investigation of all ongoing police corruption. Thus the threat of premonitory control implied by scandal may be sufficient to produce a decline in the level of organization in police corruption, at least in the short run after scandal. Until the "heat is off," all organized forms of corruption may be put in abeyance, although less organized (and therefore less vulnerable) forms of corruption may persist. In addition to punishing the corrupt police department as a deviant actor, scandal may also deter police corruption among the individual actors participating in it.

In the long run after a scandal, the most important deterrent may be the internal systems of social control of corruption within police departments. The crucial variable is the *methods* of control used by internal control systems. Highly organized corruption is only vulnerable to detection by premonitory methods of control. Post-monitory methods of control are ill-suited for detecting organized corruption, precisely because organized corruption, by definition, is cooperative. Cooperative actors are far less likely to try to mobilize postmonitory control against each other. Postmonitory control is more suited to detecting less organized forms of corruption, particularly when a victim is created by a corrupt act, a victim who will try to mobilize control. Even then, however, the inferiority of the evidence produced by postmonitory methods makes postmonitory control less effective at punishing less organized corruption than premonitory control is at punishing more organized corruption. Given the relationship between the organization of police corruption and its vulnerability to control, it is reasonable to predict that only premonitory methods of control can produce a long-term decline in the quantity of organization in police corruption.

In summary, there seems to be a reasonable theoretical basis for two propositions about the consequences of social control for the organization of corruption. One is that the quantity of organization in corruption will always decline in the short run after a scandal, regardless of the methods used by internal control systems. The other is that the quantity of organization in police corruption activities will stay at a low level in the long run after scandal only if there is an internal system of social control using premonitory methods. Put another way, the second proposition holds that the quantity of organization will return to its pre-scandal level—even if the department's leadership remains honest—if merely postmonitory methods of internal control are employed. And if that occurs, then the department will once more be vulnerable to external social control: the mobilization of scandal.

Part II

Social Control

3. The Mobilization of Scandal

Police corruption in all four cities had existed for many years before the scandals occurred. Why, then, did the scandals happen when they did, and not earlier? One general answer is that scandals are "accidents": freak coincidences resulting in the public exposure of secret deviant behavior. A night watchman's unexpected diligence, for example, is often given credit for starting the Watergate scandal. But on closer examination, the making of almost any scandal seems to be far more deliberate than accidental. Scandals do not just happen; they are socially constructed phenomena involving the cooperation and conflict of many people.

This chapter analyzes the mobilization of scandal over the four corrupt police departments.[1] It shows why the scandals happened when they did and why they were a successful form of mobilizing external social control. The chapter begins by considering the general characteristics of scandal that distinguish it from other forms of social control. The structure of the four police corruption scandals is then described in terms of the principal stages of development and roles played in the making of scandal. Finally, the developmental process of the scandals is examined by identifying the conditions associated with scandal moving from one stage to another, especially to the final stage of the police department being labeled a deviant organization.

1. An earlier version of this chapter was presented at the Annual Meeting of the American Sociological Association, Chicago, 1977.

SCANDAL AS SOCIAL CONTROL

Dictionaries and colloquial usage define "scandal" in two very different ways. According to one definition, scandal *is* deviant behavior. According to the other definition, scandal is a social *reaction* to deviant behavior, a reaction of disapproval and outrage. The first definition is used, for example, when reporters are described as "uncovering" or "revealing" a scandal. The second definition is used, for example, when an official is said to have resigned under the pressure of a scandal. The ambiguity of a term that means both crime and punishment must be resolved for purposes of analysis. This study adopts the second definition, using "scandal" to refer only to public *reactions* to disclosures of police corruption, and not to police corruption itself.

The definition of scandal as a negative public reaction to deviance is more useful for this study because such reactions can constitute social control: a punitive sanction designed to deter future deviance. Not all deviance, however, is scandalous. Neither are all scandals punitive. Certain conditions seem to be required in order for police corruption to be scandalous and for police corruption scandals to be punitive.

Conditions of Scandalous Deviance

Scandal differs from other social reactions to deviant behavior in three important respects. First, the social reaction that constitutes scandal is one of intense outrage and anger, rather than of mere disapproval.[2] Second, the deviance that is subjected to a scandalized social reaction is usually a surprise to the group reacting to the deviance, something that is not part of their assumptions about what is normally likely to occur. A third characteristic of scandal is perhaps most important in differentiating it from all other forms of social control.

2. Arnold A. Rogow and Harold Lasswell, *Power, Corruption, and Rectitude* (Englewood Cliffs, N.J.: Prentice Hall, 1963), p. 74. See also John A. Gardiner, *The Politics of Corruption* (New York: Russell Sage Foundation, 1970).

Scandal is generally a social reaction to deviance committed by an occupant of a role invested with social *trust*.[3] The socially trusted role of the deviant explains both the intensity of the disapproval and the surprise that the deviance could ever occur. For a trusted actor to break important rules is a "breach of faith," a betrayal of trust that those investing the trust expected not to occur. Violations of *personal* trust occur with predictable frequency in our society. Spouses commit adultery, bank tellers embezzle, and children lie to their parents. When these violations of personal trust are discovered, the reaction of those who had invested the trust in the trust violators is similar to that of a scandal: outrage, surprise, and a feeling of betrayal. Spouses, bank supervisors, and parents may all display a scandalized reaction as individuals to violations of their personal trust in other individuals. At the societal level, however, such personal trust violations are not surprising, nor do they produce social reactions of outrage and feelings of betrayal. Personal trust violations are not scandalous, precisely because the nature of the trust violated was personal, not social. Scandal is a social reaction to a violation of socially invested trust in an institution or role.

Societies seem to invest more trust in those roles and institutions closer to the center of the society.[4] Such central institutions as a society's law, government, and religion symbolize the identity of the society itself. Deviance in these central positions suggests something negative about the entire society, something the society may be unwilling to accept. It suggests that the society itself is deviant from its own standards of conduct. The unac-

3. See Albert J. Reiss, Jr.'s discussion of fiducial roles in the Foreword to Antony Simpson's *The Literature of Police Corruption: Volume 1. A Guide to Bibliography and Theory* (New York: The John Jay Press, 1977).

4. See Edward Shils, *Center and Periphery* (Chicago: University of Chicago Press, 1975); and Jack D. Douglas, "A Sociological Theory of Official Deviance and Public Concerns with Official Deviance," in *Official Deviance*, ed. Jack D. Douglas and John M. Johnson (Philadelphia: Lippincott, 1977), pp. 395–410.

ceptability of this suggestion may be the source of the social outrage that is scandal.

Collectivities, of course, may differ in their standards of conduct. In American society, there is substantial variation across different regions, states, and cities in the "real" standards of conduct that the collectivities hold for their own behavior, often regardless of what the relevant laws establish as appropriate standards.[5] These standards apply by implication to those roles and institutions at the center of the collectivities. And just as they differ across communities at the same point in time, these standards of conduct may differ within communities at different points in time. Behavior is not inherently scandalous. Scandalous behavior is that which a collectivity so labels. What is scandalous in New York may not be so in Chicago. What is scandalous one year may not have been scandalous the year before.

As representatives of the law, a central symbol of society itself, the police arguably occupy a central place in the collectivities they serve. Unlike such public officials as judges and legislators, however, the police occupy their position of trust as an organization rather than as individuals. The deviance of one lone judge has often caused a scandal, but the deviance of one police officer generally produces little social reaction in any but the smallest communities. Police corruption per se is generally not scandalous, because it is merely an individual form of deviance by those whom the collectivity does not invest trust in as individuals. A corrupt police department, however, *is* scandalous, because the collectivity does invest trust in the police department as an organization.

In order to be labeled corrupt, of course, a police department must be shown to be in violation of its collectivity's standards of conduct. This is a problem of both evidence and definition. The problem of evidence centers on the status of those who charge a police de-

5. Daniel Elazar, *American Federalism: A View from the States* (New York: Thomas Y. Crowell, 1972).

partment with being corrupt, as well as on the extent of
the evidence offered. The problem of definition is more
difficult, because collective standards of conduct are
often unclear or unarticulated. The attempt to make a
scandal over police corruption is often a process of
defining exactly what a collectivity's standards of conduct are. Indeed, the making of scandal may even
change the standards of conduct, as the currently frequent references to a "post-Watergate morality" suggest. Attempts to make a scandal produce not only a
conflict over whether the rules have been broken, but
they may also produce a conflict over what the rules
should be.[6] In a community that has never objected to
police being paid not to arrest prostitutes, a scandal over
such corruption may create a new standard against
police collusion with prostitutes, as well as demonstrating that the police organization is deviant in relation to
an ex post facto application of the new standard.

The most difficult condition to achieve for making
police corruption scandalous may be the interpretation
of police corruption as organizational rather than individual behavior. In the four cities studied, this condition
was satisfied by the discovery of evidence that the police
department had failed to police itself properly. When
presented with evidence or allegations that police officers had committed corrupt acts, either as individuals or
as part of an organized arrangement, superior officers
in all four police departments failed to investigate the
charges thoroughly enough to satisfy the public. A central aspect of the social trust invested in the police as an
organization is that no social resources are routinely allocated to check on police behavior externally. Police
departments are trusted organizationally to control the
conduct of their members. Failures of internal control

---

6. In the scandal over the financial affairs of President Carter's
first Budget Director, Bert Lance, for example, the norm that a
Budget Director should not have his personal debt service tied to the
prime interest rate was proposed for the first time. See, generally,
New York Times, August 15–October 1, 1977.

are betrayals of that trust.[7] If the organization does not show any interest in controlling its members' deviance, then the organization itself appears to be corrupt.

Conditions of Punitive Scandals

Attempts to make a scandal over deviance, like other ways of attempting to punish deviance, do not always succeed. In order for a scandal to be punitive, it must succeed in creating a collective definition of the deviance as scandalous. To be punished by scandal, deviance must not only satisfy the conditions of being scandalous, it must also be subjected to widely shared agreement that the conditions have been satisfied.

Scandal is a public act of labeling an actor's identity, a ceremony of status degradation. The label that scandal attempts to apply to its subject is a new identity, a morally inferior status unworthy of trust. The new identity is applied by an unmasking of the old identity, a revelation that the deviant's identity has not been what he claimed it to be, but has really been deviant all along.[8] Rather than saying the deviant is *now* unworthy of trust, the scandal shows how the deviant has in fact not been worthy of trust for some time. A scandal over police corruption is an attempt to show that the police department has long been breaking rather than enforcing laws, creating crime rather than controlling it.

A scandal is punitive when the new identity is successfully applied, when the label of deviant is made to "stick." The label sticks in the sense that people generally respond to the deviant in terms of the label. The more people respond to the deviant in terms of the label, the more punitive the label is. The degree to which scandal stigmatizes its subjects depends on the

7. I am indebted to Dr. Jack Katz for both the notions of failure of self-regulation as a condition of scandal, and the division of labor in the making of scandal.

8. Harold Garfinkel, "Conditions of Successful Degradation Ceremonies," *American Journal of Sociology*, Vol. 61 (March 1956), pp. 420–424.

degree to which the stigma is behaviorally applied to the subjects by other people. The behavioral application need not always be focused directly on the subjects of scandal; families of the subjects may also be the targets of the stigma. At the height of the Knapp Commission hearings in New York, for example, the police commissioner was told that many police officers were keeping their children home from school because of the ridicule they received from fellow students—jokes and taunts about the dishonest occupation of their fathers.[9] Similarly, wives of the subjects of scandal have committed suicide in response to the stigma applied to them.[10] Yet many of the business executives convicted of crimes related to the Watergate scandal or the subsequent wave of scandal over corporate bribery abroad have apparently retired without stigma, living comfortably in terms of their social relations as well as material comforts.[11] For those who have resources to avoid people who would treat them as stigmatized, stigma can be avoided almost entirely.

Scandals come in different sizes. There are several senses in which the size of a scandal varies, but perhaps the most consequential is the variation in the number of people who acknowledge the stigma directed by scandal at its subjects. A little scandal, in this sense, is one that creates very little stigma, one that results in very few people acting as if the subject of scandal had been labeled deviant. A big scandal is one that produces a

9. Kennedy School of Government, *The Knapp Commission and Patrick V. Murphy (B)* (Cambridge, Mass.: Harvard University, mimeo, 1977).

10. See, e.g., "Rep. Young's Wife is Apparent Suicide: Mother of 5 Found Shot to Death—Texas Lawmaker Was Linked to Sex Scandal by Secretary," *New York Times*, Friday, July 15, 1977.

11. As another example, see the description of the Netherlands' Prince Bernhard's life a year after he was forced to resign from numerous high posts because of the collective outrage at his having taken bribes from the Lockheed Corporation. See "Bernhard, a Year after Disgrace over Lockheed, Shows No Scars," *New York Times*, July 5, 1977.

widely shared definition that its subject is deviant. A
little scandal, therefore, is hardly punitive at all, while a
big scandal is very punitive. All four police departments
studied here experienced a little scandal about two years
prior to the big scandal that led to reform. The little
scandals met all the conditions for creating a scandalized
reaction to disclosures of police corruption, with one
major exception: they all failed to demonstrate the organizational nature of the deviance. In some instances,
there were even allegations to the effect that corruption
was fostered by the organization. But merely claiming
that deviance exists is not sufficient for creating a big
scandal. Satisfying the conditions for deviance to be
scandalous and for scandals to be punitive depends not
only on the nature of the information about the deviance that is publicly disclosed, but also on the structure
and process of scandal as collective behavior.

THE STRUCTURE OF THE SCANDALS

The scandals over police corruption, both big and little, shared a common structure in relation to both the
stages of development and the key roles in the making
of scandal. The stages of development corresponded
closely to the division of labor, with one key role dominating each stage. The stages and the roles provide the
structure within which the process of scandal takes
place. The timing of each stage's appearance and the
recruitment of people to fill the roles seem to have an
important effect on the final outcome of the process of
scandal.

Revelation

The first stage of the scandals was the revelation of
facts showing that police corruption existed as an organizational form of deviance. The information revealed at this stage was new to the public record, exposing behavior that had generally been kept secret. The
revelations may have been no surprise to people knowl-

edgeable about police practices, including everyone from cab drivers to honest mayors. Some facts had even been alleged before in recent years. But as public fact, the revelations and their supporting documentation created a window in a wall of secrecy and suggested that there were even more facts to find.

The revealers were both internal and external to the police department. In New York and Central City, the decision to reveal corruption was a cooperative action by officers in the zealot fringe, four in New York and almost thirty in Central City. In Oakland and Newburgh, the decision to reveal corruption was made by victims of corrupt acts perpetrated by the evil fringe in those police departments. In Newburgh, the victim was a large corporation, Sears, Roebuck and Company. In Oakland, the victim revealing corruption was a lone individual, a local merchant widely known for his drinking habits.

New revelations were made after the initial ones in all four cases. Additional facts were often brought to light at strategic times in the conflict over whether the organization was deviant. The scandals varied in the extent to which subsequent revelations occurred. The revealer role in the subsequent revelations was usually filled by someone other than those who had made the initial revelations. But without the initial revelation, the scandal process would not have begun in the first place. The explanation of the initial revelation, then, is one of the most important problems in understanding the process of scandal.

Publication

Revealers do not usually have the resources to make their revelations known to the general public. Those in control of the news media do have the required resources, and it is their decisions that dominate the publication stage. It was not necessary in all four cities for revealers to go to the news media in order to have their revelations published for the view of the general public. In Newburgh, the victim revealing corruption went directly to the state police, whose investigation led to criminal indictments. The indictments were reported as news, and those reports were the first publication of the victim's revelations of police corruption. But in the other three cities, publication preceded any prosecution. Indeed, publication was often sought as a means of creating pressure for prosecution.

Publication decisions can theoretically be made by any mass communications medium, including radio and television as well as newspapers. Yet the three decisions to publish revelations that preceded prosecution were all made by newspapers, and not by the electronic media. In fact, only one police corruption exposé of which I am aware was "published" through the medium of television.[12] Whether the primary role of newspapers in this stage reflects the muckraking tradition of the print media or the bias of television news for more visual events, it is clear that the newspapers were the only medium to show much interest in the revealers' willingness to talk.

It is important to distinguish editorial decisions from decisions made by reporters. The revealers generally made contact with reporters, but it was the editors who decided whether the revelations would be made public. The reporters in two cases played a key role in pressing for publication, but the editorial decisions always dominated the publication stage. Editorial decisions, in turn, may have been constrained by the publishers' role in the community, relationships to political officials, and other factors. The editorial page's political positions were also a possible constraint upon the news editor's judgment. But whatever the constraints may have been, the decisions to publish revelations seem to have rested with the news editors. As in the case of the revelations them-

12. Television Station WHAS–TV in Louisville created a police corruption scandal in 1970–71. See Robert H. Williams, *Vice Squad* (New York: Thomas Y. Crowell, 1973), pp. 35–41.

selves, publication of revelations usually occurred more than once. After the first publication decision was made, however, the subsequent decisions to report revelations appear to have been fairly routine, subject to whatever standards of verification had been established for publishing police corruption stories.

Defense

The defense stage usually appeared immediately after the publication stage. The defenses of the police departments against attempts to label them corrupt followed various strategies, from denial of the charges to attacks upon the motives or reliability of the revealers. A less public form of defense was the attempt to prevent any more revelations, either by silencing the revealers (through physical violence in some cases) or by scaring any potential new revealers from joining in the revelations. A successful defense at this stage might have terminated the scandal, preventing further revelations and minimizing the stigma of the revelations already made.

The defender role can be filled publicly by almost anyone who has access to news media. The public figures who played the defender role varied on a continuum of personal interest to disinterest in the police department's reputation. The chief police executive, the police union president, and high police officials all played the defender role in at least one of the cities, but their close personal interest in the department was always clear. Mayors and prosecutors had somewhat less stake in the police departments' reputations, but enough so that their defense of the police could have appeared to have been self-interested. More disinterested actors playing the defender role were city council members and leaders of civic groups, although the political party affiliations of even these disinterested actors often affected the credibility of their defense. Like most of the stages of scandal, the defense stage usually appeared numerous times.

Dramatization

A dramatization is a public interpretation of the published revelations of police corruption as serious cause for public concern. No new information was introduced at this stage, but the already known facts were dramatized as evil. The known facts may have implied that the police department was organizationally corrupt, but the dramatizations explicitly interpreted the facts in this fashion. Dramatizations lend extra weight to revelations in labeling the police departments as deviants.

The dramatizer role was filled by the same kinds of people who filled the defender role, with the usual exception of police officials. Mayors, prosecutors, city council members, and civic group leaders each played the dramatizer role in at least one of the scandals.

Prosecution

The prosecution stage is the consideration by a prosecutor and grand jury of the evidence revealed by the scandal for possible criminal indictments and trial. The decision to prosecute or not, and how many charges to bring against how many people, was generally made by the local prosecutor himself; federal prosecutors were almost entirely uninvolved in the four scandals. The local grand jury's domination by the prosecutor even became an issue in the Central City scandal, but public criticism did not alter the prosecutor's complete power to decide whom to prosecute.

Prosecution decisions are, however, constrained both by the legal standards of evidence and by the prosecutor's political alliances. Prosecutors in Central City and Newburgh were members of the political elite dominating the police department. Such alliances made extensive prosecution of police corruption seem unlikely, but they did not prevent the prosecution of Newburgh police officers. The prosecutor there did resign halfway through the investigation, but he never attempted to block the prosecution of the cases developed by the state police. If he had, he might have been investigated himself. Moreover, there is a certain amount of political risk in failing to prosecute police corruption. The prosecutor in Central City who scorned the evidence of police corruption was defeated at the polls six months after the scandal, ending a twelve-year career.

In New York and Oakland, the prosecutors were not politically allied to the elected officials responsible for the police. They were, however, operationally allied to the police in the performance of their routine tasks—tasks vital to their own political survival. The prosecutor in Oakland was less dependent on the police for making big cases because he had his own staff of non-police investigators. But the five district attorneys in New York all relied heavily on police officers to conduct their investigative legwork. Both before and after the scandal, the claim was made that the district attorneys in New York would never be eager to prosecute police officers as long as they depended so greatly on police cooperation.[13] Even so, the district attorneys there did prosecute some cases developed from revelations made in the scandal.

Labeling

Attempts to label the police departments as corrupt and attempts to thwart the application of the label were made at every stage of the scandals. Labeling was the final stage of the scandals, the stage at which the label had been successfully applied. The key role in the labeling stage was one that had been important but passive in every prior stage: the audience. The audience for a police corruption scandal was the general community that each department served. Revelations were directed at that community, publications were read by it, defenders and dramatizers sought to persuade it, and prosecution occurred in its name. The labeling stage was the community's verdict, the judgment of the audience about the meaning of the morality play of scandal. If the

13. Knapp Commission Report, pp. 13–15.

labeling stage had not appeared, the implicit verdict would be not guilty: the police department is not a deviant organization. But since the audience generally seemed to agree that the police department was corrupt, the label was successfully applied. The organizations were stigmatized, and the scandals were punitive. Whether scandals over police corruption ever reach this final stage may depend on the process of scandal—that is, on the conditions affecting the transition of scandal from one stage to the next.

THE PROCESS OF THE SCANDALS

While the four scandals all had common stages of development, the exact order in which the stages appeared and reappeared varied from city to city. The recruitment of key public figures into the various roles also varied. Despite the differences, however, there did seem to be some general conditions common to the appearance of each stage of scandal, conditions that comprised the process by which the scandals developed from revelations to labeling.

Conditions of Revelation

The revelation stage of scandal is the one most often interpreted as accidental, explained as a "mistake" in the organizational strategies for controlling information about deviance. But in the four police corruption scandals studied here, the conditions of the appearance of the revelation stage were firmly rooted in the social organization of the corrupt police departments. All four disclosures can be linked to structural failures of internal control, failures associated with conflict over organizational goals. In Central City and New York, the failure of internal control lay in not controlling the zealot fringe. In Oakland and Newburgh, the failure of internal control lay in not keeping the "evil fringe" within safe limits. In all four cases, the failures of internal control were associated with either internal or external conflict over whether the police department should be corrupt.

The zealot fringe in both New York and Central City became alienated from the departments only after a four-year process of trying to work for change from within. In both cities, the alienation of the zealots may have been speeded up by the apparent increase in police corruption related to narcotics sales. But there was also a failure of the "system" in both cities to "cool out" the zealots' complaints. Instead of trying to pacify the zealots by, for example, assigning them to such corruption-free units as the police academy, the response of the two departments was to punish the zealots for making trouble. By rejecting the legal standards for police conduct that the zealots supported, the upper levels of the two departments made the zealots all the more dedicated to those standards, and all the less dedicated to the police departments' norms of silence.

The role of the newspaper reporters was important to the revelations occurring in New York and Central City, quite apart from the reporters' role in the publication stage. In New York, a *New York Times* police reporter had taken an interest in police corruption and had let his police contacts know that he would be interested in doing a story on any revelations police officers might make. The reporter was also gathering evidence from other sources, particularly those who paid bribes to police. One of the reporter's police contacts was a friend of Frank Serpico, the officer who had taken his complaints of corruption to numerous police officials without obtaining satisfaction. The reporter's interest served as a basis for the friend to persuade Serpico and two other officers to make revelations to the reporter. Whether the revealers would have sought out the reporter if he had not announced his interest is unclear.[14]

14. Peter Maas, *Serpico* (New York: Viking, 1973); and David Burnham, *The Role of the Media in Controlling Corruption* (New York: John Jay Press, 1976).

A team of investigative reporters in Central City played a similar role in seeking out the revealers. The revealers—twenty-eight of them at first, and more later on—were ready to talk, but they had not taken any initiative to do so. Some of the zealots' actions (such as the federal arrest of a police-protected bootlegger in 1972, initiated by a police zealot) had stimulated the reporters' interest in police corruption, so the revealers cannot be seen as entirely passive in making their revelations. Nor can internal conflict alone account for all of the initial revelations in Central City. Discussions of merging the city and county police departments had created friction between the two organizations since 1970, and since 1972 the county police had been raiding vice establishments corruptly protected by the city police. After the investigative reporters contacted the county police about city police corruption, the county police actively interrogated the prisoners of city police housed in the county jail. A number of revelations of police corruption came from the prisoners, who were allegedly promised more lenient sentences by the county police in exchange for information about police corruption, real or invented. But despite the reporters' initiative and the interest of the county police in having the city police labeled as deviant in order to discourage the merger, it is probably fair to say that the revelations of the city police zealots were the most crucial factor in mobilizing the scandal. Without the inside story of the zealots, the other revelations did not constitute evidence that the police department was organizationally corrupt.

The revelations in Oakland and Newburgh were initiated by victims of police corruption, but the police departments themselves made the victims' revelations almost inevitable. If the two departments had kept the evil fringe from engaging in forms of corruption that created victims who knew that the police were their victimizers, then there would have been no victims to make revelations. While it is true that the Newburgh police did not confront their burglary victims directly, the sheer frequency of the Newburgh police burglaries relative to the size of the city probably made it impossible for the victims not to discover the identity of the burglars. The Newburgh police did confront directly the narcotics dealers they shook down, but probably assumed that the criminal status of those victims would keep their accusations from being taken seriously. In the context of the respectable burglary victims' complaints, however, the testimony of the narcotics dealers was eventually taken quite seriously.

The "accident" that led to the initial revelation of police corruption in Newburgh was a result of the poor information control strategies characteristic of an evil fringe led by the chief himself. One of the several police burglaries at Sears had been camouflaged by a police radio broadcast that a "normal" break-in had occurred there. An officer uninvolved in the corrupt activities and working in a different part of town heard the radio message before going into a diner for supper. He commented to a friend that "they're really ripping off Sears." A Sears saleswoman overheard the remark and drove right over to the store, only to find police officers carrying out merchandise. She notified the Sears security force the next day. The security force asked the police chief for an investigation. When the chief did nothing, Sears mobilized a state police investigation of the burglary and then of the entire department.[15] Corrupt officers made revelations in exchange for leniency, and other victims of police corruption contributed further revelations. The implication of the chief in any one of the corrupt acts was sufficient evidence that the department was incapable of policing itself and organizationally in violation of its public trust.

Revelations of police corruption in Oakland were made several times in the early 1950s.[16] All of the pub-

15. Interview with Thomas Wohlrab, Deputy Commissioner, Newburgh Police Department, February 1, 1976.
16. *Oakland Tribune*, May 5, 1952; January 16, 1953; April 7, 1953; April 10, 1953; and March 12, 1954.

lished revelations, however, were met with at least a
token response by police managers showing some effort
to control police misconduct. But the revelation in 1955
of the police department's failure to investigate a brutal
extortion and kidnapping by police officers was the first
evidence suggesting that the Oakland Police Department was organizationally corrupt. The victim of the
corrupt acts by members of Oakland's evil fringe told
his experiences to several people, one of whom told a
reporter. Although the victim had been threatened
with violence by police if he did not keep his story quiet,
the victim did confirm the story to a reporter. The reporter then contacted the new city manager, who also
took on a revealer role, focusing the facts provided by
the victim.

The city manager called a press conference to an-
nounce the facts that the victim had revealed. In announcing the facts, he stressed the seriousness of the
failure to investigate the charges properly, rather than
just the seriousness of the charges themselves. The
manager chose that public occasion to reprimand the
police chief for not having notified the city manager's
office of the case.[17] In announcing his order that all
complaints of police misconduct be forwarded immediately to the city manager's office, the manager implied
that the police department was incapable of policing
itself. The victim may have revealed police corruption,
but it was the manager who revealed the evidence suggesting that the department was organizationally corrupt.

The manager's actions stemmed from a conflict over
organizational goals for the police department. An Oakland native, the new Oakland manager had been the
highly successful manager of nearby Richmond, keeping its shipyard-based economy from dying in the
changing national economic conditions after World War
II. When a long-term "caretaker" city manager in Oak-

17. *Oakland Tribune*, January 4, 1955.

land died, the new manager was hired to undertake an active approach to developing Oakland's own faltering economic base. What the city council may not have known when it hired the new manager was that he had plans to reform the police department, to make it more honest as well as more efficient. He could not undertake drastic changes without strong justification, however, so he waited for an opportunity to create a justification. The extortion case and its improper internal investigation gave the manager just the opportunity he was waiting for: evidence for labeling the police department as deviant and in need of reform.[18] In the conflict between his own goals for the police department and the existing goals of the dominant coalition of politicians and police officials, labeling the police department as deviant was a weapon the manager used to win the conflict.

Similar conflicts of goals seem to have fueled the revelations in the other cities. The Newburgh revelation stemmed from a conflict between Sears, Roebuck and the police department about the purpose of the police: preventing burglaries or committing them. The Central City and New York revelations stemmed from conflict within each department over the character of the police organization and the implications of that character for the identity of its individual members. Moreover, in all four cases, the conflict over goals widened after the initial revelations were made. More and more actors participated in the conflict, and their participation often came in the form of new revelations. The Knapp Commission in New York, for example, was not created until some time after the zealots made their revelations. But it was the revelations of the Knapp Commission, and not the revelations of the zealots, that ultimately provided the facts (as well as the dramatizations) that led to the final stage of successful labeling. In both the initial and the subsequent revelations, then, the central condition for the occurrence of the revelations seems to have been

18. Interview with Wayne Thompson, former city manager of Oakland, May 9, 1975.

conflict. The more intensive the conflict over police organizational goals, the more likely it seems that revelations will occur.

Conditions of Publication

Publication of the revelations of organizational police
corruption in Oakland, New York, and Central City was
linked in every case to some involvement of newspaper
personnel in the conflict over police department goals.
This involvement in the conflict began before the making or the publication of the revelations. The personnel
involved in the conflict ranged from a reporter in New
York to an editor in Central City to a publisher in Oakland. In each case, some participant in the internal
decision-making of the newspaper was predisposed to
see the police department labeled as corrupt in order to
have new police organizational goals adopted. No employee of a Newburgh paper seems to have been
involved in the conflict over police goals, and the publication stage appeared there purely as a result of the
prosecution stage. The Newburgh newspapers made no
independent decision to publish revelations of police
corruption unconnected to ongoing legal processing of
the revelations.

The involvement of the publisher of the *Oakland Tribune* in the conflict over police department goals was
sought out by the new city manager. The publisher had
a strong interest in the manager's program for economic development, and was one of the manager's
strongest behind-the-scenes supporters. He had committed himself to providing supportive press coverage
for any of the manager's efforts to revitalize the city.
When the manager joined in the mobilization of a scandal over police corruption, the *Tribune* supported the
effort with extensive press coverage. The manager
asked that *Tribune* reporters be assigned to play a revealer role, seeking out new facts about police corruption, and even about general administrative problems of
the police department. Stories as routine as friction be-

tween the patrol and detective branches of the police department were turned into front-page news. When there was nothing new to report, the facts that had been revealed already were restated as an overview story. The problems of the police department made headlines almost every day for three weeks. As the city manager later said, "If the story had gotten off the front pages, I never would have been able to change the police department."[19] When the story did slip off the front page in the second week of the scandal, the scandal was revitalized by a reporter's new revelation of corruption in the elite detective branch, additional evidence that the problem of corruption was organizational rather than individual.

The involvement of the managing editor of the major Central City newspaper in the conflict over police organizational goals was stimulated by the interests of four of his best reporters, and perhaps by the climate of investigative journalism created in the aftermath of the recent successes of *Washington Post* reporters Carl Bernstein and Bob Woodward in uncovering the Watergate story.[20] The publisher of the newspaper had been and remained a strong supporter of the mayor, but the newly hired managing editor was guaranteed a free hand in setting news policy. One of his first acts was to allow four reporters to undertake long-term investigations of major problems in the city, in order to produce more complete coverage of the problems than is possible on a day-to-day basis. Freeing the reporters from their normal assignments, the editor approved the team's request to work on police corruption, an area that the little scandal had made to look promising. When the initial inquiries began to show results, the managing editor allowed the team to work almost full-time on the police corruption story for over six months. By the conclusion of their investigation, the team had

19. Ibid.
20. See, e.g., Bob Woodward and Carl Bernstein, *All the President's Men* (New York: Simon and Schuster, 1974).

gathered enough information for a copyrighted series of front-page stories lasting almost two weeks. Followup stories and new revelations stimulated by the stories kept police corruption in the headlines for almost a year. Curiously, the editorial page took little notice of the stories, even though the stories themselves portrayed the department as thoroughly corrupt. The involvement in the conflict over police organizational goals appeared to be limited to the middle levels of the newspaper, and did not extend, as in Oakland, to the top of the news organization.

The involvement of the *New York Times* in the conflict over police organizational goals was located even further down in the hierarchy of the newspaper. The principal police reporter had decided on his own to look into police corruption after doing a series of stories on police "cooping" (sleeping on duty).[21] When he found the zealot police officers willing to make revelations, he arranged a meeting between his editors and the revealers. The editors were not enthusiastic about publishing the revelations. They told the reporter and the police revealers how delicate the subject was and that "there would be enormous difficulties in publishing such a story."[22] The revealers brought along a high middle-management police official to confirm their statements, without whose presence "nothing would have happened," according to the reporter. In the end, the editor approved the story but decided not to print it until a "hook to hang it on" developed. Only when the reporter seized the publication role was the story published: he dropped hints to a top aide in the mayor's office that a "blockbuster" story on police corruption was about to be published (which was untrue), and the mayor appointed an investigative committee in order to steal the thunder of the *Times* story. The zealots' revelations finally were published two days later, along with the additional information gathered by the reporter.

The decision to publish revelations of organizational

21. Burnham, *The Role of the Media in Controlling Corruption*.
22. Maas, *Serpico*, p. 255.

police corruption is more than a yes-or-no choice. Once
a decision is made to publish the story, a number of
additional decisions must be made. How much newspaper column space to devote to the story, where in the
newspaper to place the story, what tone to adopt,
whether to draw conclusions from the facts, and whether to run follow-up stories are all decisions that can have
major consequences for the outcome of the scandal process.[23] Each of those decisions may yield a greater or
lesser quantity of stigma applied to the police department. The more involved the newspaper was in the
conflict over police organizational goals, the more the
decisions seemed to be made in the direction of stigmatizing the police. Where the newspaper was least involved in the organizational goal conflict (New York),
the tone, conclusions, and follow-up stories were the
most restrained. Where the newspaper was involved in
the conflict at the highest level of management (Oakland), the tone and conclusions were the most negative,
and repetitious follow-up stories were the most
frequent.

The involvement of newspaper personnel in the conflict over police organizational goals may not be a necessary condition for publication of revelations of police
corruption. Other cases may be found in which there
was no interest in police corruption among newspaper
personnel until, for instance, zealots sought out the
newspaper as a means of publishing their revelations.
Merely judging from newspaper accounts, this may
have been the case in Cincinnati and Albany in recent
years.[24] But in Oakland, New York, and Central City,
research into the origins of the publication decisions
shows that a condition common to those decisions was
involvement by newspaper personnel in the conflict
over whether the police department should be corrupt.

23. See, generally, Leon Sigal, *Reporters and Officials* (Lexington,
Mass.: D. C. Heath and Co., 1973).
24. See, e.g., John J. McGlennon, "Bureaucratic Crisis and Executive Leadership: Corruption in Police Departments" (Ph.D. dissertation, Johns Hopkins University, 1977), pp. 133–155.

Conditions of Defense

Three of the four scandals included a public defense
of the police department against the early attempts to
label it corrupt, but each defense was short-lived. The
condition common to the three scandals in which a defense occurred was some vulnerability in the status of
the revealers.[25] In the fourth case, Newburgh, the un-
questioned legitimacy of the criminal indictments was
associated with almost no attempt to defend the department from the deviant label. When the Newburgh
chief was suspended from duty, a group called "Concerned Citizens for the Preservation of Law and Order"
was formed to organize a testimonial dinner on behalf
of the police department, with a planned attendance of
six hundred people. At that time, a straw poll conducted
by a local newspaper showed strong public support for
the police chief.[26] But after a patrolman testified in
court about one of the burglaries at Sears, public opinion changed radically and the conditions of defense
evaporated. The testimonial dinner was canceled, according to a spokesman, "for lack of people participation."[27] The legitimacy of the criminal process and the
invulnerability of Sears as a major revealer removed the
apparently necessary condition for a defense to be
made. Not even the police officers themselves, let alone
any other public figures, attempted to make a public
defense of the department against the deviant label.

The Oakland Police Department found it difficult to
make a defense against the label because one of the
primary revealers of the organizational corruption was
the department's superior, the city manager. The extortion victim was vulnerable to attack because he was a
known inebriate, but he had only revealed allegations of
individual police corruption. It was the city manager
who was responsible for pointing out the organization's
failure to police itself properly. The police chief re-

25. Albert J. Reiss, Jr., Lectures, Yale University, 1973.
26. *Newburgh Evening News*, January 25, 1972.
27. *Newburgh Evening News*, May 25, 1972.

mained silent, but the head of the detectives denied that any Oakland police officers could commit any criminal acts, implicitly claiming that the revealer was lying.[28] The strong role of the manager in the revelations seems to have kept any other public figures from defending the police from the deviant label.

In Central City, the active role of the young police zealots in revealing corruption seems to have favored a widely based defense of the police department against the deviant label. The defense began with the police chief claiming that the zealots were inventing their revelations because they were disgruntled by their failure to be promoted—an ironic charge, since one of the revelations was that promotions could only be obtained by paying the Republican Party several hundred dollars. Supporters of the police department on the city council also defended the department by attacking the motives of both the revealers and the newspaper. They claimed that the scandal was fabricated as a way of selling more newspapers.

The clearest attack on the status of the revealers was found in New York, where the incumbent police commissioner defended the department by labeling the sources of the revelations as "prostitutes, narcotics addicts and gamblers, and disgruntled policemen."[29] The *New York Times* responded by refuting the commissioner's claim that the revealers were of a socially or morally inferior status. An editorial note near the report of the commissioner's defense reported that no addicts or prostitutes had been interviewed for the story, but that architects, restaurant owners, contractors, social scientists, and police officers decorated for heroism had been the sources of the revelations.[30]

While the vulnerability of the revealers' status was a common condition for the appearance of a public defense, there were also other strategies for defending the

28. *Oakland Tribune*, January 15, 1955.
29. *New York Times*, April 29, 1970, p. 1.
30. Ibid., p. 1.

police departments. One of these strategies was to attack the legitimacy of the manner in which the revelations were made, irrespective of the truth of the revelations. This strategy was an indirect attack upon the status of the revealers, implying that their methods were deviant even if their motives were not. The Central City police officials and their public supporters attacked the propriety of making criminal allegations in the press instead of in the grand jury room. Even the mayor of Central City, who generally played a dramatizer rather than a defender role, announced that anyone who had information about police corruption should present it to a grand jury. Most revealers refused to do that because of their mistrust of the prosecutor in control of the grand jury, but the symbolic invocation of the criminal justice process as the proper way to make allegations probably hurt the credibility of the revealers' claims. In New York, the methods of the Knapp Commission were denounced as a "civil liberties disaster" by a civic group usually hostile to the police, the American Civil Liberties Union. The use of hidden microphones and double agents to gather evidence, as well as the presentation of accusations in public hearings where the accused had no opportunity to defend themselves were labeled by the civil libertarians as violations of due process.[31]

The most significant strategy for defending police departments from the deviant label was the denial of organizational deviance by the admission of individual deviance within the organization. Police officials and other defenders claimed that there are always a few rotten apples in a barrel, but that does not mean that the whole barrel is rotten. Those attempting to apply the label, of course, were claiming that the whole barrel was indeed rotten, and that the problem was organizational deviance rather than deviance by individual members of the organization. The less evidence of organizational deviance that is revealed, the more likely it may be that the "rotten apple" defense will be invoked. Even reform

31. *New York Times*, October 23, 1971, p. 21.

police executives invoked the rotten apple argument, but they generally did so after the department had already been successfully labeled as a deviant organization.

The public defense of the police departments in the three cities where it appeared failed to thwart the application of a deviant label. One key reason may have been that the defenders were for the most part closely allied to the interests of the departments they defended. Their lack of impartiality may have made their defenses unconvincing. Another reason for the failure may have been that the defenses seemed to disappear after the initial response to the publication of the revelations of organizational corruption. The continuing disclosures of organizational deviance made defenses increasingly more dangerous for the defenders' own reputations. (Where the disclosures of organizational deviance did not continue to grow, however, defenses became more frequent; a reform public safety director in Central City labeled the revelations of organizational deviance as "Mickey Mouse stuff" six months after their publication.) But perhaps the major reason for the failure of the public defenses was that the municipal executives, both mayors and managers, failed to take on a defender role. Where they have taken on that role in other cities, the defense has been successful in thwarting the deviant label.[32] That is not to say what is cause and what is effect; mayors may only defend police departments when they expect the defense will succeed. In Oakland, New York, and Central City, the municipal executives may have calculated their potential losses from defending the police as greater than their potential losses from not joining the attack on the police.

Defenses made by those too close to the control of the police department can backfire. A hasty denial of corruption charges without the appearance of a careful and thorough investigation can provide even more evidence

32. McGlennon, "Bureaucratic Crisis and Executive Leadership," pp. 139–144.

that the police department is not interested in policing itself. While the chief in Central City was busy denying the revelations, the mayor was busy forming an "elite" police squad to investigate the revelations under his own personal direction. In New York, the police commissioner's vigorous denials of the corruption charges led to the disbanding of an investigating committee of which he was a member, and the formation of the Knapp Commission, the group ultimately responsible for the labeling of the department as deviant.

The private defense from further revelations also failed in the three cities. The little scandals of earlier years in the three cities had been successfully terminated by control of information after the initial revelations, but the information control strategies failed to work during the big scandals. Perhaps because the conflict over goals was more intense, perhaps because the news media took more interest, or perhaps because the investigative strategies were different, revelations continued to be made in the three cities after the initial revelations. The new revelations often appeared at critically important points in the development of the scandal, keeping the momentum of labeling going by providing fuel for dramatizations. The failure of covert defenses against more information leakage may have done even more harm than the absence of a continuing vigorous public defense. And as the increasing evidence gave more credibility to the revealers, the conditions of defense and the defenses themselves both disappeared.

Conditions of Dramatization

The revelations of organizational police corruption in all four cities were dramatized by various public figures. The condition common to all four dramatizations, just as for the revelations, was conflict over the organizational goals of the police department. Some dramatizers even changed sides in the conflict, publicly attacking the corrupt character of the department after having previously ignored corruption. This was true, for example, of the mayors in New York and Central City, both of whom were aiming for higher elective office at the time the revelations were first published. Once the conflict came out into the open, the numerous political figures in each city had to decide which side they would choose in the conflict. Their choices seem to have been determined by their assessment of who would win the conflict.

The mayor of New York may have sought to dramatize or to postpone the corruption issue by creating an independent investigatory commission. Whatever his intention,[33] the result was the creation of the most successful dramatizer in any of the four cities. The Knapp Commission took its dramatizer role very seriously, defining it in those terms from the very outset. Its entire purpose was to show the audience of New York City that the police department was a corrupt organization.[34] The revelations it sought out and the televised public hearing format for presenting them were all calculated to apply the deviant label to the department. The commission employed its revelations strategically in order to make the most dramatic use of them. When, for example, a city official claimed that there was no organized corruption in the police department,[35] the Knapp Commission revealed the next day that its agents had observed a large group of police officers stealing $15,000 worth of meat from a warehouse in the early hours of the morning, while the agents made repeated but unsuccessful calls to the local precinct supervisors to have them investigate the police burglary in progress.[36] The revelation refuted the defense that corruption was merely individualized, and dramatized the unwillingness of the department to police itself.

33. The district attorney of New York County, Frank Hogan, later admitted that he had nominated the "wrong man" to the mayor to head the commission. *New York Times*, October 12, 1972, p. 1.
34. Kennedy School of Government, *The Knapp Commission and Patrick V. Murphy (B)*.
35. *New York Times*, February 9, 1977, p. 1.
36. *New York Times*, February 10, 1977, p. 1.

The Knapp Commission's dramatizations occurred in a community in which there had been intensive conflict over police organizational goals and conduct for a number of years. Police treatment of minority groups, police brutality, and police effectiveness in fighting crime had been major issues ever since the beginning of the then current mayoral administration in 1966. There was a large audience already receptive to the Knapp Commission's dramatizations, and the size of the audience grew after the dramatizations were made. In Oakland and Central City, however, the existing conflict over police organizational goals was quite limited. The city manager in Oakland and the zealot-revealers in Central City had to create a conflict out of an almost complete consensus that the police departments were not only adequate, but among the "finest in the country." In creating the conflict, they relied on existing support for the norms that the police had broken. The brutal nature of the extortion in Oakland and the connection of the Central City police with narcotics traffic may have been the keys to widening the conflict beyond its originators. While the communities may have been tolerant of some forms of police corruption, they were not tolerant of the particular forms that were revealed. Much the same could be said of Newburgh, although the dramatizations there occurred after the indictments of 23 percent of the department, and were somewhat superfluous by that point.

The counter examples of no dramatizations occurring where there is insufficient conflict over police organizational goals can be found in the little scandals in all four departments. The facts of corruption revealed in these precursors of the big scandals were often as serious as the facts revealed in the big scandals themselves. But without any conflict to fuel a dramatization of the facts, the little scandals did not succeed in labeling the police departments as deviant.

Conditions of Prosecution

Criminal prosecution received a great deal of publicity in the Oakland and Newburgh scandals, but not in the Central City and New York scandals. In both New York and Central City, the criminal prosecutions that did occur encompassed a very small part of the corruption that had been revealed, while in Oakland and Newburgh the criminal prosecutions encompassed virtually all of the revealed corruption.

The variation in the extent of prosecution is not consistent with the differences in the constraints upon the prosecutors. The prosecutors in Newburgh and Central City were linked to the political elite controlling the police, yet one prosecuted the police (in Newburgh) and the other did not. The prosecutors in Oakland and New York were all independent of the elected officials in control of the police, yet the Oakland prosecutor undertook extensive prosecution of police corruption and the New York prosecutors did not.

The variation in prosecution is, however, consistent with the victim or non-victim nature of the revealed corruption. Police corruption for which there is an identifiable victim to give testimony is a much easier kind of crime on which to gather evidence. As the case of Newburgh shows, it may even be impossible not to prosecute such crimes once the evidence has been gathered. But crimes without victims are much more difficult acts on which to gather evidence. It is one thing for a revealer to describe patterns of corruption in a police department; it is quite another to provide the evidence necessary for conviction of individual police officers and officials for taking bribes voluntarily offered to them, since the bribe-givers have no incentive for testifying. Prosecution may have occurred where it did because the crimes revealed produced victims. The police crimes revealed in New York and Central City were mainly victimless. Even if the prosecutors in those two cities had been eager to prosecute the large portion of the police department allegedly participating in corruption, they would have been unable to do so without a long and expensive investigation. No such time and expense was necessary in Oakland and Newburgh, where the victims provided the ready evidence needed for a speedy prosecution. Since many prosecutors seem to "contract"[37] with police departments to ignore police misconduct in exchange for police support of prosecutorial work, the presence or absence of victims seems to be the best explanation for the presence or absence of prosecution, regardless of the nature or intensity of the conflict.

Conditions of Labeling

The conditions of an audience labeling a police department as corrupt are the conditions of a successful, punitive scandal. The conditions include the appearance of the revelation, publication, and dramatization stages. Other stages are not essential. Extensive prosecution may contribute to the labeling of the department as corrupt, as it did in Oakland, or it may be virtually the sole condition for labeling the department as corrupt, as it was in Newburgh. But prosecution is not a necessary condition for labeling a police department corrupt, as the cases of New York and Central City demonstrate. The appearance of a defense in three of the cities also did not prevent the label from being applied, although more sustained defenses by more defenders might have done so.

The conditions of labeling a police department corrupt do not depend upon which stages appear so much as on what happens during each stage. A defense may backfire, a dramatization may fail to stress the organizational nature of the deviance, or a revelation may turn out to be patently untrue. Timing may also be an important factor in leading to successful labeling. The initial revelations in New York petered out into a little scandal because they were not followed by any further major revelations (although they were followed by the creation

37. See p. 22.

of the Knapp Commission, which provided the big-scandal revelations almost two years later). A loss of momentum in the process of building a steadily more convincing case that the police department is corrupt may thwart the successful application of the label. A successful defense, a lack of dramatizations, or even a low-key approach to publication of the revelations may result in the failure of scandal to label the department as corrupt.

To the extent that general conclusions can be drawn from such limited evidence, three conditions seem to be associated with successful labeling of police departments as corrupt. One is the publication of revelations of failures of the departments to police themselves, evidence that the police organization has violated the public trust that it would exercise internal control. A second condition is that the revealers be credible, or at least endorsed by a highly credible public figure; some association of the revealers always seems to be of higher status than the police department itself, such as reporters, city managers, or blue ribbon commissions.[38] The final condition seems to be that the revelations be dramatized as serious by public figures who can claim to represent a large portion of the community. Leaders of marginal civic groups may dramatize corruption or defend the department, but their statements are not as important, for example, as those of congressmen unaffiliated with the local political elite, or of leaders of the major professional associations. To the extent that a police department can (1) demonstrate its vigor in policing corruption internally, (2) label the revealers as unreliable sources of information, and (3) escape the attacks of major public figures, it may be able to avoid being labeled as corrupt. Where a police department fails to take these steps, the conditions of successful labeling may be met, and the police department may be punished by the stigma of scandal.

38. Reiss, Lectures.

4. The Response to Scandal

Once labeled by scandal as deviant organizations, the four police departments faced a crisis of organizational direction and survival. Such crises generally seem to produce direct outside intervention in the conduct of organizations. Just as a corporation facing bankruptcy loses control of its affairs to courts and creditors, the police departments that were labeled corrupt lost control of their affairs to powerful actors in their environments.[1] The three police departments already held captive by their environments came under the control of a different set of outside actors, the victors in the conflict of scandal. In all four cases, the direct intervention of outsiders shaped the police departments' response to scandal.

That response consisted of three major decisions. One was to change the leadership of the department. Another concerned the question of how to deal with the corrupt past of the department, in both public imagery and administrative policy. And the third decision concerned the selection of new policies for internal control of corruption activities. Only the first decision had a common result in all four departments, and only the first decision was made entirely by outsiders, who seem to have had progressively less influence on the second and third decisions. The selection of policies for internal control of corruption was probably the most important decision for determining the future of corruption in the departments, yet that decision was subjected to almost

1. James D. Thompson, *Organizations in Action* (New York: McGraw-Hill, 1967), p. 155.

no direct outside intervention. The direct intervention of outsiders may have shaped the organizations' response to scandal, but it did not determine the response completely.

CHANGING THE LEADERSHIP

When the subject of a scandal is an individual, the symbolic sanction of disgrace is often accompanied by removal of the subject from his trusted role. For example, an American president subjected to scandal was replaced by another president. But when the subject of scandal is an organization, it is generally impossible to remove the organization from its trusted role. Although the colorful history of the American police does include several instances in which an entire police department was disbanded by legislative fiat in response to scandal, such responses hardly seem possible today.[2] The growth of public employee unions, civil service protections, and other constraints on personnel actions has made it generally impossible to fire all the employees of a government agency en masse. Instead of removing the entire membership of the organization, the typical response is to remove the organization's leadership.

In the public eye, the leadership of a police department may consist of only the chief police executive and perhaps his closest aides. The actual control of a police department, however, includes all those actors participating in the dominant coalition. In some instances, the police executive may even be excluded from the dominant coalition. The public definition of new leadership in the four police departments had important symbolic consequences, and the actual makeup of the dominant coalition had important instrumental consequences for

2. Both the New York City and "Central City" Police Departments were legally abolished, and all of their members dismissed, in the nineteenth century. For an account of the events in New York, see James F. Richardson, *The New York Police* (New York: Oxford University Press, 1970), Chapter 4.

each organization's behavior after the scandal. The power of scandal as an agent of change is clearly demonstrated by the outside intervention it produced for changing both the chief police executive and the dominant coalition.

Changing the Police Executive

Two of the four incumbent police executives were removed shortly after the big scandal developed. One other resigned after the big scandal, and the fourth resigned in anticipation of a big scandal. These technical differences in the manner of changing the police executive, however, do not conflict with the interpretation that outside intervention caused all four police executives to depart.

The clearest case of outside intervention causing the changing of the police executive was Newburgh. The Newburgh police chief, who had directed the police burglaries, was suspended by the city manager in anticipation of his being indicted. The chief remained under suspension while the criminal charges were prosecuted, and was dismissed upon his conviction in accordance with civil service regulations. The outside intervention of the criminal justice process, then, removed the incumbent chief, and the outside intervention of the electorate produced a majority of "reformers" on the Newburgh city council in the first election after the big scandal. Not content to let the former chief's deputy become the next permanent chief, the city council changed the structure of the office of police executive from tenured civil service chief to untenured, appointive police commissioner. This change allowed the city council to direct the city manager to recruit an "outsider" to become the new police executive. An aide to the local prosecutor who had helped prosecute the chief and the other police officers was hired as the first "reform" police executive, and a professional police administrator from the midwest was hired a year later when the first police commissioner resigned. The outside intervention produced a change not only in the individuals who occupied the role of police executive, but also in the *kind* of person who could occupy the role. The mayor of Central City had tended to exclude himself from police department affairs in the six years prior to the big scandal. His few attempts to exert control over the department had generally been rebuffed. Even though the mayor's office routinely forwarded letters from party headquarters recommending police officers for promotion, the mayor was not involved in the day-to-day running of the police department. When the big scandal erupted just after the mayor began a campaign for higher elective office, two of his major political supporters, the governor and the Central City newspaper, put substantial pressure on him to take an anti-corruption stance. When the chief hastily attacked the revealers and tried to keep any other police officers from talking to reporters, the mayor decided to change the top leadership of the department. He fired the safety director (a nontenured political appointee), demoted the chief to his permanent civil service rank of major (in which he would serve out his remaining years until reaching eligibility for retirement), and asked the assistant chief (who was already eligible for retirement) to retire. A former federal law enforcement agent who was running for county sheriff was appointed as the reform police chief and served for the remaining two years of the mayor's term of office. The change in leadership did little to help the mayor's campaign, however: he lost both his home territory and the general election by a landslide.

Like the Central City mayor, the Oakland city manager did not feel he could intervene in police affairs without strong provocation. Unlike the Central City mayor, however, the Oakland city manager placed reform of the police department high on his list of priorities and actively helped to create the provocation for intervening in the department. Even so, the city manager did not fire the Oakland police chief, despite his legal authority to do so. Instead, he helped to create enough public pressure so that the chief would resign voluntarily. After a few weeks of the scandal, the chief went on sick leave for a heart condition and then resigned a few weeks later. Under civil service regulations, the new chief had to be appointed from the ranks of captains already in the department. The new chief had been an Oakland officer for twenty years, but he was an outsider to the social life and norms of the police department. A former varsity rower at the University of California at Berkeley, he was not a typical Oakland police officer in appearance, outlook, or behavior.

The case of New York is the hardest to fit into the pattern of changing the police executive through outside intervention. The revelations published in April of 1970 did not seem to result in labeling the police department organizationally corrupt, but they did entangle the incumbent police commissioner in a public dispute over his and the revealers' objectivity. The dispute led first to the disbanding of the committee of public officials that the mayor had created to investigate the revelations, and then led to the creation of the independent Knapp Commission. The police commissioner's conflict of interest was cited as the main reason for the change, which occurred three weeks after the revelations were published. By midsummer, the Knapp Commission had become a clear threat to the department, and the police commissioner had lost a battle with the city investigations commissioner over forwarding all citizen complaints of police corruption from the police department to the investigations department. Several weeks later, the police commissioner resigned.

The resignation of the New York City Police Commissioner was not a direct result of outside demands for his resignation, although there had been substantial public criticism of his failure to act aggressively against corruption. More important, he did not resign in the wake of a big scandal labeling the police department as organizationally corrupt. Rather, he resigned in what may have been anticipation of the Knapp Commission's labeling the department corrupt, and perhaps in anticipation that direct outside intervention would result when such labeling did occur. In any case, his resignation allowed the mayor to appoint a new commissioner in October of 1970 with a mandate to clean up corruption. The new commissioner had one year to establish a record of performance as a reformer, which he did successfully enough to avoid taking any of the blame for the organizational corruption revealed by the Knapp Commission hearings in October of 1971. Despite these slight departures from the patterns evident in the other three cases, it is not unreasonable to conclude that the incumbent police executive in New York would not have resigned if there had been no public criticism of his internal control over corruption.

The symbolic consequences of changing the police executive might help a police department to remove (or in the case of New York, temporarily avoid) the deviant label. The appointment of a new police executive symbolizes a public repudiation of the department's previous corrupt character and a new dedication to the achievement of the legitimate goals mandated for the police department by the legal system. The new police executive presents a new identity for the police department, making it, in effect, a different organization from the one that had been corrupt. The public statements of the new executives all seemed to be directed to creating a new organizational character:

> By far the vast majority of the men in the Oakland Police Department are men of which the City of Oakland should be very proud. . . . However, this department has many problems of which we are aware. . . . I am sure that we are taking the right step to straighten out our department. That is our prerogative and duty.[3]

3. *Oakland Tribune*, February 13, 1955.

Except for your paycheck there is no such thing as a clean
buck.... Let the word go out to every precinct station-
house, to every detective squad room, to every command
and to every man on every post: we will not tolerate dis-
honesty in any form.[4]

We've got to start talking about honesty, integrity ... and
we will take whatever action is necessary. If it means criminal indictments, so be it. There will be no sacred cows in the
Central City Police Department. Make no mistake about
that.[5]

The appointment of the new police executives may
have helped to create a public image of a new police
department, but the effort was not always successful. In
Central City, the continuation of new (if minor) revelations after the appointment of a new police executive
seemed to negate the idea that new leadership equaled a
new organizational identity. In New York, the most
convincing revelations of organizational corruption
came a year after the appointment of the new police
executive. The new executive's own actions during his
first year paradoxically contributed to a public image of
pervasive corruption in the department, because of the
commissioner's severe and highly visible steps to bring
the corruption under control. The Oakland and Newburgh executives, however, were aided by the fact that
all of the major revelations of organizational corruption
had occurred by the time they took office. Their implied
claims for an overnight transformation of the department's character were not contradicted by any public
evidence of continuing organizational corruption.

None of the four departments, of course, actually
achieved an overnight change in organizational character. Even with the adoption of new goals, the process of
achieving the compliance of the organization's membership with these goals was slow and arduous. But before
the compliance attempts could even begin, the domi-

4. *New York Times*, October 28, 1970, p. 28.
5. "Central City Clarion," March 16, 1974.

nant coalition had to adopt the new legitimate goals. The police executive by himself does not comprise the dominant coalition of any police department. Changing the police executive through outside intervention was only the first step in changing the entire police leadership, the full dominant coalition running the department.

Changing the Dominant Coalition

Since a dominant coalition is a process and not an entity,[6] changing the coalition was not simply a problem of getting rid of certain people. While it usually was important that certain individuals be removed from the scene, it was more important to change the way in which the police department was governed, the process by which certain types of people were included in or excluded from the governance of the organization. This change was no easy matter. One of the hardest tasks of both outside actors and the new police executives seeking to change the police department was simply figuring out exactly how the department was run: locating and defining the dominant coalition in order to change it. Once they did locate the coalition, they changed it through both formal and informal means.

The dominant coalition of the Oakland Police Department seemed to include, on most issues, four key police officials and an unknown number of politicians. The officials were the three precinct commanders and the commander of the detectives. These four positions held almost complete control over the day-to-day operations of the department and reported directly to the chief. When the reform chief was appointed, he confronted the same dominant coalition that had existed under his predecessor. With the full support of both the city manager and the electorate, the new chief put an end to this concentration of power through formal policy changes. His first step was to abolish the precinct commands, ending the fiefdoms of the precinct captains

6. See p. 9.

by centralizing the command of patrol operations from headquarters. Instead of having complete command of a geographic area twenty-four hours a day, seven days a week, each captain now had temporary command of the entire patrol force for only the eight hours each captain was on duty; only the chief had twenty-four hour control of any area of the city. The second step was to reorganize the command structure of the police department, but that required the approval by the voters of a change in the city charter. Instead of having all captains reporting directly to the chief, the proposed charter amendment provided for the nontenured appointment of three deputy chiefs from the tenured ranks of police captain. The proposal was to allow the chief to select his own middle managers, rather than being stuck with whoever passed the civil service test for captain. The three deputy chiefs were each to head a major division: patrol, investigations, or support services. The referendum on the proposal was held several months after the scandal, and the voters approved it by a substantial margin.[7] The closing of the precinct stations and the creation of a new stratum of top managers allowed the new chief to exclude from the new dominant coalition both the police officials and the politicians who had participated in the old dominant coalition. By centralizing command, all outside influence was forced to come through an unreceptive chief.

A similar structural change was undertaken in Newburgh, where the city council changed the police leadership structure from civil service to untenured positions. The structural change was also a vehicle for paying a much higher salary to the police executive, which permitted the city manager to recruit a more competent police executive. The doubling of the police executive's salary and the provision for three appointive deputies at similarly high salaries constituted a significant step in a city that has a steadily shrinking tax base and very high

7. *Oakland Tribune*, April 20, 1955.

unemployment. The need for change there was not so great as elsewhere, however, for the dominant coalition of the department was shattered by the criminal prosecution. The politicians controlling the police reportedly ceased their involvement in police corruption as soon as the indictments were handed down.

The dominant coalition of the Central City Police Department included the four deputy chiefs, a few captains and lieutenants, and the major political party officials. The incumbent chief's power in this dominant coalition was so unstable that he spent a fair amount of time trying to keep his deputies from gaining enough political influence to take his job. When the incumbent chief was replaced in the big scandal, the dominant coalition remained almost unchanged. The new chief spent several months learning how the dominant coalition worked—suffering at the same time from their efforts to undercut his power. After five months in office, the new chief shuffled some of the top commanders, but he apparently did not break their hold on the department nor their linkages to the politicians. Only after a full year did the chief banish the top commanders to meaningless positions (even while they maintained high rank) and appoint two key aides who were loyal to him. Significantly, the loyalty of the internal policing unit commander was always questionable. But the old dominant coalition was indeed broken up, if not destroyed, with the strong outside intervention of the mayor. The major personnel changes at the end of the first year were preceded by the mayor's interviewing almost all of the top officials in the department to see why they were not supporting the fight against corruption. With stigmatizing headlines and pictures of most participants in the dominant coalition, the outside intervention of newspapers also contributed to the breakup of the old dominant coalition.

The dominant coalition of the New York City Police Department has historically been located at the level of command intervening between the precinct commanders and headquarters.[8] The sheer size of the organization and of the city itself has always made tight central control difficult, if not impossible. A policy of increased centralization of command, pursued for the twenty years prior to the big scandal, had failed to achieve central control over either legitimate or illegitimate police activities. The police commissioner was largely at the mercy of his field commanders. Although the commanders served at the pleasure of the commissioner, few commissioners had ever been able to gather enough information about their commanders to control them. Moreover, few commissioners had ever been willing to demote the field commanders for failing to implement the goals set at headquarters. The formal structures for exercising control over the field commanders were available, but no police commissioner had ever used them. The rapid turnover of New York City police commissioners had allowed the permanent cadre of field commanders to maintain their long-run power despite any temporary disputes with the current commissioner; since 1898, the average tenure of the commissioners had been approximately two years.[9] The reform executive in New York served only two and a half years, but he still managed to outlast most of his field commanders. Ninety percent of the commanders above the rank of captain retired during the reform administration.[10]

The reform commissioner in New York did not define the problem with the field commanders as personal involvement in corruption. His greatest concern was their tradition of ignoring, or at least not checking for, corruption among their subordinates. A very few

8. Wallace S. Sayre and Herbert Kaufman, *Governing New York City* (New York: W. W. Norton, 1960), p. 288.
9. Allan N. Kornblum, "The Moral Hazards" (Ph.D. dissertation, Princeton University, 1973), p. 325.
10. Lawrence W. Sherman, "Controlling Police Corruption: Scandal and Organizational Reform" (Ph.D. dissertation, Yale University, 1976), p. 145.

high-ranking commanders, in ranks up to assistant chief inspector, were suspected of having participated in corruption arrangements until as late as 1971. But according to one internal investigator, "the bosses stayed away from the money as soon as the salaries started to climb" in the late 1960s. The potential financial losses from detection of corruption became greater than the potential gain, except for the extremely lucrative area of narcotics corruption.

The problem was therefore defined not as making the commanders honest, but rather as making them take the initiative in implementing the goal of honest law enforcement. By long tradition, corruption control was the exclusive responsibility of headquarters investigating units, and not an appropriate concern for field commanders. Indeed, the field commanders even criticized "headquarters" to their subordinates whenever a police officer was arrested for corruption. The reform commissioner broke up this dominant coalition supporting corruption by putting new people into the field command positions and by changing the means of enforcing managerial standards.

The policy of managerial turnover was hardly subtle. The reform executive, even before he took office, announced that a "new generation of commanders" was required to run the department. In his first speech to the commanders, he publicly told them to end corruption or face demotion. More important than public exhortation, however, was a financial threat. Demotion in rank would mean retirement later at a lower pension than would immediate retirement at the highest rank attained, since pension was calculated solely on the basis of the final year's salary. In private, many individual commanders were specifically threatened with demotion if they did not retire. Some threatened age discrimination suits, but most went quietly and avoided stigma. The process was later described as "blood letting," but it did pave the way for adoption of new organizational goals.

The reform police executive in New York took the initiative to break up the dominant coalition, but not without outside prodding. The unknown threat of what the Knapp Commission would do was a constant stimulus for strong action against corruption throughout the entire first year of the reform administration, the year before the Knapp Commission created the big scandal labeling the department as organizationally corrupt. The existence of the Knapp Commission provided the justification for the "blood letting," without which an even more severe crisis of morale would have resulted. As the commissioner later acknowledged, he would not have been able to move as fast or as far in changing the top command of the department without the outside pressure of the Knapp Commission.[11]

In Central City, the initiative for breaking up the dominant coalition was more clearly external. The mayor publicly called on the top police commanders to retire for the good of the department, and he also undercut the power of party officials to meddle in public affairs. The attempt to remove key participants in the dominant coalition, however, failed because the structural weapons available in New York were not available in Central City, which lacked the pension threat available in New York. Under Central City law, the pensions of commanders would always be computed in the same way as the pensions of patrol officers, and they could only be increased by longevity, not attainment of higher rank. Although demotion from deputy chief to major, for example, meant a reduction in salary, only earlier retirement could produce a reduction in pension. Not even the ex-chief could have been forced from the department, especially since he still had three more years to serve until he would be eligible for pension.

The available evidence does not permit a conclusion as to whether a punitive scandal always results in outside intervention to change the leadership of a corrupt

11. Interview with Patrick V. Murphy, former Police Commissioner, New York City, April, 1976.

police department. In all four of the present cases, however, the dominant coalition was changed, and new goals of honesty were adopted. Goals are not automatically achieved, and the change in organizational leadership was only a first step towards reducing corrupt activity in the police departments. The next step was coping with each organization's history of corruption as an obstacle to reform.

COPING WITH THE PAST

The corrupt past posed a dilemma for the reform leadership. Many officers still in the department had committed serious crimes, and they were linked to active or temporarily dormant social networks of criminals, politicians, or other corrupt police officers. Yet a vigorous effort to investigate past corruption produced still more revelations of organizational corruption that detracted from the department's new identity as an honest organization. Confronting the past might have hurt the appearance of the organization's integrity, but ignoring the past might have hurt the reality of the organization's integrity. Some reform executives chose one path, and some chose the other, but all of them tried to avoid the dilemma by encouraging rapid turnover among the rank and file.

Investigating the Past

The new police executives in Central City and Newburgh chose the path of investigating police corruption activities that had occurred prior to their taking office. Both of them had good reasons to do so, but both failed in the attempt.

In Central City, the reform executive took office without the benefit of any indictments having been handed down against police officers. The scandal had succeeded solely on the strength of allegations reported in the newspaper, and the paper expected the reform executive to have most of the implicated officers prosecuted. But the police "truth squad," formed by the mayor before the reform executive was appointed, arrived at a different version of the "truth" from that of the revealers. Given the crude methods the squad employed,[12] direct testimony was very hard to obtain, and gathering legal proof of specific acts—in contrast to journalistic evidence of general patterns—was virtually impossible. But even with more sophisticated methods, it would have been difficult to obtain testimony about the corrupt acts, which were for the most part consensual in nature. As the analysis of investigative methods will show, consensual corruption is generally vulnerable to detection only while it is ongoing, and not after it has ceased to occur.

Whatever the reasons, the lack of all but a very few indictments left the entire Central City Police Department under a cloud of suspicion. The informal accusations of the media remained unadjudicated, either formally or informally. To say in public that internal investigators could find no evidence is not to say that the charges were untrue, notwithstanding the legal presumption of innocence. The department was left in a state of limbo, with the innocent stigmatized and the guilty uncertain of their fate. Worst of all, the preoccupation with the past diverted attention and energy away from the current corruption and other managerial problems. The past in Central City continued to be a burden on the present and future.

The prosecutions of the Newburgh police officers probably removed a higher percentage of corrupt officers than in any of the other three departments. Even so, the potential for continuing corruption was maintained by a number of other officers who were rumored to have been corrupt but who escaped prosecution. The "uncaught" possessed the skills, predisposition, and linkages to corruption networks necessary to engage in corruption. While the scandal may have deterred them from taking regular bribes from gamblers, they knew

12. See Chapter 6.

where to find the gamblers if the "heat" of scandal were to die down.

Taking office after a year of criminal prosecutions during which the department was under the command of an acting chief, the first Newburgh "reform" executive announced his intention to find out about all those who were guilty. He devoted most of his one year tenure to that effort. As a former assistant district attorney in the office prosecuting the Newburgh officers, his skills seemed suited to the task of investigating the history of individual officers. Yet he failed to uncover any new evidence or to produce criminal charges, succeeding only in prolonging the personal agony of the scandal for the officers (honest or otherwise) who had been present during the pre-scandal period. His successor abandoned the investigations and made a speech focusing on the future. The second reform executive's speech was widely interpreted in the department as an "amnesty" policy.[13]

Amnesty

An amnesty policy places a higher priority on the future behavior of police officers than on their past behavior. It gives the members of a once-corrupt police department a second chance en masse. It does not pardon any individual officers for specific misdeeds, nor does it promise that cases against once-corrupt officers will not be prosecuted. It is simply a statement by a police executive of how he will allocate his resources, particularly his resources for internal investigations. An amnesty policy is a strong hint that the police executive will not try to investigate the past.

The Oakland case provides the clearest example of an amnesty policy, although several sources reported that it was implied in New York as well. When the reform chief took over, he was well aware of the extent of past cor-

13. Interview with James Taylor, former Newburgh Police Commissioner, October 8, 1975.

ruption. Because he had long been isolated from organized corruption by his job in the relatively corruption-free Traffic Division, however, he had no direct personal knowledge of the details of organized corruption. Since no one was confronting the reform chief with any allegations that had not already gone to the grand jury, he made a speech to his commanders in which he implied amnesty for past sins. "From this day forward," he said, "we will have complete honesty."[14] Shortly thereafter, the head of a newly created internal investigation unit told a police fraternal society that all future investigations of police officers would be followed through, and no cover-ups would be tolerated.[15] Most of the subsequent attention of both the department and the news media was focused on the "new look" of the department and its reforms, rather than on the adjudication of past sins.

The drawback of an amnesty policy is that it does not destroy the personal linkages between corrupt police officers and other participants in corruption. These networks may continue despite the scandal. Or if the networks cease to operate because they are deterred by the scandal, they may become reactivated at some future time. The more officers with such linkages who can be separated from the department, the less potential there is for a continuation or future resurgence of corruption. Yet amnesty does not preclude a high rate of separation. Other means besides criminal or departmental prosecutions are available for ridding the department of many, though not all, of those who may try to maintain corrupt activities. By encouraging or inducing the retirement of the group of older officers presumably more wedded to corrupt traditions, the new leadership can change the membership of the department through turnover.

14. Interview with Lieutenant Garrett F. Kyle, Oakland Police Department, May 2, 1975. See also the formal grant of amnesty to corrupt police in Hong Kong reported in the *New York Times*, November 8, 1977, p. 2.
15. *Oakland Tribune*, February 23, 1955.

Turnover

All four departments attempted to get rid of "old blood" and hire an infusion of "new blood" after the big scandals. The success of the attempts depended both on the retirement of older officers and the availability of funds for the hiring of new recruits. All four succeeded in increasing the retirement rate somewhat, but two of them (Central City and New York) were prevented from hiring large numbers of new recruits because of municipal fiscal crises.

Two departments laid particular stress on turnover. The more overt effort of the two was Central City's attempt to rid the department of its older officers. The reform executive publicly announced a policy of encouraging early retirements. Even though many officers said they did not want to retire while the "cloud of scandal hung over the department," the rates of retirement and resignation did increase slightly.[16]

The Oakland police executive employed less public but more substantial inducements for the older officers to retire, with better results. He was so strict about the personal appearance and work habits of his officers that many men of the "old school" were made to feel uncomfortable, quite apart from any issues of corruption or control. The peak of these new demands came during the first reform year, 1955, when the chief called two full dress inspections of the entire department. Officers who had not worn uniforms for years were forced to buy new ones; guns had to be cleaned and shoes had to be shined. Many officers quit before the inspections, and others quit after being reprimanded for their appearance at the inspection. Perhaps in combination with fears about detection of corruption, this policy seemed to explain the doubling of the normal number of officers retiring or resigning in the first year of reform.[17]

Because the data on the four cases extends for different numbers of years after the big scandals, it is hard to

16. Sherman, "Controlling Police Corruption," p. 135.
17. Ibid., p. 137.

make exact comparisons among the departments. Even so, the contrasts are apparent. Eighty percent of the Oakland police force that had been hired before the scandal was still there five years later, while in New York 78 percent was still there after four years. In Newburgh, a mere 41 percent of the pre-scandal personnel were still employed four years after the scandal, the most substantial turnover of any of the four cases. Even though 23 percent were removed by criminal conviction, the "natural" turnover of 36 percent was still higher than the 20 percent in Oakland and the 22 percent in New York. Because of a hiring freeze, Central City had no turnover until late in the second year after the scandal. Because of the destruction of records in some cities, comparisons of these rates with prior five- or four-year periods are not possible.[18] But the comparisons among the four cities are instructive for the analysis of changes in corruption presented in Part III.

The value of turnover as a corruption control policy is only as good as the assumption on which it is based: that older officers are more likely to be corrupt than officers hired in their place. Certainly the assumption makes sense in terms of the older officers' knowledge of past and potential corruption networks. The question is whether new officers would be just as likely to develop similar networks. Given three conditions, the answer should be no. First, if organized corruption is under control at the time the new recruits enter, they cannot tie into active corruption networks, which would be an easier process than trying to develop new networks of their own. Second, if the new officers are socialized in a way that makes them value honesty and fear punishment for corruption, they will presumably be less likely to take advantage of the corruption opportunities they may find. Third, if older officers who can teach the skills necessary for corruption activities are no longer present, or if those who remain are unwilling to trust the

18. See the discussion of the limitations of the method used to calculate this data in Sherman, "Controlling Police Corruption," pp. 135-143.

new recruits, then the new recruits will not be taught the skills necessary for pursuing corrupt opportunities in a low-risk fashion.

All three conditions were apparently present in the Oakland Police Department. No new officers were hired until the end of the first reform year, by which time a deputy chief had announced that organized corruption had been brought under control and payoff arrangements had been stopped.[19] The first class of recruits was selected from a pool of applicants generated by a nationwide campaign, including visits to college police science programs at Michigan State University and the University of California at Berkeley. The law requiring applicants to be residents of Oakland was repealed, and a one-in-ten survival rate among the applicants gave the class an aura of being the "finest in the country." On their first day at the training academy, the chief made a two-sentence speech to them: "Gentlemen, welcome to the Oakland Police Department. If you do anything wrong, I shall personally escort you to the gates of San Quentin."[20] The presence of several former Oakland policemen in nearby San Quentin prison gave considerable weight to the speech. Specially selected training officers guided the rookies during their first year in the field. According to members of recruit classes during the reform period, most older police officers would barely speak to the rookies, much less teach them the techniques of corruption or introduce them into corruption networks.

There is some evidence that the conditions of control of organized corruption, new processes of recruit socialization, and limited contact with presently or once-corrupt officers were met in Newburgh, which may have made turnover function as a corruption preventative. On the other hand, the small size of the department made some contact with older officers inevitable, which may have countered the effects of rapid turnover.

19. *Oakland Tribune*, November 17, 1955.
20. Interview with Raymond P. Brown, former Deputy Chief,

The rate of turnover in New York was remarkably similar to Oakland's, if slightly faster. The meaning of the figures, however, was entirely different. Organized corruption flourished long after the reform administration took over in October of 1970, lasting until at least mid-1972.[21] The formal process of recruit socialization in police academy courses was not changed until 1972. Older officers seemed to show little reluctance to teach recruits the methods of corruption, an initiation rite of long standing.[22] To compound matters, two very large recruit classes had been hired in 1968 and 1969, years said by many insiders to have been the two most corrupt in the recent history of the department. These 6,700 recruits, comprising over one-fifth of the department as of January 1970, were socialized just at the time that the informal taboos against heroin corruption had broken down and some police officers had begun selling drugs. The attitudes and corruption skills developed by these recruits would stay with most of them and with the department until their retirement twenty years later.

This historical legacy created a far more immediate problem for New York than dealing with past sins. The problem was how to confront a present and a likely future of ongoing corruption. In retrospect, one stroke of fortune was that budget restrictions severely limited the number of new officers hired during the two years it took the reform executive to bring organized corruption under control. When large numbers of recruits were again hired, they confronted a different environment (although most of these recruits were soon laid off by further budget cuts).

Turnover may have helped create a new organizational climate at the critical point of a new dominant

---

Oakland Police Department, May 5, 1975.

21. See Chapter 9.

22. Edward Droge, *The Patrolman: A Cop's Story* (New York: New American Library, 1973); and Leonard Shecter and William Phillips, *On the Pad* (New York: G. P. Putnam's, 1974).

coalition's attempt to impose new organizational goals. Turnover could not, however, serve as a substitute for internal corruption control policies. Turnover aided those policies by providing a pool of new officers loyal to the legitimate goals of the department who would serve as anti-corruption spies. But without the use of effective policies for bringing organized corruption under control, the past corruption of the department may soon become irrelevant because of ongoing corruption, and new officers may become as corrupt as the old. The reform police executives all had to confront the past, but only in order to move on to dealing with the present and future corruption conditions in their departments.

SELECTING CONTROL POLICIES

The selection of an organizational goal does not mandate a particular strategy for achieving the goal. A dominant coalition adopting the goal of honest law enforcement for a police department must still select the policies by which it will attempt to achieve that goal. Some policies for achieving honesty may be more effective than others. Whether corruption declines or survives in a police department adopting a goal of honest law enforcement may depend on the kinds of policies selected to control corruption.

Corruption control policies in the four police departments fell into two categories. One category was the line management of the department's performance of police tasks, including policies of supervision, evaluation of performance, and incentives. The other category was the detection of corruption activities and punishment of corrupt police officers by internal policing and judicial systems. In comparing control policies among the police departments, both categories can be divided into two different approaches: premonitory and postmonitory. Premonitory policies deal with corruption by anticipating its likely occurrence, and by using information about corruption activities to prevent them or intercept them while they are still in progress. Postmonitory policies fail

Line Management		
Internal Policing	Postmonitory	Premonitory
Premonitory		New York
		Oakland
Postmonitory	Central City	Newburgh

Figure 2 Corruption Control Policies
in the Four Police Departments

to anticipate corruption, and only deal with corrupt acts after they have already occurred. While many disparate policies must be lumped together to produce such generalizations, Figure 2 shows the basic differences among the four cases in the corruption control policies they adopted after the scandals.

The reform administration in Central City responded to corruption entirely after the fact in its investigative policies and most of its managerial policies. The second post-scandal police executive in Newburgh developed an aggressive management style for identifying and thwarting corruption opportunities, but the formal investigation apparatus there was only mobilized by after-the-fact complaints, not advance intelligence. The reform executives' corruption control policies in New York and Oakland included an information-seeking, corruption-anticipating strategy for both line management and internal policing. These differences seem to have produced very different consequences for police corruption activities, as later chapters will suggest.

It is difficult to account for these differences with existing theories of social control strategies. One theory suggests that premonitory strategies will be employed to control deviance wherever victims are not created by the deviant acts.[23] All four departments had experienced "victimless" corruption, but only two of them adopted a

23. Albert J. Reiss, Jr. and David J. Bordua, "Environment and Organization: A Perspective on the Police," in *The Police*, ed. David J. Bordua (New York: John Wiley, 1967), p. 41.

completely premonitory strategy. Another theory suggests that premonitory strategies are more likely to be employed wherever there is a conflict between those in authority and those not in authority over the norms being enforced.[24] All four police departments had a clear conflict between the rank and file and the reform executive, yet not all of them employed a premonitory strategy. A third theory suggests that organizations in which employees exercise discretion in decision-making will monitor them to insure that they are exercising that discretion properly.[25] All four police departments allowed their employees the discretion normally found in police work, yet only two of them tested their members to see if the discretion was being used corruptly.

Differences among the four reform police executives also fail to account for the differences in the policies they selected for controlling corruption. In many ways, the reform executives were quite similar. All four were college graduates, and all four had held managerial positions in other law enforcement agencies. The differences that did exist among them did not match the differences in their control policies. Two of the executives were "outsiders" who had not previously worked for the department they headed, and two were "insiders." While it might be reasonable to predict that outsiders are more likely to employ premonitory strategies, the only postmonitory strategy was adopted by an outsider. Two of the executives were appointed by city managers, and two by mayors. While it might be reasonable to predict that mayoral appointees are less likely to adopt premonitory strategies, the most clearly premonitory strategy of all was adopted by a mayoral appointee (in New York).

What may account for the differences in corruption control policies are the differences in organizational capacity at the time the reform executive was appointed.

24. Donald J. Black, "The Mobilization of Law," *Journal of Legal Studies*, Vol. 2 (1973), pp. 140–141.
25. Thompson, *Organizations in Action*, p. 122.

Police departments, like other kinds of organizations, vary widely in their competence for performing certain tasks. The proverbial Scotland Yard inspector called in to investigate a small-town murder too difficult for the local constabulary to handle illustrates the differences in capacity among police departments. The source of differences in police organizational capacity may be the differences in recruitment policies or in the kinds of tasks a police department has previously been called upon to perform and for which it has therefore been forced to develop a capacity.

One task that police departments vary widely in their capacity to perform is the investigation of complex, highly organized, clandestine crimes. This category of crimes can only be policed through covert, premonitory methods.[26] Some departments, particularly seaport cities, apparently developed this capacity in order to control foreign espionage between the World Wars. In the 1950s and '60s, those departments expanded that capacity in order to focus on the Mafia families in their cities, as well as on "subversive" or radical political organizations.[27] For some reason, however, many other departments, even large ones, failed to develop any kind of intelligence-gathering capacity, and remained almost entirely postmonitory in their approach to all crimes under their jurisdiction.

Corruption in all four police departments at the time of the scandals was complex, highly organized, and clandestine. Where the capacity to police that kind of crime was already present in police departments in the pre-scandal period, the goal of controlling corruption was met by applying that capacity to corruption. In effect, Oakland and New York used no methods for policing corruption that had not been used previously for policing something else. Newburgh and Central City also used their available capacities, but those cities had

26. Reiss and Bordua, "Environment and Organization."
27. Anthony V. Bouza, *Police Intelligence* (New York: AMS Press, 1976).

developed almost no premonitory policing capacity for any kind of crime. The latter two cities policed corruption as they policed virtually every other kind of crime: with overt, reactive, postmonitory strategies.[28]

One slight modification of this pattern should be noted. In Central City, a federally funded project had helped to develop premonitory investigative strategies in one small unit for a few years before the scandal. The recent development of narcotics traffic in the city had also stimulated some premonitory activity in the narcotics squad. The premonitory capacity that did exist, however, was unavailable to the reform executive because of its alliance with corruption. The reform executive observed that the best investigators in the department were suspected of having participated in corruption activities, and that the most trustworthy investigators were usually the least competent. One implication of the Central City situation is that a premonitory capacity must not only be present in the department in order to be used against corruption, but it must also be *available* to the dominant coalition and supportive of the coalition's legitimate goals.

A second difference in capacity among police departments is the capacity for managing police tasks, for making the rank-and-file officers conform to certain standards and goals for performance. Every department has some capacity for line management control, no matter how poor. Yet most police management is clearly postmonitory, from the sergeant who reads an arrest report after the suspect is apprehended to the chief who meets with black community leaders after a riot. The capacity for closely monitoring the performance of subordinates and for identifying and preventing problems is a rare thing in American police departments. The reasons for the presence or absence of this

28. Lawrence W. Sherman, "Police Corruption Control: Environmental Context versus Organizational Policy," in *Police and Society*, ed. David H. Bayley (Beverly Hills, Calif.: Sage Publications, 1977), pp. 121–124.

capacity are unclear, although the background and education of police supervisors provide one possible explanation.

According to the interview evidence, none of the four cases had actually used a premonitory approach to management before the scandal. In two of them, however (New York and Oakland), the capacity for premonitory management was apparently available. In both cities there was a young generation of ambitious and better-educated officers just under the middle-management level who were eager to adopt a "tight" management approach. By opening up key management positions to this cadre and demanding accountable performance, the reform executives in New York and Oakland made use of a latent capacity which had never before been tapped. Central City followed the same pattern in filling two of the top jobs, but that change was far less sweeping than the changes of command personnel in Oakland and New York. Newburgh used lateral entry—an illegal method in most police departments—to import a middle-management capacity (three new deputy commissioners) along with the reform executive, all of whom had been schooled elsewhere in tight management control.

Over a long period of time, the capacity for a premonitory approach to both investigations and line management can probably be developed in any police department. But one thing reform executives do not have is time. Regardless of how long a reformer ultimately lasts, the pressure for taking some kind of action is greatest in the immediate wake of the scandal. Building up the department's capacity might be feasible as a long-term strategy, but the immediate response to scandal cannot await the hiring of new recruits and training them to become a new generation of managers, or to become skilled enough to successfully perform premonitory investigations. In the short run, a reform executive can only use whatever capacity is immediately available.

A larger sample of cases might easily falsify this hypothesis about organizational capacity. Many police departments may have the capacity for premonitory control of corruption but refuse to use it because of concerns for morale or political pressure. Other departments may in fact develop a premonitory capacity overnight in the wake of a corruption scandal. On the limited basis of the four present cases, however, the capacity hypothesis seems to account for the differences in control policies used by the departments, all of which adopted the goal of controlling police corruption.

One factor that apparently had no influence on the selection of control policies was the intervention of outsiders. Outside intervention forced the departments to adopt new goals and accept a new dominant coalition. To a lesser extent, external conditions shaped the decision on how to cope with the past. But the selection and implementation of control policies were completely internal. In the wake of scandal's external control, internal control was left entirely up to the deviant organizations. Yet no decision was more important to the prospects for reforming the corrupt police departments.

5. Preventive Control

Two kinds of internal control policies were used in the four departments. The next chapter examines policies for punitive control, those designed to detect and punish corrupt officers. This chapter examines the managerial policies for preventive control, those designed to prevent police corruption by removing the conditions and opportunities that facilitate it.

Two strategies of preventive control were evident in the departments studied. One strategy was aimed at the police departments' internal administrative practices. The other was aimed at their political and task environments. The strategies for changing the organization and for changing its environment both attempted to change the conditions that the police executives defined as being conducive to corruption.

CHANGING THE ORGANIZATION

Several distinct approaches for changing the organizational conditions conducive to corruption were used in the four police departments: internal accountability, tight supervision, and abolition of procedures encouraging corruption. New York employed all three of the approaches, Oakland used two, and Newburgh and Central City each used only one. The tactics used to implement the approaches varied among the cities employing them, but the intended organizational consequences of each approach were always the same.

Internal Accountability

Police departments often pay lip service to the ideal of being accountable to the community. At the same time, they are often reluctant to hold their own members internally accountable for tolerating misconduct. Prior to the scandal in each of the four cities, police supervisors were not held accountable for the behavior of their subordinates, and police officers were not held accountable for the behavior of their colleagues. The reform executives in New York and Oakland changed that situation.

Internal accountability is the policy of holding organizational members responsible for the acts of others as well as for their own actions. Its use in a police department is no different from holding a corporate vice-president responsible for the performance of his division. An internal accountability policy seeks to diffuse the responsibility for control of misconduct both vertically and horizontally throughout an organization, in order to increase the chances that someone will try to stop the improper or inadequate performance of tasks. It is analogous to the concept of "vicarious liability" long established at civil law, which holds employers liable for their employees' negligent acts without regard to the employer's diligence, control or knowledge.[1]

A prerequisite of internal accountability is a clear communication of standards to which the employees will be held accountable. This "sending out the message" was done by all four reform executives in the first days of their administration as part of the establishment of a new identity and new goals for the organization. Only in New York and Oakland, however, did the reform executives use the "message" as the basis for an internal accountability policy. The New York executive directed his policy of accountability primarily at the command ranks, and he articulated it in clearer terms than did any of the other reform executives: "I will hold each of you [captains and above] accountable for the

1. Alan M. Dershowitz, "Increasing Community Control over Corporate Crime: A Problem in the Law of Sanctions," in *White Collar Crime*, ed. Gilbert Geis (New York: Atherton Press, 1968), p. 151. See also Patrick V. Murphy and Thomas Plate, *Commissioner* (New York: Simon and Schuster, 1977), p. 147.

misdeeds of your subordinates. . . . With bold leadership you can—you must—create a climate in which corruption is unthinkable."[2]

The Oakland executive directed his accountability policy towards the lower ranks, a more appropriate target in a department having only three commanders with responsibilities comparable to those of a captain in New York. Since the Oakland executive knew and trusted his commanders personally, he could concentrate on making the first-line supervisors accountable for the conduct of the rank and file. He did not clearly articulate his expectation of accountability, but he did make his standards of integrity clear by a dramatic personal example. Three days after his appointment, he attended an annual civic club dinner for the "policeman of the year." In keeping with tradition, $1,000 worth of presents were displayed in front of the head table for later presentation to the award winner, an officer who had been shot in a holdup. The chief was called up first to receive a gold watch in honor of his present appointment. When the microphone was turned over to him, the chief refused to accept the gold watch, announcing that it was against the policy of the Oakland Police Department for officers, or chiefs, or even the "policeman of the year" to accept gifts. Moreover, the chief announced his intention to refuse a $1,500 diamond-studded badge which the department traditionally gave to new chiefs. As the stunned crowd dispersed, a newspaper photographer snapped a picture of the spurned gifts for the next day's front page.[3]

The reform executives in both Oakland and New York moved swiftly to enforce their policies of internal accountability. In one of his first official actions, the Oakland reform executive punished the commander of detectives with a sentence of five days without pay for failing to thoroughly investigate a corruption allegation. Some months later, he suspended a sergeant for failing

2. *New York Times*, October 28, 1970.
3. *Oakland Tribune*, February 18, 1955.

to investigate a prisoner's complaint that officers had taken money from the prisoner.[4] Another sergeant was suspended for letting one of his patrolmen work while intoxicated.[5] Patrolmen were also held accountable for crimes committed in their presence. One officer was turned in by his peers for stealing fifty dollars at the scene of a burglary. Other officers proved very cooperative in internal investigations after two of their colleagues were dismissed for refusing to take a lie detector test.[6]

In New York, the reform executive immediately enforced standards for the personal integrity of commanders, but he did not move to enforce their accountability for the behavior of subordinates until some months later. Taking office in October 1970, he demoted two inspectors in November for not cooperating with a grand jury's investigation of their alleged personal corruption.[7] Not until the following April, however, did he take any action against a commander for failure to control corruption. When the Knapp Commission revealed a meathouse burglary that its agents had discovered and the failure of the precinct desk officers to respond to the agents' anonymous calls reporting the burglary in progress, the executive punished the commander of the precinct in which the burglary occurred.

Once the accountability campaign in New York began, it moved forward swiftly. In May 1971, the commissioner warned the commanders that they weren't moving fast enough and that the FBI was investigating corruption in the department.[8] Two more precinct commanders were removed a week later. In June, a division commander (supervising several precincts) was

4. *Oakland Tribune*, March 4 and October 18, 1955.
5. *Oakland Tribune*, October 28, 1955.
6. Interview with Thomas Rogers, former Deputy Chief, Oakland Police Department, May 2, 1975.
7. *New York Times*, November 17, 1970, p. 17.
8. *New York Times*, May 13, 1971, p. 1.

transferred and charged with failure to have a corruption complaint investigated properly. After removing several other high officials from command over the summer, the commissioner again warned all the commanders publicly that he was "fed up" with their inadequate response to his demands to control corruption. Telling them to get on his team or get out, he warned that a shakeup was imminent. Just before Labor Day, a new chief of patrol was promoted over seventy-two more senior officers, an unheard-of break with tradition. The next day, almost 10 percent of the more than seventy precinct commanders were removed in one fell swoop, with three lieutenants and four sergeants charged with laxity of supervision. The actions came after an investigation of twenty precincts for officers sleeping on duty. The following day, one assistant chief retired and three inspectors were demoted.[9]

The costs of the accountability policy in New York were substantial. The commissioner was attacked by city councilmen for "image-making" in anticipation of the upcoming Knapp Commission hearings, and for holding "one-a-day press conferences" on police corruption "instead of" fighting crime. The president of the patrolman's union claimed the commissioner was "destroying the department" and called on him to resign. The *New York Times* reported a "backwash of bitterness among police officers," and the commissioner was booed at a promotion ceremony by the wives of newly promoted sergeants.[10]

The most important criticism was that the accountability policy itself was unfair and unreasonable. The commanders argued that with hundreds or, in some cases, thousands of officers under their command, they could not humanly prevent every act of misconduct. The commissioner addressed this complaint by clarify-

9. *New York Times*, May 13, June 21; August 23, 31; and September 1, 2; all 1971, all on p. 1.

10. *New York Times*, September 1, 1971, p. 44; September 3, 1971, p. 1; September 4, 1971, p. 14.

ing his policy. In a message to all 3,700 sergeants and superior ranks, he defined accountability as holding commanders responsible for "conditions they can realistically affect."[11] This definition was later emphasized by a departmental survey asking all commanders to specify the nature and kinds of corruption they suspected existed in their commands, and to describe the steps they were taking to deal with each kind of corruption. One commander claimed that there were no payoffs from unlicensed food wagon peddlers in his precinct, when in fact the Internal Affairs Division had evidence that at least one peddler had complained about shakedowns to that commander to no avail. When the commander was punished, he became a classic case for the accountability principle: despite clear knowledge of possible corruption conditions, he had refused to take action. Moreover, he had covered up the facts in an official report.[12]

This story illustrates an important point about any policy of accountability. Unless the police executive has independent sources of information about corruption conditions, he will be unable to take action against commanders who ignore them. The general problem of obtaining information about corruption will be considered later, but it is worth noting here that one important source of information is generated by the accountability policy itself. In one of his accountability speeches, the New York reform commissioner set a goal of every officer taking action if he suspected a colleague of corruption.[13] After the shakeups of September 1971, one sergeant commented that "the men hate [the commissioner], but right now a cop would lock up his partner, with all the pressure that's on him."[14] The statement may have been an exaggeration, but the trend it implied

11. *New York Times*, September 21, 1971, p. 41.
12. *New York Times*, November 28, 1972, p. 34.
13. *New York Times*, May 13, 1971, p. 1.
14. *New York Times*, September 20, 1971, p. 1.

was correct. Some officers had occasionally reported corruption even before the scandal. But after the accountability shakeups and Knapp Commission hearings in the fall of 1971, the number of corruption complaints filed by officers against other officers—excluding those from "field associates" specially recruited to this task at about that time—began to climb steadily.[15] In 1972, 4.6 percent of the 3,077 corruption complaints received by the internal policing unit were made by police officers. In 1973, 12.1 percent of the 3,387 complaints were from police officers, a threefold increase.[16] New York, incidentally, was not the only one of the four cities in which peer control occurred. In Central City, 12 percent of the misconduct complaints during the first year of reform came from within the department, with over half of them from patrol officers.

This finding is of revolutionary significance for the field of police administration. The police code of silence has been accepted by many police administrators as an inevitable fact ever since August Vollmer first described it in his 1931 Wickersham Commission report.[17] But it is clearly not as inevitable as had been thought. Whether through fear of punishment for nonreporting or through other means, police officers can indeed be made to exercise peer control to hold their colleagues accountable to professional standards.

Tight Supervision

Supervision in organizations is often described as falling on a continuum from "tight" to "loose." The usage of the terms in police departments suggests that super-

15. Although not without reprisals against those who "squealed." For a harrowing account of the harassment that forced one officer to retire after testifying in court against his colleagues, see the *New York Times*, July 3, 1977, p. 1.

16. Lawrence W. Sherman, "Controlling Police Corruption: Scandal and Organizational Reform" (Ph.D. dissertation, Yale University, 1976), p. 158.

17. Cited in William A. Westley, "Secrecy and the Police," *Social Forces*, Vol. 34 (1956), pp. 254–257.

vision is tighter when it places a greater proportion of a subordinate's work *time* or work *product* under the direct surveillance of a supervisor. The reform executives in Oakland, New York, and Newburgh all attempted to increase the tightness of supervision over both the work time and work products of subordinates.

Of the three executives adopting this policy, the reform chief in Oakland was the most vigorous in implementing it. While pounding his desk in a staff meeting, he once told his commanders, "I want control, control, control."[18] Much of his control was personal. His closing down of the outlying precinct houses, thereby centralizing operations in a new headquarters building, was ostensibly done for the purpose of cutting costs, but he told one aide that his real reason for the change was to make it easier to "keep an eye on everybody." He delegated very little decision-making authority to his deputies, and often drove the streets at night observing police responses to radio-dispatched calls.

The Oakland chief used his accountability policy to force every supervisor to tighten up supervision. He even ordered the use of specific techniques for supervision. Much more paperwork was required of the supervisors in order to record facts and responsibilities in case any suspicion might arise at a later date. Sergeants were required to file daily activity reports for each of their subordinates. Detectives were required to file monthly reports of their investigative activity. New procedures were established for receiving prisoners' property, receiving complaints against police officers, and recording property found on dead bodies. Written reports on these tasks were generally required with signatures of approval necessary from several levels of supervision. In effect, supervisors were forced by the forms to at least think about the corruption potential of their subordinates' tasks.

Research on other organizations suggests that there

18. Interview with John Giudici, former Captain, Oakland Police Department, May 1, 1975.

was probably some subversion of the purpose of the forms[19] and much variation in styles of supervision among individual supervisors and between the different functional divisions.[20] But all Oakland sources agreed that supervision in general became tighter under the reform chief than it had been before. The tactic for implementing that strategy was increased centralization and bureaucratization, a mountain of paper work, and a proliferation of rules.

In contrast, New York in 1970 had already become more bureaucratized than Oakland has ever been, and as centralized as New York's geography permitted. The New York Police Department was "drowning in paperwork," according to its members. It boasted a rule book almost one foot thick. Some strategy other than bureaucratization was required for tightening supervision, since department supervisors had become quite skilled at outwardly complying with control forms while evading their intent.[21] Centralization had become part of the corruption problem. Since most authority for dealing with corruption was located at headquarters, no one in the field who knew about corruption felt that he could properly do anything about it.

Decentralization (but not debureaucratization) with internal accountability became the reform executive's principal strategy for tightening supervision. At every level of supervision, more flexibility in decision-making was authorized for the allocation of manpower and other resources. Accountability was applied not just to corruption control, but to crime control and police services as well. So much decision-making power was

19. E.g., Peter Blau, *The Dynamics of Bureaucracy* (Chicago: University of Chicago Press, 1956).

20. Larry L. Tifft, "Comparative Police Supervision Systems: An Organizational Analysis" (Ph.D. dissertation, University of Illinois at Champaign-Urbana, 1970).

21. There was even a bureaucratic division of labor in New York for evading the intent of the control forms. Every precinct had a clerical officer who processed all paperwork, and most of them were paid by other officers to disguise corruption activities by filling out the forms "right." See Knapp Commission Report, pp. 166–169.

pushed down the hierarchy so far and so fast that friction often developed between adjoining ranks about who had the authority to do what. The "neighborhood police chief" program, for example, by giving sergeants 24-hour-a-day scheduling power, came into conflict with the "operations lieutenant" program giving lieutenants power to reshuffle task assignments during their 8-hour shift.[22]

A central element of decentralization in New York was the allocation of more corruption control resources to field commanders. This innovation had actually begun in the last month of the prior administration, but it was refined during the reform administration. The resources varied from an entire investigating squad at the borough command level (which encompassed about fifteen precincts) to an "integrity officer" in each precinct. While the most serious or complex corruption investigations were reserved for the central Internal Affairs Division (I.A.D.), almost all corruption complaints were farmed out to the decentralized units for resolution.[23] The field internal policing units could even decide not to investigate, but the central unit reviewed the field units' findings on every case and returned the case to the field units when further work was necessary.

Although the field units were used primarily for reactive investigations of citizen complaints, the field commanders could use their anti-corruption resources in any fashion they chose. In the later years of the reform administration, field units sometimes engaged in covert, premonitory "integrity tests" and proactive surveillance of likely misconduct situations. In effect, then, decentralization gave both the field commanders and those who evaluated the commanders similar resources for

22. Lawrence W. Sherman, Catherine H. Milton, and Thomas V. Kelley, *Team Policing: Seven Case Studies* (Washington, D.C.: Police Foundation, 1973), p. 31.
23. One sample of New York City corruption investigations in 1972 found that 97 percent were conducted by field units. See John C. Meyer, Jr., "The Nature and Investigation of Police Offenses in the New York City Police Department" (Ph.D. dissertation, State University of New York at Albany, 1976).

learning about and coping with corruption conditions. The establishment of two separate information systems, one local and one central, seemed to increase the probability that information about a given corruption situation would be captured. It also increased the tightness of supervision.

Quite apart from what supervisors do or are expected to do, one apparent way to increase the tightness of supervision is to increase the number of supervisors. The reform executive in New York convinced the city budget director and the mayor of the value of this approach at a time when a hiring freeze and other austerity measures had been invoked. By the end of the reform administration, the number of line officers per supervisor had dropped by 31 percent, from 7.8:1 to 5.4:1. The change was particularly marked at the level of first-line supervision; the absolute number of sergeants rose by over 40 percent.[24]

Yet a low ratio of line officers to supervisors hardly guarantees close supervision in any absolute sense. The ratio in Central City for the five years before the scandal was slightly above 3:1, about half of the ratio at the *end* of the New York reform administration. A somewhat greater tendency to use supervisory ranks in such line jobs as detective may account for the very low ratio in Central City, but the difference is still substantial. The style of supervision in Central City, however, was reportedly just as lax before the scandal as it had been in pre-scandal New York.

It is unclear whether the increased proportion of supervisors in New York actually increased the tightness of supervision. In the area of first-line patrol supervision, my personal observations at the time suggested that little if any change in practice resulted from the presence of more sergeants. In some instances, for example, two sergeants would ride in the same patrol car, whereas before the increase a sergeant would always ride with a patrol officer. In the supervision of the

24. Sherman, "Controlling Police Corruption," p. 164.

most corruption-prone tasks, however, the reduced span of control at the first-line level did seem to make a difference.

In contrast to patrol supervision, vice enforcement supervision in New York employed new supervisory methods as well as more supervisors. Gambling enforcement teams were reduced in size from fifteen officers under one lieutenant to six officers under one sergeant. Narcotics enforcement teams were made even smaller. Both narcotics and gambling enforcement, centralized into an Organized Crime Control Bureau, were shifted to a format of "directed investigations." Instead of the investigators deciding which cases to work on when, their supervisors dictated the daily tasks. No arrests or searches were to be made without the advance approval of a higher supervisor *and* the on-site presence of the first-line supervisor. While none of these methods could prevent corrupt collusion between supervisors and subordinates, they made the policy of holding the supervisors accountable into a fair and reasonable expectation.

The policy of supervisory presence at arrests was also adopted for a few corruption-prone patrol tasks: enforcement of construction site laws, Sunday closing laws, and gambling laws. Precinct commanders were instructed to identify the locations in their precincts most prone to corruption, such as corners frequented by prostitutes, taverns hosting gambling operations, and construction sites. A corruption control manual issued to all commanders provided a checklist for identifying these locations. The precinct commander or his aide was expected to give frequent but irregular surveillance to the corruption-prone locations, as both a deterrent and an information-gathering device.

Such elaborate procedures for increasing supervision were unnecessary in Newburgh, where both the population and the number of police officers are smaller than in one New York precinct. Instead, the Newburgh commissioner and his deputies (in the second reform administration) accomplished much the same thing as

New York's line supervisors did by personally directing narcotics and gambling cases, and by undertaking surveillance of police activities at all hours of the day and night. The one elaborate procedure that was employed in Newburgh was the installation on every patrol car of a tachograph, a device that records the movements and speed of a car in relation to elapsed time. The tachograph can tell when and for how long a car was stopped, information which can be useful both as a deterrent to sleeping on duty and as a tool for reactive corruption investigations.

Abolition of Corrupting Procedures

There are numerous formal procedures in most police departments that inadvertently encourage corruption. These procedures either imply levels of productivity that are all but impossible to achieve by legitimate means, or the procedures may create pressure for a de facto financial contribution from officers which they often try to "earn back" in corrupt ways. For example, detectives may be required to use personal autos for investigative work with little or no compensation for mileage. Vice investigations may require the purchase of information from informers, but funds for paying informers may be insufficient or unavailable. While such corrupting procedures could be found in all four cases, only the reform administration in New York formally recognized them as such and attempted to cope with them. For that matter, even New York's policies in this area were somewhat contradictory.

The reform administration in New York recognized the corrupting nature of arrest quotas in vice enforcement. The practices of basing promotions of vice investigators on the quantity of their arrests, and of evaluating vice enforcement supervisors on the arrest productivity of their subordinates, ignored the difficulty of gathering evidence on vice crimes in a legal fashion. The result was often perjury in trial testimony and in affidavits for search warrants. Institutionalized lying to achieve legitimate enforcement objectives paved the way for lying to cover up corruption.[25] The reform policy addressed the problem of developing new methods for evaluating vice enforcement workers on criteria other than arrest productivity. The enforcement priority was placed on the successful prosecution of a few big cases rather than on making weak arrests in a larger number of cases.

Yet the New York reform administration did not acknowledge the corrupting pressure caused by evaluating field commanders on the basis of the reported crime rates in their commands. This procedure was largely due to public pressure for crime control, and was, admittedly, modified to take the social context of the command into consideration; if social conditions "worsened" over a year in a precinct, for example, an increase in reported crime was not held against the commander. Yet evidence of such illegal practices as "canning" (not recording a citizen crime report) and "downgrading" (recording the report as a less serious offense than the citizen had described) was uncovered by both the police Inspections Division and the press. Given the absence of any clear direction for the field commanders on what they were supposed to do in order to reduce crime, this corrupt response (for the personal gain of promotion if crime reports did not increase) to a legitimate demand was quite predictable.

In the required use of police officers' personal funds, however, the reform policy in New York was consistent. "Buy money" for purchasing narcotics incidental to arrest was greatly increased, reducing the incentive to steal cash from narcotics pushers in order to make future "buy-and-busts." Funds for informers were increased and rigidly controlled, reducing the incentive for officers to keep back a portion of any seized narcotics for paying informers. Personal use of autos in surveillance work was reimbursed on a per-mile basis, instead of on a "going rate" basis related to the number of

25. See, e.g., Jonathan Rubinstein, *City Police* (New York: Farrar, Straus and Giroux, 1973), p. 383. See also Murphy and Plate, *Commissioner*, pp. 230–232.

arrests each investigator made.[26] The reform policy was to advance $200 to each investigator at the beginning of each month, the expenditure of which would then be accounted for by daily expense reports.

Central City's reform executive adopted similar policies for eliminating inducements to corruption, but not for that reason. Informers' fees allowances were increased threefold in Central City, and narcotics "buy" money was made more readily available. These two changes were the only examples of preventive control that could be found in Central City. Neither Newburgh nor Oakland made any effort to abolish corrupting procedures.

CHANGING THE ENVIRONMENT

All of the resources and many of the pressures for the four police departments to become corrupt had some connection to their organizational environments. Although certain elements of their environments were responsible for creating a new dominant coalition and imposing new goals, other elements persisted in preferring the police departments to be corrupt even after the scandals. Three of the reform executives tried to change those elements of their organizations' environments that could foster a return of organizational corruption. The two major environmental elements posing this threat were the task environment with its resources for corruption, and the political environment with its pressures for corruption. The attempt to change external conditions is classified as an internal control policy because the initiative for changing the environment came from within the organization.

Changing the Task Environment

The resources for corruption in the departments' task environments were largely unchanged by the scandals. Gambling and other vices persisted, and the "honest"

26. Allan N. Kornblum, "The Moral Hazards" (Ph.D. dissertation, Princeton University, 1973), p. 258.

citizens and merchants who wanted to pay for special consideration from the police seemed to have been unaffected by the scandals. The reform executives in Oakland, Newburgh, and New York all tried to eliminate as many resources for corruption as they could.

The reform executives in New York and Oakland both tried to eliminate gambling as a resource for corruption. The methods they used for accomplishing that goal, however, were as different as the task environments in which their departments were located. Gambling was in decline in Oakland when the reform executive took office,[27] and it had never reached the scale of the major industry that gambling was and is in New York. It was feasible, then, for the Oakland reform executive to eliminate police corruption related to gambling by eliminating gambling itself. The crackdown on gambling was given a major share of departmental resources, and from all accounts was extremely successful. No exceptions were made to the absolute ban on gambling. To this day, church bingo cannot be found in Oakland, nor charity bazaar gambling, nor any of the other exceptions usually made to the gambling laws in many cities.

In New York, on the other hand, the demand for gambling was so great, and the locations at which it thrived so numerous and mobile, that it would have been pointless to try to wipe it out altogether or even to reduce it substantially. In order to remove gambling as a resource for corruption, the reform police executive virtually eliminated gambling *enforcement*. He did not refuse to enforce the law, which would have been a violation of the city charter; he merely ordered the patrol force to refrain from initiating any gambling arrests. They could still make arrests in response to citizens' complaints, which were relatively rare. And investigators were still allowed to initiate arrests against high-level gambling "bankers." But the enforcement powers necessary for maintaining the precinct gambling

27. Giudici, interview.

"pad" were abolished, putting gambling out of reach as a resource for corruption.

The distribution of proactive enforcement powers within the police departments played an important role in the elimination of other resources for corruption. The New York reform executive adopted a policy towards Sabbath law and construction code enforcement similar to the one towards gambling, restricting the proactive authority of line patrol officers. Only in response to citizen complaints could officers take enforcement action in these areas, and then only in the presence of a supervisor. By restricting the discretionary authority of line officers in relation to their tasks, and by trying to minimize the frequency with which certain corruption-prone tasks were performed, the policy tried to remove those pervasive offenses as resources for corruption. Whether the policies were successful is unclear. Much publicity attended the changes, and citizen complaints of corruption in these areas did decrease. Nonetheless, some complaints of Sabbath and construction shakedowns kept coming in, so the policy probably failed to "dry up" these opportunities for corruption completely.[28]

In contrast, Central City expanded, rather than contracted, line enforcement authority in order to remove resources for corruption. Curiously, the policy change occurred in relation to the "little" scandal and before the reform administration took office. Up until 1972, only vice and narcotics officers were permitted to make vice or narcotics arrests. Any shakedowns in those areas were effectively monopolized by the officers holding the necessary enforcement authority. Some months before the little scandal occurred, the mayor ordered an end to any restrictions on the arrest authority of any officer. By breaking up the enforcement monopoly of special squads, the mayor destroyed their ability to guarantee protection from arrest. It is unclear, however, why the

28. For a critique of the policy, see Knapp Commission Report, pp. 149–151.

change was made when it was. Indeed, this pre-scandal reform exposed vice protection arrangements to younger, zealot officers, and may have given them much of the information they later revealed when generating the big scandal two years later.

Changes in enforcement policies may have been effective in insulating the organization from certain portions of the task environment, but they did not have a direct impact on the environment itself. Equally important were policies directed at changing the behavior of key actors in the police task environment: the corrupters and potential corrupters of the police, and the victims and potential victims of police corruption. One method for achieving this goal was used in common by the reform executives in Oakland, New York, and Newburgh. All three made concerted appeals to the public, largely through speeches to civic and trade groups.

The reform executive in Newburgh encouraged the public to report any knowledge or hints of police misconduct to him personally, rather than passively tolerating the existence of police corruption. In the evenings, the executive left a telephone answering machine on in his locked private office to receive any citizen complaints. He guaranteed a full investigation of any complaints, even anonymous ones, and met with many community groups and leaders to seek out information on police misconduct.

In New York, the greater size of the department required a less personal approach to generating public complaints than in Newburgh, but the methods were essentially the same in both cities. The New York Police Department publicized a telephone number that was set up to receive calls on corruption twenty-four hours a day, seven days a week. Following the Knapp Commission's charge that the public did not file corruption complaints because it had no faith in the willingness of the police to investigate such charges, the department initiated a strong public relations campaign to encourage more complaints.

The reform chief in Oakland did not seek to encourage complaints from the general public, although his successors did so some ten years later. Instead of addressing the self-perceived victims of corruption, the chief encouraged people who voluntarily gave money to the police to define themselves as victims of police power and traditional business practices, and to resist being victimized. His first target was the tavern owner. In a speech to a trade group encompassing three-fourths of the tavern owners in Oakland, the chief urged them to stop giving free drinks to policemen, and to stop serving any policemen in uniform, on or off duty. While many Oakland barkeepers had always been willing to buy the "deterrent presence" of uniformed officers in their establishments with free drinks, the trade group voted to cooperate with the chief's request.[29] The chief then moved on to other merchants in his efforts to stop an even more venerable tradition, the annual giving of Christmas gifts to policemen. His attack on the practice began with a front-page news headline reporting that seventeen captains and lieutenants had pledged to set an example by refusing to take any Christmas gifts.[30] The chief distributed letters to many merchants, stressing that if they all cooperated in not giving gifts, none of them would be left at a relative disadvantage in the good will of the police. The letters left unspoken the substantial saving of money the merchants would gain by heeding the chief's request.

The reform executive in New York also tried to "kill Christmas," as his aides put it, but New York's size and local culture made the effort more difficult than in Oakland. The reliance on patrol sergeants to distribute anti-Christmas-gift handbills to the hundreds of thousands of New York merchants weakened the effort somewhat. Some merchants, receiving the handbill from the same sergeants who had "collected" the year

29. *Oakland Tribune*, March 16, 1955.
30. *Oakland Tribune*, December 6, 1955.

before, interpreted the message as a demand for even bigger gifts. Other sergeants, particularly those belonging to the corruption groups called "Sergeants' Clubs," delivered the handbills to the nearest sewer grate and went on with their regular Christmas "collections." Both Oakland and New York officially acclaimed their anti-Christmas-gift campaigns a success, but several sources in both cities conceded that the practice had only been reduced and not eliminated.

"Killing Christmas" in Newburgh was complicated by a city ordinance which permitted city employees to accept gifts and rewards of up to twenty-five dollars. When the police union cited the ordinance as an objection to the reform executive's no-gift policy, he went to the city council and successfully demanded the repeal of the ordinance. The attendant publicity was apparently welcomed by many merchants in that economically declining city, and they used it to excuse their break with tradition.[31]

By far the most systematic attempt to change the task environment in any of the four cities was the bribery arrest campaign in New York. In the wake of the command shakeup of early September 1971, and one month before the Knapp Commission created the big scandal, the reform commissioner turned his public attacks away from indolent police commanders and launched an attack on the police-corrupting public. In a speech to the city's chamber of commerce, he announced that it "takes two to bribe." He told the businessmen that police officers would no longer respond to bribery attempts by saying, "You can get into trouble for talking like that." Instead, he put the public on notice that the new response to bribe offers would be, "You are under arrest." On that same day he issued a teletype message to all officers ordering them to arrest any briber, whoever the person, whatever the occasion, including hotel man-

31. Interview with James Taylor, former Police Commissioner, Newburgh, New York, October 8, 1975.

agers, restaurant owners, merchants, building superin-
tendents, housing contractors, tow-truck drivers, and
motorists.[32]

The rank and file responded immediately with a
dramatic increase in the number of bribery arrests. The
commissioner held several press conferences at which
he praised officers who had spurned large sums. Some
of them were even promoted to detective. The incentive
of promotion almost proved too successful, for the
number of bribery arrests quickly outpaced the number
of promotional openings. Perhaps because of changing
perceptions in the likelihood of promotion, the monthly
bribery arrest figures varied erratically for the rest of
the reform executive's administration. Nonetheless, a
much higher bribery arrest rate was sustained overall.
In the eight months prior to the introduction of the
policy (which is as far back as the department's statistics
go), the mean number of bribery arrests per month was
about fourteen. In the next four months, the mean
monthly total was almost seventy, a fivefold increase.
For the rest of the reform administration, the mean
monthly bribery arrest total was about fifty-seven.[33]

The Oakland police fell upon a bribery arrest policy
more by chance than by plan. In the fifth and final year
of the reform administration, a group of gamblers from
San Francisco approached an Oakland police captain
with a proposal for paid protection of a gambling room
they wished to establish. The captain played along with
the offer rather than taking any immediate action, and
went right to the chief to tell him of the proposal. The
chief decided to seize the opportunity to build a strong
case against the six would-be bribers, one that could
guarantee criminal convictions and prison sentences.
With the approval of the city manager, who notified the
publisher of the *Tribune* in advance just in case anyone
should accuse the police of real rather than feigned

32. *New York Times*, September 18, 1971, p. 34.
33. Internal Affairs Division Records, New York City Police Department, 1971–74.

complicity in the gamblers' scheme, a detailed agreement was worked out and a down payment was made.[34] The key transactions were tape-recorded and were witnessed by three high police officials. The gamblers were arrested, and a wave of publicity followed. The case was so strong that the wealthy gamblers did not even go to trial, accepting prison terms through plea bargaining.

Changing the Political Environment

The greatest obstacle to reforming a corrupt police department is a corrupt political environment. In New York, there was admittedly minimal participation of the political environment in police corruption even before the scandal. But in the other three cities studied, the linkage of politics to police corruption was substantial in the pre-scandal period.

Many academics and police administrators have expressed strong pessimism about the possibilities of changing corrupt political environments. Yet in two of the cases studied, there was a dramatic change in the integrity of the political environments. In Newburgh and Oakland, the police executives not only severed the linkage between politics and corruption, they also reduced political corruption in general.

The Oakland reform executive almost refused his promotion to chief because he assumed the job would be attached to corrupt political "strings." His first question of the city manager was: "How many commitments had to be made?" The manager, who had announced the reform chief's appointment without even advising the city council, replied: "Only two." That was because two Roman Catholic officers were to be promoted when eligible, instead of being passed over—a traditional practice in that Protestant-dominated department. The reform chief was surprised at the answer, having fully expected to be asked to allow gambling and prostitution

34. Interview with Wayne Thompson, former City Manager of Oakland, May 9, 1975.

operations to continue. But he demanded that the manager provide a written guarantee of the no-strings terms of appointment.[35]

The Oakland Police Department has a relatively high degree of *legal* autonomy from politics. The council-manager plan of government included statutes forbidding the council members from any interference in the police department. In practice, however, there had been great council involvement in the enforcement policy of the department. A councilman had been accused of receiving payoffs from a gambler via a police bagman as recently as two years before the big scandal.[36] But the reforming city manager and chief invoked the autonomy granted them in statute and plotted a radically new course for the department. No open confrontation ever developed between the city council and the chief over enforcement policy or any other issue. Indeed, the council backed up some of the most unpopular enforcement decisions, such as a gambling raid on the politically powerful Labor Temple. With the business elites on the side of police reform and legalistic vice enforcement, the council seemed to accept the new police policies as inevitable.

Moreover, some council members were reportedly afraid of the reform chief and his highly developed intelligence network. Quite apart from ending any involvement in police corruption, these politicians allegedly put an end to their involvement in other forms of corruption as well. All sources agree that the reform chief established a new moral climate in Oakland's municipal affairs by his avowed insistence on enforcing all the laws—against *any*body. The political weakness of the council no doubt made the moral climate easier to achieve there than in a strong, "machine"-run city. Even so, a change in the morality of a political elite is a rare achievement under any circumstances. The value of the achievement for controlling police corruption in Oak-

35. Ibid.
36. *Oakland Tribune*, April 7, 1955.

land was underlined by an important finding: virtually all of the corruption that reportedly persisted under the reform administration was initiated within the ranks of the police, rather than in the political or task environment. Extortion and theft, but not bribery, were the only forms of corruption surviving the change in the environment of the Oakland Police Department.

By the time the second reform executive arrived in Newburgh, two years of scandal and investigations had apparently put an end to the politically coordinated protection of vice operations. While two major politicians escaped prosecution only by their timely deaths, police officers were the only officials to have been punished up to that time. The executive confronted a massive morale problem, part of which was due to the injustice his officers felt at the politicians having gotten off free while the police took all the blame for corruption.

Both federal and state investigations of political corruption in Newburgh and Orange County seemed to have been closed at that point. The reform executive, after identifying some key sources of evidence, went to the (Republican) U.S. Attorney in New York City to ask for a new probe of (Republican) political corruption in upstate Orange County.[37] His request was granted. By early 1976 the Republican county chairman was convicted of a corruption-related federal felony, and a reformer-dominated city council seemed firmly entrenched in Newburgh. For reasons quite separate from the corruption investigations, the reform police executive was elevated to the position of city manager, and his handpicked deputy became police commissioner.

The changes in the political environment in both Oakland and Newburgh occurred in the context of a council-manager structure of government. Arguably, a police executive serving at the pleasure of a mayor could have more difficulty than one appointed by a city manager in challenging the political status quo. But in any

37. Taylor, interview.

form of city government, a post-scandal period is a time of flux; the nature of the status quo itself is unclear. Depending on the nature of the scandal, old commitments, debts, and favors might be excusably put aside if the equivalent of a "post-Watergate morality" seems to be ascendant. Under just such conditions, the police executives in Oakland and Newburgh seized the initiative in enforcing a new morality in the political environment of their police departments.

A Note on Pride

A common hypothesis in discussions of police corruption control is that the more pride police officers have in their department, the more "resistant" they will be to corruption. In examining the managerial side of reform strategies in the four cases, very little of the reform executives' attention was found to have been directed at building pride. Instead, the thrust of the strategies in every case was directed at removing "temptation" and building fear. As one official in the New York Police Department put it: "We have to continue to be tough because a lot of cops stopped being corrupt out of fear of being caught, not out of sudden idealism."[38]

The closest things to a pride-building strategy were the various efforts to improve the physical appearance of police officers and their equipment. Even these seemed to lower morale rather than raise it, at least in the short run, because the demands for spit-and-polish appearance were backed up by threats of punishment. On this evidence, then, it would seem that pride should be regarded as a consequence of long-term reform efforts, rather than as a cause: the more a police department resists corruption, the more pride its officers may have in the department. Fear of detection would seem to be causally prior to pride in integrity, at least in police departments in which corruption was once widespread.

The managerial policies described above were internally

38. *New York Times*, July 4, 1976, Section IV, p. 4.

generated strategies for preventing corruption by removing the internal and external conditions conducive to it. Some of the four departments used more of these preventive strategies than others, and in those departments the strategies may have had a more lasting impact on the conditions conducive to corruption. Since efforts to prevent corruption constitute a premonitory strategy for corruption control, the departments using more of these preventive policies can be classified as adopting a premonitory strategy for managerial control of corruption. Of the five managerial policies for preventing corruption (internal accountability, tight supervision, abolition of corrupting procedures, changing the task environment, and changing the political environment), New York and Oakland adopted four, Newburgh adopted three, and Central City adopted one. Since only Central City used less than half of the policies identified among the four departments, only Central City is classified as having adopted a postmonitory approach to managerial policies for corruption control. That is not to say that these five policies are the only ones that can be employed to prevent corruption, although they may be the most effective.

Managerial policies for preventing police corruption, no matter how effective, cannot completely eliminate opportunities for it. Fear of detection and punishment may also be necessary for deterring corrupt responses to the opportunities that do remain. While managerial personnel may play some role in detection and punishment, by far the greatest symbolic threat to corruption activities is the internal policing unit. While internal policing policies are also managerial decisions, they are qualitatively different from the strategies discussed above. Removed from the day-to-day operations of the department, internal policing is as separate from a police department as the police are from the life of their community. And like a police department, its greatest power is punishment, as the central agency of punitive control.

6. Punitive Control

The punitive control policies adopted after the scandals were practical applications of the deterrence hypothesis. The policies were attempts to increase the detection and punishment of corrupt acts in order to deter all officers in each department from engaging in corrupt acts. The task of detecting and gathering evidence on corrupt acts was assigned to separate units for internal policing.[1] The four departments differed substantially in the ways in which their internal policing units detected and gathered evidence on corruption. This chapter attempts to show how the differences in internal policing methods might account for the differences among the four departments in their punishment rates.

Like the preventive control policies implemented through line management and environmental change, the punitive control policies can be classified roughly as premonitory or postmonitory. Much of the work of all internal policing units is of necessity postmonitory, given the large volume of citizen complaints about corrupt acts alleged to have already occurred. In fact, the

1. Separate units for internal policing are relatively rare in U.S. police departments, even among the larger ones. In 1965, only 10 of 27 police departments (37%) in cities of 100,000 or more that responded to a mail survey claimed to have separate internal policing units. See Ronald A. LaCouture, "Summary of Findings of a Study of Inspection and Control Measures in Use in Selected Law Enforcement Agencies," in Gerald P. Foster, "Police Administration and the Control of Police Criminality: A Case Study Approach" (D.P.A. dissertation, University of Southern California, 1966). Of the four present cities, only New York differentiated internal policing from line management prior to the scandal. After the scandal, all four departments reorganized the internal policing task and greatly increased the manpower resources allocated to it.

vast majority of corruption cases in all four departments after the scandal was postmonitory, but the organization and methods of the four internal policing units clearly varied in the degree to which they were intended to anticipate and intercept any corruption still occurring after the scandal. Two of the departments had internal policing units with a capacity for detecting and investigating corrupt acts as they occurred or in advance of their occurrence. Even though the capacity was used on relatively rare occasions, it was nonetheless available. Moreover, the premonitory capacity of the internal policing units was well known to the officers in the departments where it was available, just as its absence in the other departments was also common knowledge. So while the typical internal investigation in all four departments was postmonitory, it may still be valid to classify some of the internal policing units as premonitory on the basis of their capacity.

These differences in the capacity of the internal policing units might account for the differences in punishment rates. The most severe punishment a police department can administer to its members is dismissal. Because of strict civil service regulations, the evidentiary standards required for dismissing an officer for cause are almost as high as the standards required for criminal conviction.[2] Strong evidence must be gathered in order to meet those standards. Premonitory methods of internal policing seem to be more likely to produce direct evidence that satisfies those standards. While premonitory methods were used only rarely, it was only the rare case that uncovered evidence sufficient for justifying dismissal. While problems of access to data prevented a detailed comparison of the outcomes of premonitory and postmonitory investigations, there does seem to be some relationship between the presence of a

2. See, e.g., *Managing for Effective Police Discipline: A Manual of Rules, Procedures, Supportive Law and Effective Management* (Gaithersburg, Maryland: International Association of Chiefs of Police, 1976), Chapter 3.

premonitory capacity and higher overall dismissal rates. The differences between a premonitory and post-monitory capacity for internal policing are evident in both the methods of detecting and the methods of investigating corruption. Following a description of the differences among the four departments in both phases of the internal policing of corruption, some data on dismissals are presented in order to explore the hypothesis that the presence of a premonitory capacity results in higher rates of internal punishment of corrupt acts.

DETECTION

Detection is the process by which control systems gain information about the violation of the rules they enforce. It is a discovery that certain violations might have occurred, might be occurring, or might occur in the future. Detection is not the process of proving "who done it," but rather the process of finding out what is done. The information acquired in the process of detection is suggestive, not conclusive. The gathering of conclusive information is the task of investigation, not detection. Detection provides the intelligence for investigations, or for making decisions about whether or not to investigate. It is the first stage in the process of mobilizing punitive social control.

There are three primary sources of intelligence about police corruption: citizens, police officers, and the probing of selected areas of police activity by internal policing units. All four departments used citizens and police as sources of intelligence, but only Oakland and New York probed selected areas of police activity. This latter source was always used as a premonitory method of detection, but the other sources could be used in either way.

Intelligence from Citizens
Every police department has some intelligence of possible police corruption thrust upon it by members of the

public.[3] Some police departments are better organized to capture that intelligence than others, and internal policing units in those departments are likely to receive more of the intelligence that citizens attempt to provide. No matter how much intelligence citizens provide and internal policing units capture, however, the social organization of police corruption activities makes intelligence from citizens very unlikely to produce premonitory detection of corruption.

Citizens possessing knowledge of police corruption may choose to present that knowledge to their police department in a variety of ways. The range of possibilities is limited only by the number of places at which the police organization is open to its environment. Letters received in the chief's office, calls received at the emergency dispatching switchboard, walk-in visits to police headquarters or district stations, and letters to other authorities that are forwarded to the police executive are the points of access to the police organization most commonly used by citizens complaining of corruption. This variety of input locations makes it difficult for internal policing units to capture and retain the information.[4] Rank-and-file officers often view corruption complaints as an attack on their department, and many officers tend to resist accepting the information presented in the complaint. In pre-scandal Oakland, Newburgh, and Central City, this resistance was tacitly approved by the dominant coalition. But in all four reform

3. See "The Administration of Complaints by Civilians against the Police," *Harvard Law Review*, Vol. 77 (January 1964), pp. 499–519; Timothy D. Naegele, "Civilian Complaints Against the Police in Los Angeles," *Issues in Criminology*, Vol. 3 (1967), pp. 7–34; Lee P. Brown, "Handling Complaints against the Police," *Police*, Vol. 12 (May–June 1968), pp. 74–81; and James R. Hudson, "Organizational Aspects of Internal and External Review of the Police," *Journal of Criminal Law, Criminology, and Police Science*, Vol. 63 (1972), pp. 427–435.

4. Lawrence W. Sherman, *The Control of Official Misconduct in Louisville, Kentucky* (Louisville, Ky.: Department of Public Safety, 1976), pp. 19–22.

systematically examine the relationship of the citizen complainants to the corruption situations they complained of, most complainants seem to have been either personally victimized by police thefts or indirectly "victimized" or offended by vice conditions which they inferred could only persist with paid police protection. Virtually all complainants seemed to define some personal interest as having suffered because of police corruption. While those citizens who make complaints constitute an unknown percentage of all those whose interests are hurt, it appears that people whose interests do not suffer from police corruption rarely make corruption complaints.

One reason why some of those whose interests are hurt do not report corruption may be fear of possible reprisal, particularly if the accused officer knows where to find the complainant. Even an anonymous complaint entails a risk of reprisal if the complainant is the only, or most likely, person to have informed the police of the corruption. For this reason, perhaps, victims rarely seem to make anonymous complaints of corruption. Wives and mothers of corruption victims, however, frequently make anonymous complaints. Their use of anonymity may stem from a desire to keep the complaint secret from the victim, rather than from the victimizer.[7] In any case, important information about corruption is often presented to the police anonymously.

Many police departments, however, tend to resist accepting anonymous corruption complaints more than they resist complaints from identified sources. In the pre-scandal period, only New York had a formal policy of accepting and investigating anonymous complaints, a policy which may have stemmed from previous corruption scandals in that city. In the reform period, New York continued this policy, and Oakland and Newburgh converted to it. Central City, however, adopted a "due

7. See Albert J. Reiss, Jr., *The Police and the Public* (New Haven, Conn.: Yale University Press, 1971), p. 86.

process" model of internal policing, in which it was held unfair to police officers to investigate them unless they knew the identity of their accuser from the outset of the investigation. This rule, of course, did not apply to the investigation of most other crimes, and there is no constitutional prohibition against investigating anonymous tips. Under strong pressure from police unions, however, many departments have gone to similarly great lengths to protect the rights of officers in internal policing procedures.[8] Whatever the reasons, a policy of ignoring anonymous complaints further reduces the amount of intelligence from citizens that reaches the internal policing units.

The same "due process" model can also exclude intelligence provided by identified complainants. In Central City, citizens complaining of police corruption were required to give formal statements, usually at police headquarters. A typed transcript of the statement was then prepared, and the citizen was required to return to headquarters to sign the statement, swearing that the facts it contained were true. If the citizen failed to come to headquarters either to make the statement or to sign it, an investigation was usually not performed. This procedure reduced the amount of information available for internal policing in two ways. First, the inconvenience of travel to headquarters during the work week (the only time the Internal Affairs Division was open) may have prevented or discouraged many complainants. Second, the requirement of signing the complaint may have frightened those who did make the journey to headquarters. Many citizens who gave formal statements in Central City never returned to sign them.

It is worth noting that citizens who report such "normal" crimes as burglary or assault do not encounter such obstacles. Crime complaints can generally be made over the telephone, and officers may be dispatched to

8. *Managing for Effective Police Discipline*, Chapter 3; and Herman Goldstein, *Policing a Free Society* (Cambridge, Mass.: Ballinger Publishing Co., 1977), pp. 265–266.

complainants' residences to take down more detailed information. Signing such complaints is often not required of the complainant when merely reporting the offense. The imposition of these special requirements on the making of corruption complaints suggests that the "real" goal of internal policing is not the sanctioning of violators, but rather the "cooling out" of people who threaten the organization. Regardless of intention, that was clearly the result in Central City.

It is unclear how much difference the quantity of corruption intelligence received from citizens makes in the ability of an internal policing unit to detect corruption. The social organization of police corruption activities keeps most citizens from becoming knowledgeable about these activities. Those who do become knowledgeable about specific details are usually either victims of or willing participants in police corruption. The information provided by victims usually produces postmonitory detection, although extortion victims do occasionally call an internal policing unit before a planned payoff meeting occurs. Consensual participants in police corruption are the citizens best able to provide premonitory intelligence of corruption, but they are also the citizens with the least incentive to do so. For the most part, then, intelligence from citizens produces only postmonitory detection of corrupt acts, on which the gathering of evidence is very difficult.[9]

Yet the organizational procedures for receiving intelligence from citizens can make a difference in the capacity of an internal policing unit for premonitory detection. Procedures that allow substantial fallout, ignore anonymous complaints, and require signed affidavits alleging corruption almost guarantee that no intelligence from citizens will produce premonitory detection. These procedures do capture some postmonitory intel-

9. For a discussion of the similar ineffectiveness of citizen complaints for detecting employment discrimination, see Leon Mayhew, *Law and Equal Opportunity* (Cambridge, Mass.: Harvard University Press, 1968).

ligence, but they are not flexible enough to deal with the urgency of premonitory intelligence; for example, anonymous tips that a payoff will occur or that police officers are committing a burglary would probably have been completely ignored with the procedures used in Central City. On the other hand, procedures that allow the capture of as much intelligence from citizens as possible are more likely to capture any premonitory intelligence that any citizens may provide, no matter how rarely such intelligence is provided. In this respect, Oakland, New York, and Newburgh had some capacity for premonitory detection of corruption through intelligence from citizens, and Central City had none.

Intelligence from Police Officers

Police officers are better sources of intelligence for detecting police corruption than citizens are. Both honest and corrupt officers, but especially the latter, have much better access than citizens do to information about corruption activities. Depending upon how the internal policing units use intelligence from police officers, such intelligence has the potential for producing premonitory detection of police corruption. All four departments employed this source of intelligence in their internal policing, but each department differed from the others in the extent to which the source was used to create a capacity for premonitory detection.

Like citizen complaints, the nature of information from honest officers may range from inferential suspicions to direct observations. Unlike citizen complaints, however, complaints from law-abiding police officers usually result from the opportunity police officers have to directly observe the behavior of other police officers. Indeed, merely accompanying officers on a full eight-hour tour of duty gave a group of citizen researchers the opportunity to observe roughly one in five patrol officers commit criminal violations of the law.[10]

10. Reiss, *The Police and the Public*, p. 156.

It is probably safe to assume that most honest police officers did not report their observations of their colleagues' corrupt acts to supervisors or internal policing units before the big scandals. Such reports did occur occasionally in New York and Central City, but they appear to have been largely ignored. Yet after the big scandals, police officers volunteered information about corruption to the internal policing units in all four cities. The internal policing units were generally receptive to the information volunteered by officers, although there were exceptions to that rule. The zealots in both New York and Central City were never very popular with any of their colleagues after they revealed corruption to the newspapers, and the internal policing officers shared the general dislike for the zealots. The hostility to the zealots was particularly damaging to detection in Central City, where the internal policing unit was oriented primarily to the allegations of past corruption that the zealots had made. Otherwise, the Central City corruption investigators clearly gave more credence to information supplied by police officers than by citizens. Police officers providing intelligence about corruption there were even spared the requirements of making and signing sworn statements.

While internal policing units in New York, Central City, and Oakland were generally receptive to corruption reports from police officers, only in New York and Oakland did they take the initiative to seek out police officers who would provide corruption intelligence. The internal policing unit in New York and the reform chief in Oakland used law-abiding officers (or so they were believed to be) to provide a steady stream of *inferential* information about possible corruption by their colleagues. Officers who volunteered information did so infrequently, and apparently only when they were fairly certain corruption existed. But officers who were questioned on a regular basis by an internal investigator provided much more information, albeit of generally lower quality than the more infrequent volunteered information. What seemed unimportant to the honest officers in the field was often very useful intelligence to the internal investigators. Under careful monitoring, honest officers in New York were even assigned by internal investigators to join corruption conspiracies in order to obtain better access to information (with all monies they received being turned over to the internal investigators as evidence). Quite apart from the value of the information these regular informants provided, the very fact that their existence was known to other police officers may have yielded a deterrent effect. Though the informants were few in number, no one was quite certain who could be trusted to keep silence.

In Oakland, the reform chief selected his friends from pre-scandal days and a few of his young college-educated recruits to serve in the role of internal informant. Reporting directly to the chief, and not to the Internal Affairs Division, the internal informants were assigned to such corruption-prone units as the vice and detective squads. Their role was never officially acknowledged, but the fact of their existence was generally suspected by the rank and file.[11]

In New York, the reform commander of the newly centralized vice and narcotics enforcement unit was the first to use "field associates," as the internal informants in New York were called. The vice commander recruited field associates from among the graduates of the in-service training course that prepared selected uniformed patrol officers for their new assignments to vice and narcotics work. By early 1972, 70 of the 400 officers newly assigned to that 925-officer bureau had agreed to serve as field associates.[12] Of course, the 330 new officers who were interviewed but not picked for the additional assignment as a field associate immediately

11. Interview with Lieutenant Garrett F. Kyle, Oakland Police Department, May 2, 1975.
12. *New York Times*, March 23, 1972, p. 37. See also Patrick V. Murphy and Thomas Plate, *Commissioner* (New York: Simon and Schuster, 1977), pp. 237–238.

spread the word that "spies" were about. Use of field associates was soon expanded to uniformed patrol by the recruitment of rookie graduates of the basic police training academy. In all the units penetrated in this manner, novices were always the target for recruiters of field associates, on the theory that officers embarking on a new assignment would be more loyal to professional ethics than officers who had already been in an assignment long enough to develop strong loyalties to their corrupt colleagues.

The Oakland program of seeking corruption information from honest officers generated no visible controversy, but the New York program was extremely controversial. Oakland had no police union in the 1950s (the chief threatened to fire any officer who joined one), but the New York police union protested long and loud against the use of "spies." The police union did not protest honest police officers reporting corruption per se. Rather, it was the crossing of the boundary between complainant and informer that infuriated the union. A police lieutenant from a Florida city who worked in the New York Internal Affairs Division on an exchange program wrote this of the field associates:

> [They] have created an uneasy aura of suspicion which has caused many nonparticipants to suffer embarrassment, humiliation and in some cases, ostracization by their peers.
>   Many officers . . . felt nothing but contempt for the individuals who volunteer for such a clandestine assignment. Many of the department personnel have now overreacted, and are not performing their assigned mission properly in the belief that their actions or non-actions will be misinterpreted by a nonqualified, biased observer.[13]

It is hard to see how an honest police officer acting as a field associate was "nonqualified" for performing the tasks of the unit to which he was assigned. But it is not

13. Middle Management Exchange Reports, New York City Police Department, 1973, unpaginated. Even the police executive called the program a "devilish" and "ruthless scheme." Murphy and Plate, *Commissioner*, p. 238.

hard to see why the use of honest police officers to spy on their colleagues generated so much anger among the rank and file and became a substantial morale problem in New York.

It is unlikely that honest officers in any of the departments, whether volunteers or "spies," reported all the information about corruption that they possessed. Even if they did, the information was limited by their own access to knowledge of corruption. Honest officers acquired reputations for being honest, particularly in the pre-scandal period. In the post-scandal reform period, information about corruption may have been controlled much more tightly than before, confined as much as possible to the participants. Even officers with reputations for corruption—or at least fraternal silence—may have been kept ignorant about the corrupt acts of others. While honest officers still had more opportunity than citizens to infer corruption or to observe it accidentally, they may still have been ignorant of much or most of the corruption activities. In particular, they usually lacked enough detailed information to produce premonitory detection of corruption activities. Without detailed knowledge, honest officers could not predict the time, place, and identity of participants in corrupt activities.

What honest officers did not know, corrupt officers did know. Participants in corruption arrangements could predict the occurrence of corrupt transactions and could identify the other participants. In addition to their own testimony, corrupt officers could provide opportunities for gathering corroborative evidence which would create a stronger case. The problem, of course, was to induce corrupt officers to betray their co-conspirators and provide the information needed for premonitory detection of corruption. The solution used in New York was to create a strong case against one member of a corruption conspiracy, and then offer him a grant of immunity or leniency in exchange for his cooperation with investigators.

Most grants of immunity are used for purposes of
postmonitory detection or investigation. It is a rare case
in the detection of any kind of crime, and not just police
corruption, that employs immunity for premonitory detection, perhaps because of the danger such cooperation
poses to those receiving immunity. The dangers attendant to being "turned around" in police corruption
are particularly substantial, since police officers have
ample opportunity to kill each other with satisfactory
excuses. A turned-around corrupt police officer risks
being discovered by his co-conspirators as a traitor, particularly if he wears a "kel" tape-recorder hidden on his
body to record conversations in which corruption is discussed.[14] It is not surprising, then, that the technique
was never used in any of the four departments before
the scandal, and was used after the scandal only in New
York.

Two assumptions had discouraged the use of corrupt
officers as a source of premonitory intelligence. One
assumption was that corrupt police officers would never
betray their colleagues in corruption. The other was
that corrupt officers were "rotten apples" who should be
expelled as soon as sufficient evidence was gathered
against them. The Knapp Commission in New York
demonstrated that the first assumption was false by re-
cruiting several corrupt officers to work for it. The
commission also argued strongly against the second assumption, claiming that corruption was organized and
that organized corruption could only be controlled by
apprehending entire corruption conspiracies, not single
police officers.

In this as in many of its recommendations, the Knapp
Commission was heeded by the New York City Police
Department. The reform administration in New York

14. See, e.g., Loudon Wainwright, "The Secret World of an
Undercover Investigator," in *Police Corruption: A Sociological Perspective* ed. Lawrence W. Sherman (Garden City, N.Y.: Anchor Books,
1974), pp. 253–262.

first heard of the Knapp Commission's success with the turn-around technique in the summer of 1971. By April of 1972, the department's internal investigators had employed the technique themselves in a large case that resulted in the apprehension of a gambling corruption group of over forty people, the largest single corruption conspiracy apprehended in any of the four cities.[15]

The use of intelligence from police officers clearly differed enough among the four departments to give some departments a greater capacity for premonitory detection than others. Three kinds of differences are apparent. First, the departments differed in their response to information volunteered by honest police officers. While Oakland and Newburgh were always receptive to this information, the internal policing unit in Central City once refused to provide an honest officer with a body microphone in order to investigate corruption of which he was suspicious. Even with volunteered information, Central City had less premonitory capacity than Oakland and New York. Second, only Oakland and New York sought out information from law-abiding officers, i.e., created internal informants or "spies." Third, only New York used corrupt officers as sources of premonitory intelligence, "turning them around" to work as spies for the internal policing units. In the use of police officers as sources of corruption intelligence, New York developed the greatest premonitory capacity, followed by Oakland and then by Central City. Newburgh did not have any intelligence of corruption supplied by police officers during the reform administration.

Intelligence from Probing

While intelligence from citizens and police officers can be used to produce either premonitory or post-monitory detection, intelligence generated by the probing of selected police activities by internal policing agents is inherently premonitory. The methods of detection used

15. *New York Times*, May 3, 1972, p. 1.

with this category of intelligence sources are designed precisely to uncover ongoing police corruption activities. Four sources of intelligence were developed by probing in Oakland and New York, two of which were also employed in Newburgh: criminal informants, wiretaps, corruption "patrols," and "integrity tests."

One of the best ways to penetrate any criminal conspiracy is to use criminal informants. Noncriminal informants, including milkmen, mailmen, storekeepers, barbers, and bartenders, may also be able to supply information about police corruption when requested to do so. But as a New York police investigating manual noted after listing these honest sources, "the most valuable source of information is likely to be a person who is now, or has been part of the criminal group."[16] Criminal informants are often unreliable, but they have the best access of anyone outside of a corruption conspiracy itself to information about the details of corruption arrangements. All of the internal investigators interviewed agreed that criminal informants were an excellent source of premonitory intelligence on corruption. In certain rare instances, internal investigators in New York paid these informants for their information. More often, as was always the case in Newburgh and Oakland, nonmonetary rewards were used to encourage informants to inform. These rewards ranged from immunity from arrest for the informants' own offenses to simple obligation for future considerations.[17]

Wiretapping of professional criminals and police officers in Oakland and New York also produced premonitory intelligence about corruption. The Oakland reform chief had his Intelligence Division regularly monitor conversations on headquarters telephones without a court order. When any wiretap information pointed to specific officers, both Oakland and New York obtained

16. "A Functional Guide to Internal Investigations," New York City Police Department, 1974, p. 20.
17. See Jerome H. Skolnick, *Justice Without Trial* (New York: John Wiley, 1966), pp. 112–138; and Jonathan Rubinstein, *City Police* (New York: Farrar, Straus and Giroux, 1973), pp. 211–213.

court orders to wiretap the officers' home phones. Newburgh did not use wiretaps, because (a) they had no occasion to, and (b) they lacked the necessary manpower, equipment, and secrecy capabilities. Central City used wiretaps illegally against the evil fringe during the pre-scandal period, but the reform administration reportedly obeyed the law in that state against any form of wiretapping.

Three of the reform administrations employed corruption patrollers: members of the internal policing units who looked for general indications of corruption activities. In Newburgh and Oakland, the police executives often drove around at night trying to monitor potential corruption situations. In New York, this task was performed routinely on carefully selected targets by members of various internal policing units. Locations known for gambling, prostitution, narcotics sales, construction, and illegal drinking were regularly observed in New York for indications of protection payoffs. In a different sense of "patrolling," the Oakland Internal Affairs Division regularly asked randomly selected bailees if the jail officers had recommended a particular bail bondsman. Similarly, accident victims were asked if traffic officers had recommended a particular lawyer for an injury suit. If they were found, both "recommendations" provided indications of possible kickbacks to police officers from the people the police recommended.

Perhaps the most controversial tactic for probing for police corruption was the "integrity test." Both Oakland and New York constructed artificial situations giving police officers the opportunity to commit corrupt acts. The tests were designed to yield the evidence needed to arrest and convict an officer who failed the "test." Based on intelligence from other sources, or on mere suspicion, integrity tests intercepted corruption as it occurred. Oakland confined this practice to its most persistent corruption problem, thefts of property from arrested persons. As early as the first year of the reform administration, Oakland's reform chief asked the dean

of the Criminology School at the nearby University of
California to supply some students to serve as actors in a
test. One by one, the students were dressed up like
bums, doused with cheap gin, and left on the street at
night. In their pockets were about twenty-five dollars in
marked bills. An internal investigator then made an
anonymous phone call to the police dispatcher, complaining of the presence of a "drunk" on the street. When
the "drunk" was arrested, his money and other personal
effects were impounded, according to standard procedure. But when the "drunk" was bailed out by another
student, the amount of money returned was ten to fifteen dollars less than the amount impounded. Evidentiary problems developed during the first several tests,
so that arrests could not be made. In the final year of the
reform administration, however, two jail officers were
caught red-handed in possession of the marked money,
dismissed, and convicted of theft. The actors in the final
test later joined the Oakland Police Department and
were severely ostracized by fellow officers.[18]

Rather than confining integrity tests to one form of
corruption, the New York reform administration used
the tactic for almost every form of corruption. Some
were random tests of conformity to procedures, such as
the infamous "wallet drop": wallets containing marked
money were dropped by internal policing officers near
randomly selected patrol officers to see if they would
turn the wallet in to the police property clerk with the
full amount of money. Other integrity tests had more
specific targets. Money left in an illegally parked car was
often used to test the integrity of certain police tow-
truck drivers against whom allegations of stealing from
towed cars had been made. Fake gambling operations
were created to see if police officers tried to establish
paid protection arrangements. Perhaps the most complex test of all was the use of an undercover officer
posing as a narcotics pusher to see if other undercover

18. Interview with George W. O'Connor, former Oakland Police
officer, October, 1975.

narcotics enforcement officers were actually paying out the total amount of "buy money" they claimed to have paid the "pusher" for narcotics in the course of building a narcotics case.

While the integrity test tactic was disliked by the rank and file in both Oakland and New York, it was again only the New York rank and file that voiced a public protest. When the tests were first disclosed in the third year of the New York reform administration, the police union claimed that roving "entrapment teams" were violating the civil rights of police officers, and they asked the district attorney to have the practice stopped. The district attorney replied that even if it was occurring in the integrity tests, entrapment is not a crime but a defense. The internal policing units denied that integrity tests constituted entrapment, since the tests only provided an opportunity, and not an inducement, for the commission of corrupt acts.[19]

The premonitory uses to which the various sources of intelligence on corruption were put in each city are summarized in Table 1. The premonitory uses are indicated if the internal policing unit in a city ever employed those approaches in the period indicated, even if premonitory detection characterized a small proportion of all internal policing activity. Most of the resources of any internal policing unit are consumed by the processing of public complaints. While ignoring such complaints in favor of other forms of intelligence might be more cost-effective, postmonitory complaint investigation is defined by most cities as a public trust which must be kept. But it may well be that the rare occasions on which intelligence was used for premonitory detection of corruption produced both an independent deterrent

19. *New York Times*, November 29, 1972, p. 49. The Detectives' Union in New York also challenged the tests of corruption complaint intake procedures described above, but their request for a restraining order was denied on the grounds that such tests are a "clearly justifiable" exercise of the Police Commissioner's official powers. *Crowley v. Codd*, Sup. Ct. N.Y. Cty., Ascione, J., *New York Law Journal*, October 28, 1977.

TABLE 1. Premonitory Detection Capacity

| | New York | |
Uses of Intelligence	Pre-scandal	Reform
Citizens		
1. Complaint intake control	−	+
2. Anonymous complaints accepted	+	+
3. No signature required	+	+
Police Officers		
4. Premonitory use of volunteers	−	+
5. Recruitment of internal informants	−	+
6. Development of "turn-arounds"	−	+
Probing Targets		
7. Criminal informants	−	+
8. Wiretaps	−	+
9. Corruption patrollers	−	+
10. Integrity tests	−	+
Total premonitory uses of intelligence	2	10

Key: + = used; − = not used.
N.A. = Not applicable.

effect and a substantial portion of the total punishment of corrupt acts.

The detection of corruption is only a necessary, and not a sufficient, condition for the imposition of punitive sanctions against corruption. Detection generally provides only the targets for investigation. Investigation must then assemble the legal and administrative evidence required for imposing sanctions. Whether or not

	City				
Central City		*Oakland*		*Newburgh*	
Pre-scandal	*Reform*	*Pre-scandal*	*Reform*	*Pre-scandal*	*Reform*
−	−	−	+	−	+
−	−	?	+	−	+
−	−	?	+	?	+
−	−	−	+	−	N.A.
−	−	−	+	−	N.A.
−	−	−	−	−	N.A.
−	−	−	+	−	+
−	−	−	+	−	−
−	−	−	+	−	+
−	−	−	+	−	−
0	0	0	9	0	5

that evidence can be assembled may depend upon how corruption investigations are conducted.

INVESTIGATION

The methods of investigation used in the four cities to gather evidence on corruption varied in three major respects. The internal policing units differed in the way they defined and treated the targets of their investigations. They also differed in the way in which they employed the central tactic of all investigations, the interview. Finally, they differed in their readiness to employ covert methods of investigation. The differences in each of these practices affected the capacity of the internal policing units to gather evidence on corruption in a premonitory fashion. The presence or absence of a premonitory investigative capacity, in turn, affected the likelihood that direct evidence of the commission of a corrupt act would be gathered.

Both administrative discipline and criminal convictions for bribery depend upon the ability of investigators to supply direct evidence of the commission of a corrupt act. Testimony reporting observations of corrupt acts is sometimes sufficient, but more than one independent source of evidence is often required. When there is oral evidence from only the accuser and the accused, the accused seems to benefit more often. Experienced corruption investigators cite the importance of physical evidence for obtaining convictions. The kinds of physical evidence most often used in corruption cases are tape recordings of conversations held during bribery transactions, and marked bills seized on the person of the defendant. The former head of the Intelligence Division of the U.S. Internal Revenue Service, which has conducted hundreds of bribery investigations, once said that he knew of no bribery conviction that was ever obtained without such evidence.[20]

The central element determining the premonitory capacity of most aspects of corruption investigations is secrecy. More specifically, the investigation must be kept secret from the target of investigation if direct evidence is to be gathered. When a case is "blown" by the target being "tipped off" that he is (or they are) under investigation, the target generally ceases his corruption activities in order to avoid being trapped in the act. Several investigative policies used by some internal policing

20. Address by Donald Bacon to the American Academy for Professional Law Enforcement, Washington, D.C., January 9, 1975.

units almost guarantee that the targets will learn that they are under investigation. To the extent that the investigative policies failed to provide the potential for maintaining secrecy, the internal policing units employing them lacked the capacity for premonitory investigation.

Targets of Investigations

The internal policing units varied in both their policies for defining their investigative targets and their policies of according certain rights to those targets. Both policies towards investigative targets affected the capacity of the internal policing units for conducting premonitory investigations, because the policies affected the secrecy of the investigations. Only the internal policing units in New York and Oakland, after the scandals, defined the targets of their investigations in broad enough terms to keep the investigations secret from all participants in corruption conspiracies. The internal policing units in New York *before and after* the scandal, in Oakland *after* the scandal, and in Central City *before* the scandal investigated officers without formally notifying them that they were targets of an investigation.

Once possible corruption has been detected, the definition of the target of an investigative effort for gathering further evidence can be either broad or narrow. Narrow definitions limit the investigative target to the officer(s) identified by detection. Broad definitions assume that other officers may be participants in the corruption activity detected, in addition to those already identified. The scope of the definition of targets has several consequences for the investigation. One consequence of a limited definition is the adoption of a criminal trial model for the conduct of the investigation: evidence is assumed to be something that already exists, and it either exculpates or convicts the "accused" officer. Witnesses are questioned directly as if they were under oath (which they usually are not), and their responses are taken at face value. If, as often happened in Central

City, citizen X denies a complaint from citizen Y that X pays off Z, the investigation is closed for "lack of evidence," and the "accused" is thereby "acquitted."

A related consequence of a limited definition of targets is an investigative preoccupation with verifying whether or not the *specific* events alleged in complaints (or detected through other sources of information) did in fact occur. If the evidence—which "speaks for itself" under this model—does not prove that the alleged events occurred, then the "trial" is over. The investigative effort does not attempt to determine if other corruption events might have occurred or might be occurring.

A third consequence of a limited definition of investigative targets is an absence of analysis of corruption patterns and trends. Each case is treated as a closed system, and the case-by-case orientation to investigations obscures the possible connections between cases.[21] The possible value of each case as an intelligence source for initiating other cases or for assisting cases initiated in other ways is ignored.

The most important consequence of a limited definition of investigative targets is that it may provide a warning signal to many other corrupt officers not defined as part of the target of the investigation. If the investigation is successful in apprehending the target, the target's co-conspirators may be able to avoid detection. The unapprehended partners, "tipped off" that they are vulnerable to detection, are given a chance to "lay low" and "cover their tracks" with defensive strategies. Most important, they probably cannot be apprehended with direct evidence of corrupt acts.

In contrast, broad definitions of investigative targets include whatever is *suggested* by the preliminary information detected, rather than just whatever is stated explicitly. If, for example, cooperation by a number of officers is suggested by the detected information, then

21. See William P. Brown, "A Police Administrative Approach to the Corruption Problem" (report prepared for the U.S. Law Enforcement Assistance Administration, 1971).

the one or two officers identified will be just the starting point for defining the target, the "tip of the iceberg." This broader definition of targets produces consequences opposite to those of the limited definition of targets: a search for any evidence of corruption, reduced concern for the veracity of the specific allegations, an attempt to construct patterns of relationships among cases, and a goal of apprehending an entire conspiracy en masse.

The broader definition of investigative targets results in a model of investigations more akin to a "fishing expedition" than to a criminal trial. The information that initiates the investigation only points out the best location for "fishing," and does not specify a particular "charge" that must be adjudicated. Evidence is assumed to be elusive and may not even exist until the investigators can create a situation in which the ongoing corruption can occur under their eyes.

A broader definition of the target allows the investigation to abandon inquiry into the specific events initially detected in order to pursue more important or more fruitful lines of inquiry on the same target. The speedy resolution of a citizen's complaint, for example, is given a lower priority than detecting and apprehending as many corrupt officers as possible. Similarly, several different cases may be integrated in order to highlight patterns of corruption and the most fruitful strategies for gathering evidence on all the officers implicated in the patterns. The broader definition encourages more analysis and less case-by-case thinking.

Finally, the broader definition of investigative targets allows investigators to refrain from immediately apprehending individual members of corruption groups, despite sufficient evidence for doing so, until the entire group can be apprehended with adequate evidence against it. This freedom offers the possibility of "turning around" the first officer against whom adequate evidence has been found, and enlisting his cooperation in return for lenience. The freedom to delay apprehension may also offer more time for surveillance. In any case, the effect of the delay is to increase the probability of punishing the entire corruption group, rather than just one member. A New York investigator publicly described his plans for this new strategy: "From now on we are going to try to take the cell rather than the individual who works within the cell, and from there work our way into the channels of organized crime as far as we can before we close in and thus perhaps get the whole operation."[22]

Within six months after that announcement, the reform administration had indeed "taken" a forty-member gambling corruption "cell." Rather than arresting the first member against whom evidence was obtained, the internal investigators "turned around" that member and used him to build a case against the whole operation.

The broad definition of investigative targets, however, is of no value for creating a premonitory capacity if there is a policy of notifying targets at an early stage that they are under investigation. The four cities differed on the point at which they would notify a target of an investigation. Under the trial model of internal investigation used during the reform period in Newburgh and Central City, all officers were notified immediately of any complaints made against them. This practice gave the suspected police officers far greater rights than the law required they be given. Oakland and New York, on the other hand, kept investigations secret from the targets for as long as possible, giving no more notification than the law required, which generally meant no notification until the targets were interrogated or arrested. If an investigation never reached the point of legally required notification, the target in Oakland or New York was never notified that he had been under investigation. This practice preserved the possibility of reopening a case if further evidence was subsequently discovered.

Both the broader definition of targets and the policy

22. William P. McCarthy, quoted in the *New York Times*, November 19, 1971, p. 26.

of notifying targets of an investigation at the end rather than the beginning of a case allowed corruption investigations to maintain greater secrecy. Secrecy afforded the opportunity to gather direct evidence of corruption activities as they were occurring. The use of these two policies, then, produced a greater capacity for premonitory investigation.

Interviews

Verbal testimony is the most commonly used form of evidence in criminal investigation. Where investigators do not observe the commission of crimes themselves, they must seek out the testimony of citizens who do. In corruption investigations, both the manner and the timing of conducting interviews with citizen witnesses to corrupt acts can affect the premonitory capacity of investigations. The manner in which the interviews are conducted can affect the willingness of witnesses to cooperate with dangerous premonitory tactics. The timing of the interviews can affect the chances of the investigation remaining secret from the investigation's target.

For various reasons, internal investigators of police corruption are often antagonistic to citizens claiming that they have witnessed police corruption. In prescandal New York and post-scandal Central City, witnesses were often treated as if they were the ones under investigation. Interviews in those cases were more like interrogations. Instead of seeking to enlist the cooperation of the witnesses in the frightening and time-consuming process of providing evidence of corruption, the internal investigators often expressed skepticism about the witnesses' stories. Investigators in New York, for example, were often reported to have demanded of the witnesses, "How did you know he was really a cop?"

The failure to enlist the cooperation of witnesses can result in a loss of postmonitory evidence. More important, however, may be the loss of potential cooperation by the witness in attempts to gather premonitory evidence. An extortion victim, for example, is often in a position to tell internal investigators when the next payoff is to be made. The investigators can then arrange to observe the transaction, and can provide the victim with marked bills to give to the extorting police officer, and a body microphone to tape-record any discussion of the transaction. Evidence of this nature is extremely valuable in obtaining sanctions. But a great risk to the extortion victim is involved in such procedures.

Regardless of how the internal investigators conduct interviews, the timing of the interviews may destroy the possibility of gathering premonitory evidence. One investigation in Central City during the reform period was a clear example of the consequences of poor timing. The internal policing unit received an allegation that a tow-truck company had been paying kickbacks to Traffic Division officers for calling the company's trucks to the scene of any accident before competing firms learned of it. The internal investigators immediately went to the tow-truck company to interview the manager, asking him directly if he paid kickbacks to the traffic officers. The manager denied the allegation, and the case was closed when no other evidence could be found to support the charge. If the interview had been delayed, other investigative tactics, such as surveillance, might have produced direct evidence of the kickbacks. By conducting the interview first, the internal investigators tipped off the corrupt actors that they were under investigation. Even if the case had not been closed, it is doubtful that any direct evidence could have been obtained after the interview.

Because Oakland and New York were more prepared to employ other tactics besides interviews, the internal investigators in those cities did not rush into an interview. In New York, internal investigators were even required to plan out an entire investigation before taking any action, in order to anticipate the possible consequences of different ways of timing the steps of the investigations. By postponing the key interviews, Oakland and New York maintained the possibility of gathering evidence on corruption as it occurred, and in that respect they had a greater premonitory capacity than the other two departments.

Covert Methods

While the policies regarding targets and interviews could either maintain or eliminate a premonitory investigative capacity, the use of covert methods was inherently premonitory. Covert investigative methods are similar to the tactics for detecting corruption by probing selected targets. Indeed, the line between detection and investigation is very thin in this area of internal policing of corruption. The analytical distinction is that covert methods of investigation follow after the initial detection of corruption (by whatever means). In operational practice, the distinction is often immaterial. Five covert methods of corruption investigation were used after the scandal in New York, four of which were used in Oakland, one in Central City, and none in Newburgh. The more such methods could be employed, the more ways of gathering direct evidence on corruption there were, and the greater the premonitory capacity of the internal policing unit using them. By definition, covert tactics are ways of gathering evidence without letting the investigative targets become aware that they are under investigation.

Visual surveillance was the most common covert tactic used in all the departments except Newburgh. It does, however, entail a certain risk of "blowing" the case. The corruption investigator's manual in New York distinguishes four degrees of surveillance, with "close" surveillance running the biggest risk of detection by the suspect. "Loose" surveillance of an officer is one way to gather more information about whom the officer is seeing, but close surveillance is required to determine the nature of his contacts with others.

If visual surveillance suggests a confirmation of the initial corruption intelligence, electronic surveillance (wiretapping or bugging) can provide a more detailed test of the hypothesis, although such surveillance is forbidden in many states. Any kind of surveillance requires a substantial commitment of personnel resources, wiretapping even more so than visual surveillance. The quality of the initial intelligence seems to have determined how great a commitment of resources was made to surveillance in Oakland and New York, the two cities using this tactic.

If a "turn-around" is developed, or if the complainant is an extortion victim, then a microphone concealed on the body of the turn-around or complainant can transmit to a nearby tape recorder statements made during corrupt transactions. The risk of this tactic blowing the investigation, however, is very high. Wary corruption suspects often pat down the body of a person they do business with in order to check for recording equipment. If any equipment is found, the wearer's life may be endangered if he does not have a backup team close at hand. For these reasons, the use of body mikes is generally confined to preplanned payoff encounters, called "meets." Newburgh did not even have the recording equipment needed for this tactic. Central City had the equipment, but its internal policing commander refused to use it for bribery arrests. New York and Oakland both obtained many sanctions with it.

The use of body microphones presumes another tactic, the faked situation. The tape-recorded payoff is not a real payoff, but a fake one staged in order to make an arrest during the commission of a corrupt act. The use of faked situations to test integrity for intelligence purposes, described above, is little different from the use of faked situations in the course of an investigation. Again, Oakland and New York used them; Central City and Newburgh did not.

Table 2 summarizes the premonitory investigative capacity of the four departments both before and after the big scandals. The results of this evaluation are somewhat surprising. While New York and Oakland both increased their capacity for premonitory investigations

TABLE 2. Premonitory Investigative Capacity

| | City | | | | | | | |
| | New York | | Central City | | Oakland | | Newburgh | |
Investigative Policy	Pre-scandal	Reform	Pre-scandal	Reform	Pre-scandal	Reform	Pre-scandal	Reform
Targets								
1. Define broadly	−	+	−	−	−	+	−	−
2. Notify last	+	+	+	−	−	+	−	−
Interviews								
3. Enlist cooperation	−	+	−	−	?	?	−	−
4. Not done first	−	+	+	−	−	+	−	−
Covert Methods								
5. Surveillance	+	+	+	+	−	+	−	−
6. Turn-arounds	−	+	−	−	−	−	−	−
7. Body microphones	+	+	−	−	−	+	−	−
8. Wiretaps	+	+	+	−	−	+	−	−
9. Faked situation	−	+	+	−	−	+	−	−
Total policies allowing premonitory capacity	4	9	5	1	0	7	0	0

of corruption during the post-scandal period, the capacity remained unchanged in Newburgh and *declined* in Central City. Central City demonstrated some premonitory capacity for investigation of the "evil fringe" (but not of other police officers) before the scandal, but became almost completely postmonitory after the scandal. On reflection, however, this finding should not be surprising. The officers most capable of conducting premonitory investigations in Central City, as noted earlier, were committed to corrupt goals for the department. Their capacity was unavailable to the new, honest dominant coalition, which was therefore compelled to rely on the postmonitory skills of the less competent but ostensibly honest investigators it could induce to work in the internal policing unit.

The internal policing unit in Newburgh was only part-time, and it never detected any ongoing corruption after the scandal. Moreover, from all reports, there was no ongoing corruption after the scandal for the unit to investigate. In a sense, then, the fact that it had no premonitory investigative capacity was irrelevant.

SANCTIONS

The preceding discussion showed why internal policing units with a premonitory capacity might be more likely to obtain sanctions against corruption than units that are exclusively postmonitory. The data necessary for a direct test of this hypothesis were impossible to locate, largely because neither police departments nor courts keep separate statistics on the sociological category of police corruption. Comparing all forms of sanctions among police departments is difficult, since even the same sanctions (e.g., suspension) can have different meanings in different departments. Two other problems complicate comparisons: the variations among and within police departments in recording either *punishments* or punished *individuals*; and the common practice of administering single punishments against individuals simultaneously for several offenses, some of which are corrupt acts and some of which are not.

One possible indicator of sanctions against corruption can be found in the annual dismissals of officers from a police department. If an internal policing unit can prove corruption occurred, the guilty officer(s) will usually be dismissed. Not all dismissals are for corruption, but most proven cases of corruption produce dismissals (unless the defendant "turns around" and cooperates with investigators). By making the tentative assumption that the number of dismissals for corruption is positively and consistently related to the number of all dismissals—as research impressions suggest—then total dismissals can be used to indicate sanctions against corruption.[23]

The greatest advantage of this indicator is that it is comparable among police departments. Data were collected for enough years for each of the departments to provide a sample just barely large enough to examine the strength of association between differences in the premonitory capacity of internal policing units and the absolute level of dismissals per 10,000 officers. While comparisons within departments over time provided mixed results due to the small number of years for each city, the total number of years from all cases provided a sample large enough for fairly clear results. Newburgh, however, had to be excluded, since it did not have any internal policing unit for four of the five years under study, and this analysis is only concerned with cases that had at least some method of internal policing.

The dismissal data are compared to internal policing

23. This indicator is not without its problems of validity. Many strong cases against corruption are never presented because the defendant resigns, either voluntarily or under pressure, before the case comes to administrative trial; those events are not included in this indicator. Many police officers are dismissed after they have been convicted of a felony. Some of those convicted were investigated by agencies outside the police department, and internal policing systems deserve no credit for their dismissal; those events could not be excluded from this indicator. Further, many dismissals are later reversed by civil service boards or civil courts, and the dismissed officers may be reinstated with back pay. Since such cases can take years, it was impossible to subtract the reinstatements from the dismissals.

scores that reflect the premonitory capacity of the corruption control units in each department in each year. The internal policing score is computed by adding the number of premonitory uses of corruption intelligence and the number of investigative policies allowing the possibility of premonitory investigation. Table 3 shows the raw data, and Table 4 shows the statistical relationship between internal policing scores and dismissal rates for all causes.

TABLE 3. Internal Policing and Dismissal Rates*

City	Year	Department size†	Total officer dismissals	Internal policing score‡	Officer dismissals per 10,000
New York	1968	27,536	20	6	7.3
	1969	29,940	16	6	5.3
	1970	31,583	39	6	12.3
	1971§	31,715	60	19	18.9
	1972	30,861	62	19	20.1
	1973	29,773	82	19	27.5
	1974	31,313	74	19	23.6
Central City	1969	1,021	2	5	19.6
	1970	1,087	3	5	27.6
	1971	1,095	1	5	9.1
	1972	1,081	2	5	18.5
	1973	1,098	5	5	45.5
	1974§	1,090	1	1	9.1
Oakland	1953	697	6	0	86.1
	1954	697	0	0	0.0
	1955§	679	5	16	73.6
	1956	626	3	16	47.9
	1957	642	2	16	31.2
	1958	666	1	16	15.0
	1959	670	3	16	44.8

*All data on dismissals and department size are taken from police department personnel records.
†Sworn officers only.
‡Score = Sum of premonitory detection and investigation policies. (See Tables 1 and 2)
§Big scandal years.

TABLE 4. Association of Internal Policing and Dismissals*

Yearly Internal Policing Scores		Yearly Dismissals per 10,000 officers		
		Under 20	Over 20	Totals
Over 10 (premonitory)	New York =	1	3	
	Oakland =	1	4	
	Central City =	0	0	
	Total‡	2	7	9
Under 10 (postmonitory)	New York =	3	0	
	Oakland =	1	1	
	Central City =	4	2	
	Total‡	8	3	11
	TOTAL	9	10	20
	Q = .81 (p ≤ .025)†			

*Strictly speaking, the sample size is not quite large enough for this test, since the expected value of two of the cells is 4.5, slightly less than the conventional minimum of five. Since strong associations tend to compensate for small sample sizes, I have chosen to violate the convention. Moreover, the simple random sampling assumption of the test used for statistical significance is not true here, since the sample was chosen arbitrarily. But as Davis advises, it is better to use an SRS significance test in such situations than no test at all. See James A. Davis, *Elementary Survey Analysis* (Englewood Cliffs, N.J.: Prentice Hall, 1971), pp. 59–60.

‡The contributions of each city to each cell in the table are specified in order to demonstrate that no one city swamps the data. The association of the aggregated data is well balanced among the cities.

†A more conservative test of significance, Fisher's Exact test, shows a P ≤ .03215. Weak statistical significance is to be expected in small samples, however, and the strength of association is still noteworthy.

New York shows the most consistent increase in sanctions during the reform period. Central City's dismissal rate *declined* during the first reform year, but so did its internal policing score, providing further evidence that dismissal rates are related to internal policing practices and not to a possible post-scandal "climate" of strict punishment. Oakland's decline in dismissals after the first reform year (1955) might be explained by the vast reduction in corruption apparently achieved during 1955.[24]

Table 4 shows a very strong positive association between premonitory internal policing scores and the dismissal rate in all twenty of the years pooled from all three cities. While the hypothesis was not clearly demonstrated within the three cities over time, the examination of the data in aggregated form lends some support to the argument. Granting the assumption of a positive relationship between dismissals for corruption and all dismissals, the data provide very tentative support for the theoretical argument that the presence of a premonitory capacity for internal policing of corruption increases the chances that internal policing units can produce the evidence required for affirmative administrative decisions to impose sanctions.

Aside from the problems of measurement associated with these data, however, there is a significant problem of interpretation. The appropriate base for dismissal rates is not the number of officers in a department, but rather the number of corrupt officers or the number of corrupt acts. Higher rates of dismissals per 10,000 officers could be a mere reflection of a much greater frequency of corrupt acts, and not a result of more effective internal policing methods. This reason alone is sufficient cause to treat the data very cautiously as merely illustrative rather than conclusive. This chapter is merely an argument, and not scientific evidence, that a premonitory capacity for internal policing yields higher

24. See Chapter 9.

rates of sanctioning of corrupt acts per corrupt act or actor. Since there are no annual data available on the frequency of corrupt acts or actors, the hypothesis cannot be tested.

In any case, this chapter demonstrates that clear differences existed among the four police departments in their policies for the punitive control of corruption. Combined with the differences in policies for preventive control, these differences may account for the differences among the four departments in their changes in police corruption.

Part III

Changes in Corruption

7. The Measurement of Corruption

Police corruption is by nature resistant to observation. Scientific attempts to measure it encounter many of the same difficulties as official attempts to detect it. In science just as in detection, somewhat unorthodox means are required to penetrate the veil of secrecy surrounding police corruption. This chapter describes the procedures by which this study attempted to measure changes over time in police corruption in the four cities. It discusses both the sources of data and the indicators of the quantity of organization in police corruption that are derived from the data. Finally, the questions to be asked of the data in the following chapters are presented.

SOURCES OF DATA

The most desirable way to measure the changes over time in police corruption might be some record or indicator of the true frequency of corrupt acts. The only indicator of corrupt acts available is the number of complaints about corrupt police behavior received and recorded by the police departments. Both the validity

and reliability of this indicator, however, are so poor as
to render it of little use. Most police corruption in most
cities is probably consensual, with both the police and
the parties to such transactions benefiting from them;
only rarely is a consensual act officially reported by any
participant.[1] The portion of the corruption that is not
consensual may be more likely to be reported, although
a victim's fear of reprisal from the police officer(s) who
made him a victim of corruption may preclude his reporting. Such selective reporting introduces error into
any estimate of rates for different types of corruption
(and their relative proportions of all corruption). The
relative proportion of reports of different types of corruption may also change over time. Scandal and reform
may increase the credibility of the internal investigation
process and thereby increase the reporting of corruption, though perhaps unevenly so across categories of
corruption. Complaints of corruption from citizens are
not unbiased estimates of the frequency of all corrupt
acts.

Rather than attempting to measure the frequency of
corrupt acts, this study attempts to measure changes
over time in the quantity of *organization* generally present in corruption activities. This measure only requires
reliable indicators of the relative proportions of corruption activities that are more and less organized. A quantitative value is assigned to different levels of organization based on the amount of cooperative action[2] present
in each of the corruption activities reported from the
various sources. Changes in the level of corruption organization are inferred from changes in the ratios of
more cooperative to less cooperative forms of corruption. The problem is to identify reliable sources of data
on the organization of police corruption.

The meaning of any report, rumor, or allegation of
police corruption is analogous to the view through a

1. See, e.g., Edwin M. Schur, *Crimes Without Victims: Deviant Behavior and Public Policy* (Englewood Cliffs, N.J.: Prentice-Hall, 1965).
2. See pp. 52–55, above.

window. Looking into one window of a building offers information about what is going on inside, but the information obtained is ordinarily assumed to be incomplete. Much of the activity inside the building may never take place within viewing range of a window, and many windows may be shuttered for much of the time. Some windows may even be false, and the picture painted on them may misrepresent the real activity behind them. Yet a systematic observer can make fairly accurate inferences by looking through as many windows in as many buildings as possible. Eventually, the observer may even acquire a fairly detailed description of how the activity inside the building is organized and how it changes over time, as long as he is careful to record the dates of his observations.

Similarly, a statement made by any source in any context reporting corrupt acts by police provides a brief glimpse of the organization of police corruption, however incomplete that glimpse may be. These windows on corruption offer many different kinds of information. The size of corruption conspiracies, the different types of corruption going on, and the nature of relationships between citizens and corrupt police are some of the features of social organization that can be seen through such windows on corruption. Temporal information may also be obtained—for example, in such statements as "This has been going on since I joined the force five years ago." Some statements may allow only a superficial view of one aspect of the organization of corruption, while others allow a highly detailed view. But the scope of the information provided by each statement is not as important as the total amount of information that all the statements make available. Each single piece of information may gather significance by reference to all the other pieces, which together may indicate how much organization was present in corruption activities at a certain point in time.

Previous research demonstrates the feasibility of studying the social organization of police corruption, with which data quantities of organization can be defined. A variety of methods have been used to discover patterns of corruption. Whyte[3] and Rubinstein[4] used long-term participant observation. Sutherland[5] used intensive interviews with a highly knowledgeable actor in police corruption (a professional thief). Investigative commissions[6] have used everything from their power to subpoena witnesses to rummaging through police files. Journalists have used police and other informants[7] to construct detailed analyses of corruption patterns. This study used newspaper accounts, criminal trials, complaints sent to the police executive, corruption investigation files, interviews with outside observers close to police affairs during the period under study, and some other sources detailed in Table 5. Most of these sources included dates of occurrence of the corruption activities they reported.

Not all of the possible sources of data were available in all four cities. In effect, changes in corruption were measured in different ways in each city. The biggest difference was in the use of internal policing files. In Central City, every citizen complaint and every allegation from any source found in the internal policing files were included in the sample of information about corruption from which the indicators of the quantity of organization were constructed. In Oakland, the internal policing files were unavailable. In New York, the files

3. William F. Whyte, *Street Corner Society* (Chicago: University of Chicago Press, 1943, 1955).

4. Jonathan Rubinstein, *City Police* (New York: Farrar, Straus and Giroux, 1973).

5. Edwin H. Sutherland, *The Professional Thief* (Chicago: University of Chicago Press, 1937).

6. Knapp Commission Report; State of Pennsylvania, Pennsylvania Crime Commission, *Report on Police Corruption and the Quality of Law Enforcement in Philadelphia* (Saint Davids, Pa.: Pennsylvania Crime Commission, 1974).

7. David Burnham, *The Role of the Media in Controlling Police Corruption* (New York: John Jay Press, 1976).

TABLE 5. Sources of Data on the Organization of Police Corruption

	City			
Source	*New York*	*Central City*	*Oakland*	*Newburgh*
Written Records:				
Newspaper stories	+	+	+	+
Writings of police officers	+	−	−	+
Citizen complaints	+	+	−	+
I.A.D. files	+	+	−	−
Chief's files	−	+	+	−
Oral Sources:				
Criminal trials	+	+	−	−
Department trials	−	+	−	−
Ex-corrupt officers	+	−	−	+
Other officers	+	+	+	+
Reform chief	+	+	−	+
I.A.D. commander	+	+	+	−
I.A.D. officers	+	+	+	−
Intelligence commander	−	+	+	N.A.
Intelligence officers	−	+	+	N.A.
Vice commander	+	−	+	N.A.
Vice officers	+	+	+	N.A.
Municipal executive	−	+	+	+
Public safety director	N.A.	+	N.A.	N.A.
Prosecutor	+	+	+	−
Other law enforcement agencies	+	+	−	−
Reporters	+	+	−	−
Other outside observers	+	+	+	−
Total sources	16	19	12	7

N.A. = Not applicable.

were too voluminous to undertake a complete census of corruption reports, as in Central City. Faced with a choice between sampling the three thousand vague and often incoherent citizen corruption complaints filed in New York for each of the five years under study there, or doing a complete census of the corruption activities described precisely and in great organizational detail by the background papers for administrative prosecutions of corrupt police officers, I chose the latter course.

The study design does not require that the data be comparable across the four cities. The object of measurement is relative changes over time in the organization of corruption within each city, and not the absolute levels of organization of corruption in each city at the same point in time. As long as each way of measuring change in corruption is internally consistent (i.e., reliable), it does not matter that a different way was used in each city. An analogous problem of measurement might be changes in the economic health of three states from 1929 to 1931; if the trends in Pennsylvania's unemployment rate, Ohio's mortgage foreclosure rate, and New York's bank closing rate were all upwards during those years, they would all indicate a similar trend for the conditions of economic health: depression. As long as unemployment, mortgage foreclosures, and bank closings were counted the same way and with the same sources of information in each year, then the trends could be compared as trends.

Yet there is some question about the internal reliability of the sources of data used to measure the organization of police corruption. Each source of data is likely to report particular categories of corruption, some of which are more organized than others. How much organization one observes in the corruption that is reported or alleged from all sources will depend in part on what the sources know, and which sources are reporting. The "turn-around" corrupt police officer, for example, is likely to report highly organized police corruption, whereas the victim of a police shakedown reports a less organized form of corruption—when he does report it. Corruption in general may be highly organized, but if the only reports of corruption come from sources having only knowledge of less organized forms of corruption, then corruption will appear to be less organized than it really is.

A wide diversity of sources of information on corruption was available in each city. In each case, the kinds of police corruption of which the sources had knowledge ranged from very low to very high levels of organization. The issue of reliability arises over whether each source was equally likely to report corruption in each year. There is a substantial possibility that reports of corruption from some sources were more likely to surface in some years than in others (i.e., were unreliable). Because of the different organizational levels of corruption reported by different sources, changes in the propensity of each source to report corruption could produce artificial changes in the overall quantity of organization observed in police corruption. That is, the trend in observed corruption organization might reflect trends in reporting rather than actual trends in the organization of corruption.

This study is primarily concerned with the *direction* of change over time in the quantity of organization in corruption, and only marginally concerned with the *magnitude* of such change. The danger of the possible unreliability of the sources, therefore, is confined to those instances in which the distortion is so great that it alters the direction of change. If the observed direction of change in the organization of corruption is opposite to that which a suspected change in the reporting rate of a particular source would produce, then the reporting change would only be distorting the magnitude of change and not the direction. If, for example, the use of "turn-arounds" increased, the observed level of corruption organization would be inflated, since turn-arounds report more organized corruption. If the observed level of corruption organization declines while the use of turn-arounds increases, then the turn-arounds would not distort the direction of change, they would merely reduce the magnitude of the observed decline in corruption organization.

Given the heavy reliance on internal policing files in Central City and New York, changes in internal policing methods obviously call the reliability of that source into question. The development of a premonitory capacity probably increases chances that internal policing will discover more organized forms of corruption, and the file data will record more organized corruption. But if the direction of change in organization is toward less organized corruption at the same time that the premonitory capacity is increased, then changes in the source of data cannot account for an observed decline in the organization of corruption. Where both the premonitory internal policing capacity and the observed level of corruption organization declined, however, as they did in Central City, then the change in internal policing as a source of data might account for the observed decline in the organization of corruption.

The greatest threat to the overall reliability of the data sources on the organization of police corruption may be the behavior of the news media. At the time of a big scandal, reporters tend to scour the recent past for information about police corruption, and they may look for organized corruption in particular. As the scandal fades from public memory, however, the media may pay less attention to police corruption. This appears to have been the case in Oakland and Newburgh. But in Central City and New York, police corruption remained a frequent topic of news stories for the entire period after the scandal that was studied in each city.

Despite these limitations and possible reliability threats regarding the sources of data, there is still a good possibility that the data provide an accurate reflection of the direction of change over time in the organization of police corruption activities in the four cities. In any case, they are the only data of which questions can be asked regarding the impact of scandal and internal control policies. In order to describe the changes in corruption organization in quantitative terms, I have constructed eight indicators of four different aspects of the organization of police corruption from the raw data.

INDICATORS OF ORGANIZATION

Police corruption activities vary in the extent to which they are products of cooperative social action. Some forms of police corruption involve more social cooperation than others. Similarly, the totality of corruption activities occurring in a police department during a given year can involve more or less social cooperation. That is, corruption activities in a police department can be more organized in general in some years than in others. Four aspects of the extent of social cooperation in police corruption can be measured with the information about corruption that surfaces from various sources: active cooperation among police officers, passive cooperation among police officers, cooperation between citizens and police, and the duration of cooperation.

Most of the indicators of the four aspects of cooperation employ the distinction introduced in Chapter 2 between corruption arrangements and corruption events.[8] Corruption events are acts of corruption that are not part of a continuing relationship between the people on the two sides of a corruption transaction. Corruption arrangements are continuing relationships between two sides of a corruption transaction. A corruption event is a single act of corruption; a corruption arrangement embraces numerous acts of corruption. The distinction between these two forms of corruption has important implications for the overall quantity of organization in police corruption activities, and greatly aids the task of measuring corruption organization.

Active Cooperation among Officers
Cooperation among police officers in corrupt activities may be either active or passive. Active cooperation

8. See p. 42, above.

consists of actual participation in corrupt activities. Passive cooperation consists of officers tolerating or not interfering with corrupt activities, without actually participating in violations of the law. Active cooperation in corruption is measured by the size of the corruption groups reported to have existed in a given year. The more officers participating in each corruption group, on average, the more active cooperation there is in those police corruption activities.

The number of officers participating in corruption events was often unclear from the information available. In the case of corruption arrangements, however, there was almost always enough information to discriminate between arrangements in which only one police officer was involved and those in which more than one officer was involved. The proportion of all corruption arrangements involving two or more officers thus provides a quantitative indication of the amount of active cooperation among police officers that exists in corruption arrangements, if not in all corruption activities.

Passive Cooperation among Officers
In certain situations, inaction can be just as cooperative as action. One form of cooperative inaction in police corruption is the failure of law-abiding police officers to mobilize social control against their actively corrupt colleagues. Another form of cooperative inaction is obeying orders not to enforce the law against civilian law violators who have paid police officials or political leaders for immunity from arrest. The first form of cooperative inaction is measured by the diversity of substantive types of corruption. The second form of cooperative inaction is measured by the highest rank level of the police department at which at least one police official is reported to be corrupt.

The more discrete types of corruption that one finds in a department at a given time, the more participation in corruption there would seem to be throughout the department. The types of corruption in which an officer can engage are limited by his functional and geographic assignment. Certain types of corruption can only be accomplished in certain assignments. It is not too gross an inference, then, to assume that the number of types reported reflects the degree to which corruption extends to many diverse units in the department. While not a direct measure of cooperative action (or inaction), more pervasive corruption implies the tacit cooperation of police officers in more units in the agreement not to mobilize social control.

The diversity of corruption is measured by two separate indicators. One is the total number of discrete types of corruption arrangements reported to have occurred in a given year. The other is the types of events. Diversity in the more organized forms of corruption, i.e., arrangements, is a better indicator of tacit cooperation, since ongoing corruption is more likely to become common knowledge among police officers than one-time events. The two indicators should move in the same direction if they are both measuring the same phenomena, so their division into subcategories allows each to serve as a check on the other.

The participation in corruption of any officer of supervisory rank generally implies at least the passive cooperation in that corruption of the officers under his supervision. Those subordinates may not receive any money from the supervisor, but they usually comply with his demands to refrain from enforcing certain laws against the lawbreakers paying for police inaction. Occasionally, a supervisor may commit a corrupt act which does not require the cooperation of his subordinates, such as selling perjured testimony in a case that the supervisor investigated personally. But such acts seem to be relatively rare, and most reports of corruption by supervisors indicate at least the tacit cooperation of their subordinates.

Because of the pyramidal structure of police department hierarchies, the higher the rank level of the supervisor, the more subordinates there are under his command. While ten corrupt sergeants may supervise more subordinates than one corrupt lieutenant, corrupt lieutenants are rarely found where the sergeants are not corrupt as well. It is not unreasonable to assume that the higher the highest rank level is at which corruption is reported, the more subordinate officers there are cooperating in the corruption. Attempts to count the number of corrupt supervisors at each rank level are subject to greater error than attempts to determine whether there were *any* corrupt supervisors at each rank level, so the latter is the preferred indicator of the extent of passive cooperation in police corruption among subordinates of corrupt supervisors.

Citizen-Police Cooperation

Citizens often seek out cooperation with the police in a corrupt relationship. For criminal enterprises such as gambling dens and brothels, cooperation in police corruption is a means of reducing uncertainty over disruptive raids which hurt profits. But other citizens, such as streetwalking prostitutes, may seek to avoid cooperation in police corruption; only under coercion do they become part of a corruption transaction. The two extremes of citizen cooperation and noncooperation are fairly clear, but it is hard to draw a line between them. No one wants to pay the police, just as no one wants to pay taxes, but all law-violators must cope with the legitimate arrest power of the police. Some citizens seek to buy off that power before it is invoked (e.g., gamblers), some citizens try to buy off that power after it is invoked (e.g., traffic offenders), and some have little choice but to be illegally exploited by the total coercion inherent in that power (e.g., victims of thefts by police during the arrest process).

The relative predominance of cooperation or noncooperation by citizens in police corruption is measured in two ways. One is the ratio of the number of types of vice protection to the number of types of police-initiated crimes. Vice-related corruption generally features the maximum cooperation in corruption sought out by citizens. Police-initiated crimes generally feature the least cooperation between police and citizens, with the latter sometimes not even knowing that they have been victims of police corruption. For example, the victim of a police burglary may not know it was the police, as opposed to a civilian burglar, who committed the crime. By dividing the types of vice protection by the types of police-initiated crime reported for each year, the indicator yields a higher value when there is more citizen cooperation in police corruption because the numerator indicates high cooperation while the denominator indicates low cooperation.

Another indicator measures citizen cooperation more explicitly and encompasses the full range of substantive corruption categories. Each type of corruption can be labeled as either consenting or victimizing. Consenting corruption denotes those situations in which a citizen has a choice of agreeing to corruption or being arrested. Victimizing corruption denotes those situations in which the citizen has no choice but is coerced into the corrupt transaction. Even a shaken-down prostitute has the option of going to jail rather than paying a police officer. If she is arrested and her money is stolen during arrest, however, the theft is coded as victimizing corruption. Consenting corruption often may not feature much cooperation between citizens and police, but it definitely features more cooperation than victimizing corruption. By dividing consenting corruption by victimizing corruption, the indicator yields a higher value when there is more citizen cooperation in police corruption.[9]

9. Both indicators of citizen cooperation in corruption use substantive classifications of types of corruption that ignore the transactional differences between arrangements and events. For example, a prostitution protection arrangement and a prostitution shakedown event both occurring in the same year are collapsed under the single category of prostitution protection, which is assigned in the first indicator to the category "vice protection," and in the second indicator to the category "consensual corruption." For a list of the categories, see Lawrence W. Sherman, "Controlling Police Corruption" (Ph.D. dissertation, Yale University, 1976), p. 273.

Duration of Cooperation

Corruption arrangements are distinguished from corruption events on the basis of continuing relationships among the same individuals, something that is characteristic of arrangements but not of events. Some corruption events may feature elaborate cooperative action. Even a highly cooperative event, however, has less total cooperation than most arrangements, because arrangements add more cooperation each time the arranged transaction is duplicated. Arrangements persist over time, but events do not. This difference makes the ratio of arrangements to events a good measure of the amount of duration of cooperation.

Two approaches are used to calculate ratios of arrangements to events. One approach is the ratio between the *number* of discrete arrangements and the number of discrete events reported from all sources. These data may or may not be a valid indication of the quantity of corruption. But since the question is not numbers of corrupt acts but the ratio between the frequencies of two distinct forms of corruption, the validity of measuring the frequency of corruption by reports of corruption need not concern us. Rather, the reliability of these data over time—i.e., whether the proportion of all arrangements that gets reported and the proportion of all events that gets reported remain relatively the same from year to year—is cause for concern.

As a check on the possible unreliability of the gross count of reports of arrangements and events, the ratio of reported *types* of arrangements to reported *types* of events is used as a second indicator of duration of cooperation. The use of types of corruption as an indicator of the total numbers of arrangements and events may be more reliable because types are more likely to be reported accurately. The "type" statement that there was (or was not) prostitution protection in a city in a given year has only a 50 percent chance of error, whereas the "number" statement that there were, for example, exactly four prostitution protection arrangements in a given year has almost a 100 percent chance of error.[10]

Both indicators of the duration of cooperation yield a higher value when there are relatively more arrangements than events or more arrangement types than event types. The relatively more arrangements, the more cooperation is indicated.

Aggregation of the Indicators

While the indicators attempt to tap different aspects of cooperation in police corruption activities, the assumption is made that all aspects of cooperation move together over time. There is no reason, for example, to assume that the duration of cooperation would change in an opposite direction from the size of corruption groups. The four aspects of cooperation are not four different dimensions of corruption organization, but rather four different ways of measuring the single dimension of how much organization—or cooperation—there is in police corruption. Each indicator, therefore, is merely a reliability check on the others.[11] Aggregation of the indicators is useful only to see how consistent the indicators are with each other, and not as a means of computing the overall magnitude of change.

In order to aggregate the eight indicators into a summary measure of the direction in which the quantity of organization changed from year to year, the modal direction of change is computed. That is, the direction in which the largest number of indicators moved (more organization, less organization, no change) is taken as the actual direction of change. Because it often happened that some of the indicators did not change at all from year to year, the modes are frequently less than

10. The "type" statement has only two possible values, present or absent; hence the 50 percent chance of error. The "number" example has *at least* five possible values: 0, 1, 2, 3, or 4 arrangements, with no theoretical limit above 4.

11. Eugene J. Webb, Donald T. Campbell, Richard D. Schwartz, and Lee Sechrest, *Unobtrusive Measures: Nonreactive Research in the Social Sciences* (Chicago: Rand McNally, 1966), Chapter 1.

half of the eight indicators. Where the modes are that low, less confidence (or perhaps none) should be placed in the reliability of the data.

In addition to the eight indicators of the quantity of organization in the totality of police corruption activities, several other indicators are used to measure selected aspects of change in corruption. Those indicators will be introduced when the data are presented. Before moving on to an analysis of the data, it is useful to summarize the facts of the cases so far and the questions to be put to the data that are presented in the next two chapters.

QUESTIONS FOR THE DATA

The four police departments studied here have been described as deviant organizations punished by a big scandal. One consequence of scandal was to change the dominant coalition in each department from support for corrupt goals to support for honest ones. The external social control of the police departments as deviant organizations produced outside intervention in their governance, converting them from corrupt police departments to police departments in which corruption existed. In the post-scandal period in all four departments, controlling police corruption was a problem of controlling individual deviance in organizations rather than a problem of controlling corrupt police departments.

The new dominant coalitions attempted to control police corruption activities with various preventive and punitive control policies. These policies were either postmonitory or premonitory: dealing only with past corruption or anticipating and searching for possible ongoing corruption. The differences in policies for punitive control seem to have been associated with differences in the number of dismissals of police officers in each department.

Three kinds of social control are evident in the summary of the four cases. Each kind of social control can produce a threat of punishment and can reasonably be assumed to have a possible deterrent effect on police corruption activities. One mechanism is scandal itself. While scandal is directed at the organization as a whole rather than at its individual members, it carries the threat of additional efforts to detect specific acts of corruption. The Knapp Commission in New York and the reporters in Central City both detected police officers committing acts of corruption. The "heat" of scandal raises uncertainties about other external social control actors, such as federal agents and local prosecutors. In addition to punishing the organization as a whole and changing the character of its dominant coalition, scandal may act as a deterrent to individual police corruption activity. However, the effects of scandal may wear off over time, producing only short-run deterrence of corruption.

A second kind of social control is the rate of dismissals of police officers (presumably reflecting the rate of dismissals for corrupt acts). The more punishment, the more deterrence of police corruption there may be. Dismissals fit the usual model of general deterrence in which the punishment of some individuals demonstrates a tangible threat to other individuals that criminal acts may result in punishment.

A third kind of social control is the set of preventive and punitive internal policies designed to control police corruption. The preventive policies may succeed in removing opportunities for and conditions conducive to police corruption, thereby reducing it. The apparatus of the punitive policies for detecting and investigating police corruption, regardless of the sanctions it produces, may deter corruption activities. General knowledge that there are "spies" about, for example, can pose a threat of punishment equal to or greater than an increase in the sanction rate. In this respect, however, it is likely that only premonitory policies pose a threat, because they may be perceived as creating a greater certainty of detection and as yielding stronger evidence than postmonitory policies.

As an exploratory study, the research design was not intended to allow clear tests of hypotheses.[12] Instead, certain questions are asked of the data, the answers to which suggest hypotheses worthy of further testing. The questions concern the nature and extent of the impact of the three different kinds of social control on the organization of police corruption. The events in each city are analyzed in certain ways that reveal the presence or absence of any apparent connection between corruption and the three kinds of social control. An attempt is also made to explore the independent effects of each kind of social control in the presence of the others.

The case of Central City provides an instance of big scandal with no premonitory control policies and no increase (in fact, a decrease) in sanctions. Any change in corruption there can be attributed only to scandal, or to the less likely alternative explanations of postmonitory control policies or some other unknown factors. The case of New York provides an instance of big scandal, premonitory control policies, and a steady increase in sanctions, but with a number of scandalizing events that can be examined for their effect on corruption in the presence of premonitory control and sanction increases. The case of Oakland provides an instance of a brief big scandal followed by a sharp change to premonitory control policies and a sharp increase in sanctions, so that the total combination of the three kinds of social control can be examined for their effect on corruption.

Unfortunately, the number of years after the scandal for which data on the organization of corruption could be obtained varied in each city. In Newburgh, the apparently complete disappearance of corruption after the big scandal meant that no data at all on corruption

12. The design fails to control for too many competing hypotheses to qualify as a valid test of the "treatment" effects of scandal and internal control policies: history, maturation, instrumentation, and multiple treatment interference are all problems in concluding anything for certain in each of the four cases. See Donald T. Campbell and Julian C. Stanley, *Experimental and Quasi-Experimental Designs for Research* (Chicago: Rand McNally, 1966).

could be found for the post-scandal period. In Central City, no data on corruption could be collected beyond the first year after the scandal. However, data could be obtained about New York for a period of three years after the scandal, and about Oakland for a period of five years after the scandal. The purpose of measuring changes over time in the organization of police corruption is to see what those changes might suggest about the questions regarding the impact of different kinds of social control:

— Does scandal produce a decline in the organization of police corruption?

— Do internal control policies produce a decline in the organization of corruption?

— Does the rate at which police officers are dismissed make any difference in the organization of corruption?

The assumption underlying each of these questions is that participants in police corruption define the more cooperative forms of corruption as being more vulnerable to social control. From the participants' perspective, an increase or mobilization of any of the three kinds of social control might make them less willing to cooperate in corruption. Judging from the available data, the assumption may well be correct.

8. Effects of Scandal

The effects of scandal on police corruption appear to vary according to the nature of the scandal. Little scandals seem to have no deterrent effect on corruption, and may even result in secondary deviation.[1] On the other hand, "critical events"[2] that are part of a larger scandal but do not comprise a scandal in themselves do seem to deter corruption. Big scandals always seem to deter corruption, if only in the short run. This chapter presents the rather scant evidence for these tentative generalizations.

EFFECTS OF LITTLE SCANDAL

Big police corruption scandals successfully define the entire police department as a corrupt organization.[3] Many big scandals are preceded by a little scandal. The time period between the big and little scandals is a strikingly uniform two years. The little scandal, which does not succeed in labeling the organization as deviant, may or may not produce an increase in sanctions. Only in New York did a little scandal produce a change in organizational control policies or leadership. A little corruption scandal occurred in all of the four present cases, as well as in the Denver Police Department (1958–60)[4]

1. Lawrence W. Sherman, "Scandal and Deterrence: The Case of Police Corruption" (paper presented at the Annual Meeting of the American Sociological Association, San Francisco, August, 1975).
2. John A. Gardiner, *The Politics of Corruption* (New York: Russell Sage Foundation, 1970), pp. 60–69.
3. See p. 65.
4. Gerald P. Foster, "Police Administration and the Control of Police Criminality: A Case Study Approach" (D.P.A. dissertation, University of Southern California, 1966).

and the New York City Buildings Department (1972–74).[5] A big scandal is often connected to a little one, in the sense that the disclosures made by the little scandal prompt various social control actors to investigate corruption in greater depth. In addition, the likelihood of a big scandal occurring may be increased by the effects of the little scandal on corruption itself, if the little scandal does in fact encourage corruption.

Some cases of little scandals suggest that if they do not produce any indictments or other threats of sanctions, they tend to be followed by an increase in the organization, and perhaps the frequency and seriousness, of police corruption. After the little 1958 scandal over police burglary in Denver, which produced no sanctions, the practice of police burglaries spread from the one precinct where burglary had begun to every precinct in the city.[6] In the New York City Buildings Department, the prices of various types of payoffs demanded by building inspectors increased after the little scandal of 1972, which produced only a few sanctions. In Newburgh, the diversity of corruption increased from five distinct types before the little scandal (with no sanctions) to eight thereafter. Similar indications were found in the three other present cases, but an overall assessment of changes in corruption fails to show that the level of corruption organization clearly increased after the little scandal in those cases.

In no case did a little scandal produce a clear decrease in the measured level of organization of corruption.[7]

5. David K. Shipler, "Study Finds $25-Million Yearly in Bribes Is Paid by City's Construction Industry," *New York Times*, June 26, 1972, p. 1, and Edward Ranzal, "City Report Finds Building Industry Infested by Graft," *New York Times*, November 8, 1974, p. 1.

6. Foster, "Police Administration and the Control of Police Criminality," p. 186.

7. But see the account of how a little scandal in the heavy electrical equipment industry put a temporary halt to price-fixing in 1949: Gilbert Geis, "The Heavy Electrical Equipment Antitrust Cases of 1961," in *Criminal Behavior Systems*, ed. Marshall B. Clinard and Richard Quinney (New York: Holt, Rinehart and Winston, 1967).

This finding may be an artifact of the measurement apparatus, however. A big scandal (two years after a little one) tends to dredge up many allegations of corruption that took place in the immediately preceding years—i.e., the period between the little and big scandals. If a higher proportion of corruption is eventually reported for the period between the scandals than for the period before the little scandal, then a real decline in corruption may be obscured by the increase in reporting. Similarly, an apparent decline in corruption after a big scandal may merely reflect a decline in reporting as public interest in police corruption wanes. In both time periods, however, the effects of reporting on the measurement of corruption organization depend not on how much corruption is reported, but on which sources are reporting. Assuming that the *relative* proportions of sources reporting highly-organized and less-organized forms of corruption do not change—even if the proportion of all corruption reported does change—then it is fairly reasonable to conclude that a little scandal does not deter corruption. Instead, the opposite might be the case if no sanctions result. Under those conditions, a little scandal demonstrates that the mere public disclosure of police corruption does not inevitably lead to sanctions. The result may be that corrupt officers are emboldened to take greater risks by engaging in more organized forms of corruption.

EFFECTS OF BIG SCANDAL

The independent effects of big scandal can be seen most clearly when it is the only kind of social control directed at police corruption. Assuming that postmonitory control policies are an inadequate or marginally effective kind of social control, a big scandal followed by no increase in sanctions and no adoption of premonitory control policies is the only kind of social control directed at police corruption. Central City provides an example of big scandal followed by a *decrease* in both the rate of dismissals and the premonitory capacity of the internal policing unit. If the organization of corruption declines despite the decrease in the other kinds of social control, then the case for the deterrent effect of big scandal is even stronger than it would be if the other kinds of social control remained constant. Almost all of the indicators of the organization of corruption suggest that the big scandal in Central City did produce a decline in the organization of corruption there.

Table 6 shows the proportion of all corruption arrangements reported in Central City that had two or more police officers participating, an indicator of active cooperation in corruption among police officers. These data are inconclusive for two reasons. One is that the decline in the size of corruption arrangements was more substantial in the year before the big scandal than in the year following it. The other more important reason is that the small number of arrangements reported for each year makes the trends over time subject to fluctuation by chance, so that none of the year-to-year changes are statistically significant. Even so, it is worth noting that the proportion of arrangements that had two or more officers during the post-scandal year was the lowest of any of the years studied.

Tables 7 and 8 show the diversity of corruption in Central City, an indicator of the amount of passive cooperation among police officers in corruption activity. Once again, the small number of types of corruption arrangements and events reported makes the changes over time subject to chance fluctuation. These data, however, do show that the most substantial decline in diversity of corruption was in the post-scandal year. Both separately and added together, the number of types of corruption arrangements and corruption events increased in the years prior to the scandal, and decreased in the first year after the scandal.

The highest rank level reported corrupt is another indicator of passive cooperation among police officers. From 1970 through 1973, the highest rank level reported corrupt in the Central City Police Department

TABLE 6. Size of Corruption Arrangements in Central City

	1970		1971		Size 1972		1973		1974–75*	
	N	%	N	%	N	%	N	%	N	%
One officer	2	14%	3	21%	4	20%	10	36%	8	47%
Two or more	12	86%	11	79%	16	80%	18	64%	9	53%
Total	14	100%	14	100%	20	100%	28	100%	17	100%

Percentage change from previous year in
percent of total that consists of two or more officers:

| | | | −8% | | +1% | | −20% | | −17% | |

*March to March, the first full year of the reform administration.

TABLE 7. Diversity of Corruption Arrangements in Central City

Types of Arrangements	1970	1971	Reports 1972	1973	1974–75*
"Gangster" protection	+	+	+	+	−
"Hit-Man" protection	−	+	−	−	−
"Fence" protection	+	+	+	+	+
Drug pusher protection	−	−	+	+	−
Burglar protection	−	−	−	+	+
Bond setting bribes	−	−	−	+	+
Bootlegger protection	+	+	+	−	−
Gambling protection	+	+	+	+	+
Illegal parking protection	−	−	+	+	−
Tavern violations protection	−	−	−	−	+
Prostitution protection	+	+	+	+	−
Traffic bribes protection (Paid to Commander)	+	−	−	−	+
Recruiting prostitutes	−	−	−	+	−
Police auto theft ring	−	−	−	−	+
Officers selling drugs	−	−	−	+	+
Police-operated gambling	−	+	+	−	+
Police fencing	−	−	+	+	−
Police burglary ring	+	+	+	+	−
Police auction embezzlement	+	+	+	+	+
Sale of promotions	+	+	+	+	−
Sale of forged licenses	−	−	−	+	−
Bail bondsmen kickbacks	−	−	−	−	+
Department materials theft	+	+	+	+	−
Charity fund embezzlement	−	+	+	+	−
Tow-truck kickbacks	−	−	−	−	+
Total arrangement types	10	12	14	17	12
Percent change from previous year‡		+20%	+17%	+21%	−29%

Key: + = Reported to have occurred that year; − = Not reported to have occurred that year.
*March to March, the first full year of the reform administration.
‡Rounded.

TABLE 8. Diversity of Corruption Events in Central City

Types of Events	1970	1971	Reports 1972	1973	1974–75*
Theft during arrest	+	−	+	+	+
Prisoner escape bribe	+	+	−	−	−
Traffic bribe	−	−	−	+	−
Tavern shakedown	−	−	−	−	−
Prostitute shakedown	−	−	+	−	+
Drug pusher "fix" of criminal process	−	−	−	+	+
Gambler "fix"	+	+	−	−	−
Shoplifter "fix"	+	−	−	−	−
Burglary "fix"	−	−	−	+	−
Rape "fix"	−	−	−	+	+
Fence "fix"	−	−	−	+	−
Assault "fix"	−	−	−	−	+
Robbery "fix"	−	+	−	+	−
Unspecified "fix"	−	−	+	+	−
Police burglary	−	−	+	−	−
Police arson	−	+	−	+	−
Police sale of stolen item	−	+	−	−	+
Police theft of auto	−	−	+	−	−
Police fraud	−	−	−	+	−
Police theft from citizens	−	−	−	+	−
Police robbery	−	−	−	−	+
Theft from department gun room	+	−	−	−	−
Sale of police records	−	−	+	−	−
Police equipment theft	−	−	−	−	+
Total event types	5	5	6	11	8
Percent change from previous year‡		0	+20%	+83%	−27%

Key: + = Reported to have occurred that year;
  − = Not reported to have occurred that year.
*March to March.
‡Rounded.

remained the same. Several sources made independent allegations that corruption payments reached the chief's office. In the first post-scandal year, however, the highest rank level reported corrupt dropped by two ranks, a 29 percent decrease on the scale of seven ranks in the Central City police hierarchy. The rank level dropped another step after the one high commander reported to be corrupt was arrested and demoted in rank.

Citizen cooperation in police corruption is measured by two different ratios. One is the ratio of the number of types of vice protection to the number of types of police-initiated crimes, presented in Table 9. The other is the ratio of the number of types of corruption in which citizens are consenting participants to the number of types of corruption in which citizens are nonconsenting, victimized participants, presented in Table 10. Despite considerable overlap between vice protection and consenting corruption, and between police-initiated crimes and victimizing corruption,[8] a comparison of Tables 9 and 10 shows that the two ratios changed in

TABLE 9. Ratios of Types of Vice and Minor Crime Protection to Types of Police-Initiated Crimes in Central City

Corruption Type	1970	1971	1972	1973	1974–75*
			Numbers and Ratios		
Types of vice protection	6	4	5	5	4
Types of police-initiated crimes	2	3	5	8	6
Ratio	3	1.33	1	0.62	0.67
Percent change from previous year‡		−56%	−25%	−38%	+8%

*March to March.
‡Rounded.

8. For a list of the types of corruption assigned to the four categories, see Lawrence W. Sherman, "Controlling Police Corruption" (Ph.D. dissertation, Yale University, 1976), pp. 374–375.

TABLE 10. Ratios of Types of Consenting Corruption to Types of Victimizing Corruption in Central City

Type	Numbers and Ratios				
	1970	*1971*	*1972*	*1973*	*1974–75**
Types of consensual corruption	13	15	16	24	15
Types of victim corruption	2	2	3	4	3
Ratio	6.5	7.5	5.3	6	5
Percent change from previous year‡		+15%	−29%	+13%	−17%

*March to March.
‡Rounded.

opposite directions for every year except 1972, the year of the little scandal in Central City, when they both declined. Contrary to the other seven indicators, the ratio of vice protection types to police-initiated crime types increased during the first post-scandal year. However, that change is based on the smallest N size of any of the indicators, making it the most subject to chance fluctuations.

The duration of cooperation in police corruption is measured by two ratios of arrangements to events, both of which are presented in Table 11. One ratio is the number of separate arrangements reported for each year to the number of events reported. The other is the number of types of arrangements reported to the number of types of events. The larger numbers of separate arrangements and events make that ratio more reliable statistically, in the sense that year-to-year changes are slightly less subject to chance fluctuations. But the types of arrangements and events, while fewer, are probably more reliably *reported* than the numbers of arrangements and events, since the information on types is less likely to be affected by changes in the *volume* of reports. The ratio of numbers of arrangements to numbers of events shows the most substantial decrease in the

TABLE 11. Ratios of Arrangements to Events in Central City

		Numbers and Ratios			
Indicator	*1970*	*1971*	*1972*	*1973*	*1974–75**
Number of arrangements	14	14	20	28	17
Number of events	7	9	10	15	17
Ratio	2	1.56	2	1.87	1
Percent change from previous year		−22%	−28%	−6%	−46%
Types of arrangements	10	12	14	17	12
Types of events	5	5	6	11	8
Ratio	2	2.4	2.3	1.54	1.5
Percent change from previous year‡		+20%	−3%	−34%	−3%

*March to March.
‡Rounded.

post-scandal year. The ratio of types of arrangements to types of events also shows a decrease for the post-scandal year. While it is not the most substantial *decrease* in the time series, the ratio of types does have its lowest value in the post-scandal year.

The N sizes of all eight of the indicators are small enough to be subject to chance fluctuation in both the magnitude and direction of change. Table 12 shows the conflicting trends in direction of the indicators for all of the pre-scandal years. While over half of the indicators changed in the same direction for two of the three pre-scandal years, the specific indicators comprising that mode shifted from year to year. For the post-scandal year, however, almost all of the indicators showed changes in the same direction. The one exception was the indicator with the smallest N sizes of the eight, and hence the one most subject to chance fluctuation. The general agreement among the indicators suggests that during the first year after the scandal the organization of corruption in Central City may really have declined.

TABLE 12. Direction of Change in All Indicators of Corruption Organization in Central City

Indicator	Direction of Change from Prior Years			
	1971	*1972*	*1973*	*1974–75**
A. *Active Cooperation*				
1. Size	−	+	−	−
B. *Passive Cooperation*				
2. Types of arrangements	+	+	+	−
3. Types of arrangements and events	0	+	+	−
4. Highest corrupt rank level	0	0	0	−
C. *Citizen-Police Cooperation*				
5. Vice protection/police-initiated	−	−	−	+
6. Consenting/victimizing	+	−	+	−
D. *Duration of Cooperation*				
7. Number arrangements/events	−	−	−	−
8. Types arrangements/events	+	−	−	−
Modal direction	No Mode	−	−	−
(size of mode)		(4/7)	(4/7)	(7/8)

Key: − = Down; + = Up; 0 = No change.
*March to March.

Assuming that the organization of corruption did decline in Central City after the big scandal, several interpretations of that change are possible. One is that big scandal alone caused the decline in corruption organization; this interpretation assumes that postmonitory internal control policies have no deterrent effect on corruption organization. Another interpretation makes no assumption about internal control policies, and attributes the change to both the presence of big scandal and postmonitory control policies. This interpretation is weakened by the decline in premonitory capacity of the internal policing system, but is strengthened by the increased visibility given to the postmonitory internal policing unit created by the mayor (the "truth squad"). A third interpretation is that the decline in corruption organization was entirely due to postmonitory controls.

The number of years studied after the scandal in Central City is insufficient to eliminate any of the interpretations. If postmonitory control stayed the same for several years and the level of organization of corruption increased, then the interpretation that postmonitory control alone produced the decline could be ruled out. If the effects of scandal are presumed to fade, then a continued low level of corruption would support the interpretation that postmonitory control alone produced the decline. In neither case, however, can we rule out the interpretation that the joint effects of postmonitory control and big scandal produced the decline.

Yet there is good reason to eliminate postmonitory control policies as a possible source of change in corruption, and to attribute the apparent decrease in Central City's corruption organization during 1974–75 to big scandal alone. On-site observations and discussions among Central City officers found little fear of the department's control machinery but a great wariness for anyone connected with the news media. A major exception to this observation was the evidence of clear respect for the polygraph test, a test to which investigated officers refused to submit, and to which vice and narcotics officers had to submit on a regular basis. Otherwise, internal corruption control policies were the butt of frequent jokes. A more persuasive reason for preferring the scandal-alone explanation is that the data reflect every corruption report from the first day of the reform administration onward. The data from the other cities suggest that new control policies may require at least a year to produce strong effects. Central City, with a longer-lasting scandal than occurred in New York or Oakland, had the most substantial decrease of any of the three cities in the magnitude of the indicators during the big-scandal year. All things considered, it is plausible to argue that scandal by itself, and not postmonitory control policies, accounted for the decrease in the 1974–75 level of corruption organization in Central City.

EFFECTS OF SCANDAL EVENTS

Both big and little scandals are comprised of numerous events. If big scandal has an overall deterrent effect upon police corruption, then the major events comprising a big scandal may also have immediately observable effects on the organization of police corruption. Such "critical events" may result in police officers immediately terminating their involvement in cooperative corruption activities.[9] While the accumulated impact of increased sanction rates and increased capacity for premonitory internal control are also possible causes of a decline in corruption organization, the sudden shock of critical events may produce a sudden decline in cooperative corruption. The case of New York provides an example of this possibly general pattern.

The formal disciplinary charges used for departmental trials in the New York City Police Department specify the months over which an accused officer or conspiracy of officers is alleged to have engaged in corruption. This information yields two dates of great theoretical interest: initiation and termination dates of the corruption activity of individual officers and of the conspiracies to which they belong. A compilation of these dates on a monthly basis indicates, *among those later officially accused*, the number of officers or groups bold enough to begin a new corruption activity relative to the number that terminated a corruption activity. Virtually all of these dates refer to corruption arrangements rather than events, and most of the arrangements had two or more members.

The gravest flaw in this indicator is that it uses enforcement data to measure, among other things, the

9. See Gardiner, *The Politics of Corruption*, pp. 60–69.

effects of enforcement. Many of the terminations counted can be attributed to the officer getting caught. These terminations may indicate the effects of scandal events on enforcement rather than on corruption behavior directly. Other terminations can be attributed to incidental causes such as a transfer to a different unit. Nevertheless, many terminations occurred voluntarily long before the corruption was detected.

Another flaw in the indicator is that the dates of *initiation* are probably quite inaccurate. The initiation date is really a statement of how far back the corruption investigators were able to gather evidence on the corruption. In some cases, the evidence extended back for over ten years. In others, evidence went back for only a month before termination. The errors in initiation dates are somewhat compensated for by the accuracy of the termination dates, the latter information being much easier for corruption investigators to obtain. Those cases failing to specify an exact termination month are omitted from the data. Terminations are more interesting theoretically than initiations, since they show how many officers were scared off (or removed from) corruption in the face of scandal events, control policies, and sanctions.

The final flaw of this indicator may be its reliability. As the detection capacity of the internal policing system improved, it should have discovered a higher proportion of the true total of corrupt activity. This should have been true for both initiations and terminations. The time lag between the two dates, however, means that any increase in the proportion of all corruption that was discovered would take effect at different times, earlier for initiations than for terminations. Compensating for this tendency was the common practice of "mopping up" all past corruption of any arrangement detected. The detection of a "sergeants' club" by premonitory means in 1974, for example, produced information about members of the "club" who had joined in 1970 and left in 1971 because of "fear of the Knapp Commission." The practice of granting leniency to apprehended

officers in exchange for historical information about the
membership of the corruption group was so common in
New York that it may well have corrected for the increase in detection capacity during the later years of the
reform administration.

The value of this indicator is that no other source
provides equivalent precision about dates. Precise dat-
ing makes it possible to observe immediate temporal
relationships between terminations and initiations and
critical scandal events, at least on a monthly basis.

Figure 3 shows the relationship between the major
scandal events in New York and the monthly number of
corruption arrangements terminated and initiated. The
graph begins with the April 1970 *New York Times* articles
on police corruption, defined as a little scandal. Not
until the Knapp Commission hearings of October-
December 1971 was the theoretical definition of a suc-
cesful scandal satisfied: public labeling of the police department as a deviant organization. Given April 1970 as
a little scandal, October-December 1971 as a big scandal,
and the events in between as major scandal events leading up to the big scandal, the termination trends in New
York are generally similar to the Central City data. Little
scandal produces little change in terminations, while big
scandal, accompanied by numerous indictments and
other well-publicized apprehensions of officers, produces a peak in the number of terminations.

In the approximately three years covered by Figure 3,
there are only five months for which as many as nine
terminations of arrangements were reported, the next
highest peak being five terminations. Of those five
largest peaks, three were preceded by big-scandal events
that tended to characterize the department as corrupt.
One peak month was preceded by a major change in
internal control policy, and another peak came just after
the reform police executive was appointed amid much
news media comment on police corruption. The executive himself immediately made a strong public statement
attacking the department's corruption—so the peak that

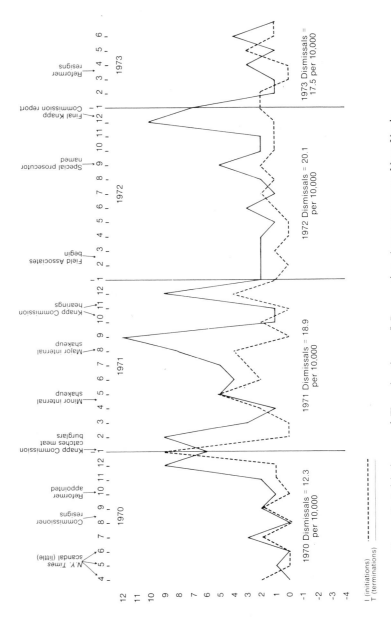

Figure 3 Initiations and Terminations of Corruption Arrangements: New York

SOURCE: Charges and Specifications, Disciplinary Records, New York City Police Department, Inspectional Services Bureau and Organized Crime Control Bureau.

followed may also have resulted, in a sense, from a scandal event. The next peak was clearly preceded by a big-scandal event: the well-publicized revelation of the Knapp Commission's discovery of a large band of police officers burglarizing a meat warehouse. The September 1971 peak followed a change of internal control policy that may have made the department appear corrupt: the punishment of a large number of commanders for failure to curb corruption. The final two peaks— December 1971 and December 1972—followed major media attention to the Knapp Commission's portrayal of widespread police corruption in its televised public hearings and its final reports respectively.

No major scandal event is omitted from the above list. All but one of the major steps of the Knapp Commission's work produced a peak in terminations. The one exception was the August 1972 release of the commission's recommendation for a special corruption prosecutor, and even that event produced a small peak of five terminations.

In contrast, only one of the major changes in internal control policy was followed by a peak in terminations: the first major "shakeup" enforcing the policy of commanders' accountability for corruption control. The very first instance of *enforcing* the accountability policy, however, also produced a small peak of five terminations in May 1971. That event was a response to the meathouse burglary: the captain in charge of the precinct in which the burglary occurred was transferred to a punishment post with a fair amount of publicity. Other major policies, such as the increased corruption intelligence capacity or the reorganization of gambling and narcotics enforcement (both implemented in early 1972), were followed by no peaks at all. This finding is not unexpected, since the new control policies were implemented gradually, in contrast to the sudden, shocking nature of a public attack on the integrity of the department. That difference is the very reason why scandal events would seem to have a short-term and immediate deterrent effect independent of changes in control policies.

Despite the apparent association between big-scandal events and terminations of corruption arrangements, another indicator suggests caution in drawing conclusions. Figure 4 uses the same raw data as Figure 3, but depicts the entry and exit of individual officers from corruption arrangements rather than the initiation and termination of the arrangements themselves. This indicator is simply a body count, and is therefore sensitive to the size of corruption arrangements, which Figure 3 is not. Figure 4 depicts more than just the size of arrangements initiated and terminated, however, because many individual officers entered and exited from arrangements at times different from the initiation and termination dates of the arrangements. Many members of "sergeants' clubs," for example, quit during the Knapp Commission hearings, but other members stayed on, keeping the arrangement going. Figure 3 is thus an indicator of the behavior of groups, while Figure 4 is an indicator of the behavior of individuals.

The patterns depicted by the two indicators differ in important respects. First, there is no peak in individual exits from arrangements after the appointment of the reform commissioner, whereas there is a peak in terminations of arrangements at that time. Second, the peak in individual exits is relatively lower after the Knapp Commission hearings than the peak in arrangement terminations is at that time. Third, the consequences of changes in internal control policy are much more visible for individual exits, notably the first big success of the "turn-around" technique leading to the arrest of forty officers in April of 1972. Fourth, the Knapp Commission recommendation for a special corruption prosecutor and the governor's implementation of that recommendation produced no effect at all on individual exits, whereas a small peak in arrangement terminations followed that scandal event.

Nevertheless, both indicators show a clear peak after

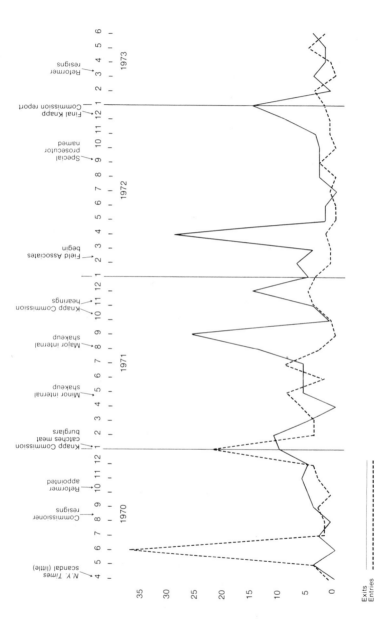

Figure 4 Individual Entry and Exit from Corruption Arrangements: New York

SOURCE: Charges and Specifications, Disciplinary Records, New York City Police Department, Inspectional Services Bureau and Organized Crime Control Bureau.

the same three out of the five big-scandal events: the apprehension of the meathouse burglars, the Knapp Commission hearings, and the final report of the commission. Even though both indicators were constructed from one potentially biased source of data, they both suggest that scandal may have an independent effect on corruption in the presence of premonitory control policies.

The general deterrent effect of big scandal also appears to be independent of increases in sanctions, at least on a short-term, month-by-month basis. Suspensions, the only kind of sanction for which there are monthly figures in New York, are perhaps a more powerful general deterrent than dismissals. Dismissals come only after a long, drawn-out trial process; the general perception of a dismissal may be that "they *finally* got Jones." Suspension in New York, procedurally comparable to a criminal indictment, resulted in the loss of badge and gun and an immediate removal from duty without pay. The general perception of suspension may be that "they got Jones." Suspensions are more shocking news, and they seem more likely than dismissals to scare other officers into both individual exits from arrangements and complete terminations of arrangements. Yet there is no significant correlation between the monthly number of suspensions and the monthly number of either individual exits or terminations of arrangements. Neither is there any significant relationship if the suspension data are lagged one month behind the corruption data. The short-term deterrent effect of scandal events seems to be independent of both changes in control policies and changes in at least this one form of sanction.[10]

10. The same is true for another type of sanction, dismissals, which show no rank order correlation (on an annual basis) with either individual exits from corruption or termination of corruption arrangements.

9. Effects of Control Policies

However great the deterrent effect of big scandals on police corruption may be, it does not seem to be lasting. The periodic repetition of punitive police corruption scandals over the last century in many diverse cities suggests that no scandal alone produces a lasting deterrent to organized police corruption. The evidence from New York suggests that the direct deterrent effects of a big-scandal event may last as briefly as one month. The Central City evidence suggests that the deterrent impact of scandal may last much longer, perhaps for a year or more. Regardless of how long the "heat" of scandal may deter corruption, however, it seems reasonable to assume that at some point the deterrent effect will wear off. When that occurs, internal control policies would seem to be the major variable affecting the level of corruption organization.

This chapter explores the effects of premonitory control policies and of sanctions over the long-term aftermath of scandal. Using the annual measures presented here, it is impossible in the short term to separate the effects of changes in control policies from the effects of big scandal. With the speculative assumption that the effects of big scandal alone last no more than two years, however, it is possible to isolate the effects of control policies after scandal's possible influence has elapsed.

The two cases used most frequently in this chapter are Oakland and New York, both of which adopted premonitory control policies. Newburgh showed such a complete cessation of corruption after the scandal that there are no post-scandal trends to analyze. The same is almost true of Oakland as well. Many Oakland measures have such small N's that ratios and percentages take on a questionable meaning. Nonetheless, the eight indicators together do suggest some meaningful patterns in both Oakland and New York.

EFFECTS OF PREMONITORY CONTROLS

Active Cooperation among Officers

The relative predominance of individualized versus cooperative corruption arrangements measures the amount of active cooperation among police officers in corruption activities. The size of corruption arrangements in both New York and Oakland seems to be more responsive to long-term changes in control policy than to scandal or to sudden changes in control policy. As Table 13 indicates, the largest percentage decrease in the size of corruption arrangements in both cities occurred not during the big-scandal year, but rather two years later. Oakland leveled off at that point, while New York continued to decline.

These strikingly similar findings suggest a pattern to search for in the data on the other indicators: the sharpest annual declines in the level of corruption organization occur only after premonitory control policies have taken hold, rather than immediately after scandal. If the other indicators show a similar pattern (which they don't), it would suggest that premonitory control policies are not only an effective long-run deterrent, but are more powerful than big scandal. An important policy implication of this pattern would be that a big scandal is not required for controlling organized corruption.[1] Great caution must be taken, however, in basing conclusions on the magnitude of changes whose measurement may be unreliable.

---

1. But big scandal may be required for justifying the use of premonitory control policies, given their controversial nature.

TABLE 13. Size of Corruption Arrangements in New York and Oakland

Indicator	Size							
Oakland (reports from all sources)								
Year	1952	1953	1954	1955	1956	1957	1958	1959
One member	3	3	3	3	1	1	1	1
Two or more members	23	23	22	21	1	0	0	0
Percent that is two or more members	88%	88%	88%	87%	50%	0%	0%	0%
Percent change from previous year in percent that is two or more members‡		0%	0%	−1%	−42%	−100%	0%	0%

	New York (official charges only)				
Year	1970*	1971	1972	1973	1974
One member	29	155	105	94	60
Two or more members	15	54	30	14	7
Percent that is two or more members	34%	26%	22%	13%	10%
Percent change from previous year in percent that is two or more members‡		−23%	−15%	−41%	−23%

*Last quarter only.
‡Rounded.

Passive Cooperation among Officers

The three indicators of passive cooperation with corruption are the diversity of corruption arrangements, the total number of discrete types of corruption arrangements and events, and the highest rank level reported corrupt.[2] The data presented in Table 14 on diversity as an indicator of passive cooperation is internally inconsistent and is also inconsistent with the data just presented on arrangement size as an indicator of active cooperation. The biggest annual percentage decreases in the number of types of arrangements, and in types of arrangements and events, occur in different years of the scandal-and-reform process in the three cases presented. The biggest decrease in Newburgh occurred in the year of the big scandal, before any new control policies were implemented. This anomaly can be explained by the fact that almost one-quarter of the department was indicted early in Newburgh's big-scandal year. The arrest and subsequent conviction of such a large portion of the department seemed to deter any recurrence of corruption in Newburgh for the two years between the scandal and the introduction of the premonitory control policies. Oakland's biggest decrease occurred the year after the big scandal, which was also one year after the introduction of premonitory control policies. These indicators suggest that Oakland's new policies took effect more rapidly there than the size-of-corruption-arrangements indicator suggests. In contrast, the biggest decrease in types of corruption in New York did not occur until three years after the big scandal, which suggests that premonitory control policies took effect more slowly there than the size-of-corruption-arrangements indicator suggests.

New York and Oakland both show peak decreases in the first year after the big-scandal year for the highest

2. For a list of the types of arrangements and events reported each year in Oakland, New York, and Newburgh, see Lawrence W. Sherman, "Controlling Police Corruption" (Ph.D. dissertation, Yale University, 1976), pp. 298–301.

TABLE 14. Diversity of Corruption in Oakland, New York, and Newburgh

				Year				
City and Type	L.S. −1	Little scandal	L.S. +1	Big scandal	B.S. +1	B.S. +2	B.S. +3	B.S. +4
Oakland	1952	1953	1954	1955	1956	1957	1958	1959
Types of arrangements	10	10	9	8	2	1	1	1
Percent change from previous year‡		0	−10%	−11%	−75%*	−50%	0	0
Types of arrangements and events	16	17	17	13	5	3	2	2
Percent change from previous year‡		+6%	0	−23%	−61%	−40%	−33%	0
New York	—	1970†	—	1971	1972	1973	1974	—
Types of arrangements		22		25	20	22	14	
Percent change from previous year‡				+14%	−20%	+10%	−36%*	
Types of arrangements and events		30		40	35	36	25	
Percent change from previous year‡				+33%	−12%	+3%	−25%*	
Newburgh	—	1970	—	1971	1972	1973	1974	
Types of arrangements		3		8	0	0	0	
Percent change from previous year‡				+167%	−100%*	0	0	
Types of arrangements and events		5		10	0	0	0	
Percent change from previous year‡				+100%	−100%*	0	0	

*Largest annual percentage decrease.
†Last quarter only.
‡Rounded.

rank level at which some kind of corruption allegedly occurred.[3] In Oakland, the sharpest drop actually occurred—as it did with many of these indicators—as soon as the reform chief took office in 1955, but 1956 was the first full year in which the highest rank level reported corrupt was lower. The mere presence of an avowed reformer seems to show as much short-term impact in Oakland as premonitory control policies (which outlasted the original reformer) show there in the long run. The mere arrival of a reform executive in New York, however, was not followed by a sharp decrease in rank level of alleged involvement. Rather, a sharp decline in New York's highest rank level reported corrupt only occurred after the big scandal and the implementation of the reformer's control policies.

Citizen-Police Cooperation

The indicators of the level of cooperation in corruption among police and citizens are two ratios: types of vice and minor crime protection to types of police-initiated crimes, and types of consenting corruption to types of victimizing corruption. Tables 15 and 16 present the data for these indicators in New York and Oakland.[4]

New York showed the biggest decrease in both indicators of citizen-police cooperation in the same year, three years after the big-scandal year. Oakland showed the effects of premonitory control more quickly. The ratio of consenting to victimizing types of corruption dropped more sharply in the first year after scandal. The ratio of types of minor crime protection to types of police-initiated crimes dropped most sharply in Oakland in the second year after big scandal. Given the far

3. For the data on highest rank level at which corruption was reported to have occurred, see Sherman, "Controlling Police Corruption," p. 304.

4. For a list of the types of corruption assigned to the four categories, see Sherman, "Controlling Police Corruption," pp. 306–308.

TABLE 15. Ratios of Types of Vice and Minor Crime Protection to Types of Police-Initiated Crimes in Oakland and New York

	Year and Ratios							
City and Type	L.S.−1	Little scandal	L.S.+1	Big scandal	B.S.+1	B.S.+2	B.S.+3	B.S.+4
	1952	1953	1954	1955	1956	1957	1958	1959
Oakland								
Types of vice protection	3	3	4	3	1	0	0	0
Types of police-initiated crimes	6	7	6	4	2	2	1	1
Ratio	.5	.43	.67	.75	.5	0	0	0
Percent change from previous year‡	—	−14%	+56%	−12%	−33%	−100%*	—	—
New York		1970†		1971	1972	1973	1974	—
Types of vice protection		10		12	9	9	5	
Types of police-initiated crimes		7		10	8	9	8	
Ratio		1.43		1.2	1.12	1.0	.62	
Percent change from previous year‡				−16%	−7%	−11%	−38%*	

*Largest annual percentage decrease.
†Last quarter only.
‡Rounded.

TABLE 16. Ratios of Types of Consenting Corruption to Types of Victimizing Corruption in Oakland and New York

				Year and Ratios				
City and Type	L.S. −1	Little scandal	L.S. +1	Big scandal	B.S. +1	B.S. +2	B.S. +3	B.S. +4
Oakland	1952	1953	1954	1955	1956	1957	1958	1959
Types of consenting corruption	12	12	13	10	3	2	1	1
Types of victimizing corruption	4	5	4	3	2	1	1	1
Ratio	3	2.4	3.25	3.33	1.5	2	1	1
Percent change from previous year‡	—	−20%	+35%	+2%	−55%*	+33%	−50%	0%
New York		1970†		1971	1972	1973	1974	—
Types of consenting corruption		24		29	25	24	15	
Types of victimizing corruption		5		7	7	7	6	
Ratio		4.8		4.1	3.6	3.4	2.5	
Percent change from previous year‡				−15%	−12%	−5%	−26%*	

*Largest annual percentage decrease.
†Last quarter only.
‡Rounded.

TABLE 17. Ratios of Arrangements to Events in Oakland

City	L.S. −1	Little scandal	L.S. +1
Oakland	*1952*	*1953*	*1954*
Arrangements reported	26	26	25
Events reported	6	7	9
Ratio	4.33	3.71	2.78
Percent change from previous year		−14%	−25%
Types of arrangements reported	10	10	9
Types of events reported	6	7	8
Ratio	1.67	1.43	1.12
Percent change from previous year‡		−14%	−22%
New York	—	*1970†*	—
Arrangements charged		44	
Events charged		22	
Ratio		2	
Percent change from previous year			
Types of arrangements charged		22	
Types of events charged		8	
Ratio		2.75	
Percent change from previous year‡			

*Largest annual percentage decrease.
†Fourth quarter only.
‡Rounded.

more extensive nature of organized corruption in New York than in Oakland at the time of the big scandal, however, even the more rapid occurrence of peak decreases in Oakland may not have been as drastic a change as that which took place in New York.

Duration of Cooperation
The duration of cooperation in police corruption is measured by the ratios of arrangements to events and

and New York

Big scandal	B.S. +1	B.S. +2	B.S. +3	B.S. +4
1955	*1956*	*1957*	*1958*	*1959*
24	2	1	1	1
6	4	2	2	2
4	.5	.5	.5	.5
+44%	−87%*	0%	0%	0%
8	2	1	1	1
5	3	2	1	1
1.6	.67	.5	1	1
+43%	−58%*	−25%	+12%	0%
1971	*1972*	*1973*	*1974*	—
209	135	108	67	
100	71	65	58	
2.09	1.9	1.66	1.15	
+4%	−9%	−13%	−31%*	
25	20	22	14	
15	15	14	11	
1.67	1.33	1.57	1.27	
−39%*	−20%	+18%	−19%	

arrangement types to event types. As Table 17 demonstrates, both indicators show peak decreases in Oakland one year after the big-scandal year.[5] The New York data on duration of cooperation are not so consistent. The ratio of the number of discrete arrangements (eventu-

5. There is an anomalous increase in the Oakland ratio of types of arrangements to types of events in the third year after the scandal, but the N's are so small (1 and 1) that the change is insignificant.

ally prosecuted) to the number of discrete events (eventually prosecuted) follows the trend shown by four of the seven other indicators, peaking in the third year after the big-scandal year. But the other indicator of duration of cooperation, the ratio of *types* of arrangements to types of events, shows two anomalies in New York. First, the peak decrease occurs *during* the year of the big scandal, just as premonitory control policies were being introduced. Second, the ratio shows an increase—counter to the general downward trend—in the second year after the big scandal. The N's are admittedly small, but large enough to be presumed reliable. One possible explanation is that the resignation of the reform police executive early in the year of the increase (1973) encouraged the return to a wider variety of arrangements. Specifically, the types of arrangements ultimately prosecuted from 1973 that had not been prosecuted from 1972 were fence protection, sale of official information, tavern violation protection, moonlighting on duty, and—something that was probably present but not detected for 1972—free meal ar-

TABLE 18. Modal Direction of Indicators of Change in Police

City	Little Scandal	L.S.+1	Big Scandal
Oakland	1953	1954	1955
Modal Direction	Down	None	Up
Percentage Size of Mode‡	50% $\left(\frac{4}{8}\right)$ *		50% $\left(\frac{4}{8}\right)$ *
New York	1970		1971
Modal Direction			No
Percentage Size of Mode‡			Mode

*These years included one indicator which did not change at all. Among the change), three or more of any one of them moving in the same direction
‡Rounded.

rangements. On the other hand, there were prosecutions of construction violation protection, after-hours "bottle club" protection, corruption among corruption investigators, corruption cover-ups, and illegal sales of firearms licenses from 1972, but *not* from 1973. It is difficult to interpret the overall increase in 1973 in diversity of arrangements relative to diversity of events in New York, since no pattern in the nature of the change is evident. In any case, the ratio increase in 1973 was followed by a decrease in 1974 to a value lower than that of 1972. The long-term trend towards more types of events relative to the types of arrangements indicates a long-term trend towards less duration in cooperation. The 1973 increase in the diversity of arrangements, then, may be only an artifact of reporting changes.

Aggregation of the Indicators

The eight indicators presented show conflicting trends in both New York and Oakland, just as they do in Central City. Table 18 shows the modal direction of change in the level of corruption organization indicated

Corruption Organization in Oakland and New York

Year and Discretion			
B.S.+1	*B.S.+2*	*B.S.+3*	*B.S.+4*
1956	*1957*	*1958*	*1959*
Down 100% $\left(\frac{8}{8}\right)$	Down 62% $\left(\frac{5}{8}\right)$	Down 37% $\left(\frac{3}{8}\right)$ *	No Change 100% $\left(\frac{8}{8}\right)$
1972	*1973*	*1974*	
Down 100% $\left(\frac{8}{8}\right)$	Down 50% $\left(\frac{4}{8}\right)$ *	Down 100% $\left(\frac{8}{8}\right)$	

three possible values for the eight indicators in these years (up, down, or no produced a mode.

each year in each of the cities, as well as the size of the modes. The modes in most years in both cities are all either extremely small or extremely large. Thus in Oakland, all that can be said with some confidence about the overall level of corruption organization is that it declined in the first year after the big-scandal year and leveled off in the fourth year after the big-scandal year. In New York, there is comparable certainty that the corruption organization level declined in both the first and third years after the big scandal.

Six of the eight indicators showed a peak decrease in Oakland in the first year after the big-scandal year (1956). Five of the eight indicators in New York showed a peak decrease in the third year after the big-scandal year.[6] In contrast to the consistency of both cities showing peak decreases in the size of corruption arrangements in the second year after the big-scandal year, the modal years for peak decreases suggest that the effects of premonitory control were felt two years earlier in Oakland's process of scandal and reform than they were in New York's.

SCANDAL, CONTROLS, AND SANCTIONS

Two major but tentative conclusions emerge from all these data. The first is that the continuing presence of premonitory control policies is associated with a continuing decline, or a stable lower level, of the quantity of organization of police corruption. This low level persists well past the time at which effects of big scandal per se can be expected to have worn off. (Data over a longer period in Central City after the big scandal and the introduction of postmonitory control policies would have provided the counter-test of this proposition: that postmonitory controls are too weak to prevent an increase in the level of corruption organization after the effects of big scandal wear off.) The second conclusion is that the implementation of premonitory control

6. For the distribution of the peak decreases, see Sherman, "Controlling Police Corruption," p. 317.

policies in New York was followed by a larger decrease in the level of corruption organization than that which followed the big scandal. Put more strongly, it appears that premonitory control policies were a more powerful deterrent in New York than big scandal was. The same may be true for Oakland, but the complete implementation of premonitory control policies there occurred in the same year as the big scandal. The simultaneous peak decline in corruption organization therefore could have resulted from either scandal or reform policies, or both.

The first conclusion could be spurious. After the big-scandal year, the primary source of data on the organization of corruption in both cities was whatever police officials had been able to detect. In New York, this source was limited almost entirely to the departmental charges against allegedly corrupt officers, including those convicted criminally.[7] In Oakland, a wider range of sources was consulted, including interviews with police officers and supervisors of the 1950s who had worked in the internal policing function as well as with those who had not. If for any reason the premonitory control policies began to erode somewhat after their initial implementation, it is possible that the data reflect this erosion of detection capacity rather than a decline in the level of corruption organization. More organized forms of corruption are easier to detect, but only if they are sought out. If internal policing becomes more post-monitory, the level of organization of the corruption it detects may decline. For example, the reported ratio of consenting corruption types to victimizing corruption types will inevitably decline if victim-complainants again become the only source of corruption intelligence, possibly obscuring a real increase in consensual corruption about which no information is being collected.

The danger of this dependence on data generated by internal policing is greatest in New York. The huge size of the corruption investigation apparatus there made it

7. Except for the indicator, highest rank level reported corrupt, which also drew on news stories and interviews.

difficult to determine exactly how premonitory it was in overall performance. The largest percentage decrease in corruption organization level occurred in 1974, the first year of a new mayoral administration and a new police commissioner. Whether that decrease resulted from the accumulated three-year impact of premonitory control policies or from a possible decline in the degree to which the control policies were premonitory is unknown. Policies are often altered under new leadership, even if only in minor ways. The difficulty of measuring the extent of premonitory control on an annual basis prevents the complete elimination of this interpretation for either New York or Oakland.

Both major conclusions could be mistaken in positing a direct effect of premonitory policies per se on the level of corruption organization. It could be the case that changes in sanction rates generated by the new control policies are an intervening variable accounting for all of the change in level of corruption organization. But as far as can be measured, there is no clear relationship between the changes in sanction rates and changes in the overall level of corruption organization. Several different approaches to examining the strength of association between sanction rates and corruption organization generally fail to produce significant results.[8]

Since changes in sanction rates do not clearly account for changes in corruption organization, the introduction of premonitory policies may be presumed to have had a direct effect on corruption organization in New York, and possibly in Oakland. That is not to say, however, that the sanction increases were irrelevant. A failure to increase sanctions may have weakened the credibility of the threat posed by premonitory controls. Sanction increases may have been an essential condition for the decline in corruption organization, but they apparently did not act as an intervening variable between premonitory controls and corruption organization.

8. Sherman, "Controlling Police Corruption," pp. 320–324.

The relationship among big scandal, premonitory controls, and sanction rates in affecting the organization of corruption is no doubt far more complex than that which a mere four cases can reveal. All three factors may be essential conditions for reducing the quantity of corruption organization, but only big scandal and premonitory controls seem to have had a direct impact upon corruption organization in the present cases.

10. Reforming Corrupt Police Departments

> What we need to learn is how and why
> some departments have changed significantly
> while others change, if at all,
> only briefly and cosmetically.
> —James Q. Wilson[1]

Police corruption may be impossible to eliminate entirely,[2] but corrupt police departments can be reformed. In addition to the four cases presented here, the cases of scandal and reform in Los Angeles,[3] Kansas City,[4] and Cincinnati[5] are often cited as evidence that police corruption can be significantly reduced. The difficult questions concern the conditions under which corrupt police departments can be reformed, the costs of reform, and the persistence of reform. This chapter offers some tentative answers to those questions.

The reform of a corrupt police department changes police corruption from organizational deviance to deviance within an organization. Reform of a department

1. "To Catch a Cop," *New York Times Book Review*, September 18, 1977, p. 34.
2. But see Herman Goldstein, *Policing a Free Society* (Cambridge, Mass.: Ballinger, 1977), p. 218.
3. See Joseph G. Woods, "The Progressives and the Police" (Ph.D. dissertation, University of California at Los Angeles, 1973).
4. See Joseph D. McNamara, "The Impact of Bureaucratic Dysfunctions on Attempts to Prevent Police Corruption," *Police Journal*, January/March, 1975.
5. See Thomas Reppetto, "Changing the System: Models of Municipal Police Organization" (D.P.A. dissertation, Harvard University, 1970).

does not necessarily mean that police corruption has been eliminated. It does mean that the department has abandoned corruption as an organizational goal. Reform also implies that there has been a reduction in some aspect of corruption, whether it is the frequency of corrupt acts, the seriousness of the types of corruption present, or the extent of cooperation among officers (and citizens) in police corruption activities. While some corruption probably persists in any reformed police department, it does so in the face of active opposition by the dominant coalition running the department, as deviance from rather than conformity to organizational goals. It is the change of organizational goals and the reduction of cooperation in corruption that is defined here as reform.

All four of the departments studied seem to satisfy this definition of reform. The case of Central City, however, is somewhat on the borderline, raising the issue of the persistence of reform as a consideration in defining reform. The Central City Police Department was taken over by a new dominant coalition supporting legitimate organizational goals, and the amount of cooperation in corruption did decline during the first year of a reform administration. But there is good reason to believe that neither the new dominant coalition nor the reduction in corruption lasted for more than two years. The field research stopped before enough time elapsed to see if that prediction was correct, so it may be best to withhold judgment on whether the Central City Police Department was reformed or not. Just as the term "reform" is often used to describe a permanent change of character in individual criminals, it seems reasonable to require at least several years to elapse before determining whether an organization has changed with enough permanence to be called "reformed." That is not to say, however, that reform is never eroded, or that eternal honesty should be part of the definition of a reformed police department. After considering the conditions and costs of achieving a reform of *some* permanence (i.e., two years or more), the vital question of *how much* permanence is considered.

CONDITIONS OF REFORM

Several necessary, if not sufficient, conditions can be identified for the reform of corrupt police departments. The conditions are found in each of the three clear cases of reform studied, as well as in several other cases about which some evidence is available. These conditions include both external and internal social control: the conditions under which social control is mobilized, and the specific kinds of social control that are employed. Ultimately, the conditions of reform are the opposite of the conditions under which police departments become corrupt; environmental pressures and opportunities for corruption and an absence of internal control must be replaced by a change in or insulation from the environment and an increase in internal control.

External Control

Some form of external social control generally seems to be essential for the reform of corrupt police departments. While it may be possible for corrupt police departments to change without the occurrence of a scandal, some form of outside intervention seems to be associated with all reported cases of reformed police departments—if only external pressure to change the departments' leadership. In all the reported cases of reformed departments that were once organizationally corrupt, the form of external social control that was employed against the departments was scandal. In order to mobilize a punitive scandal, three conditions seem to be necessary: failure of information control within the corrupt police department; participation of other organizations in a conflict over organizational goals; and manipulation of public appearances in a way that exposes the police department as a deviant organization.

In all of our four cases of punitive scandal, there was a breakdown in the internal control procedures of the corrupt police departments as deviant organizations. In two cases, the breakdown was a failure to control a zealot fringe that opposed the deviant goals of the organization. The zealots' violation of the departments' code of silence on deviant police conduct provided the revelations necessary for setting a scandal into motion. In the other two cases, the breakdown was a failure to control the excessive corruption of an evil fringe—corruption that created victims. The victims then provided the revelations necessary for setting the scandal into motion. In all four cases, the breakdown of internal control in the corrupt police departments was a failure of information control, a loss of secrecy about the deviant organizational conduct.

Equally important was the readiness of other organizations to use the revelations of corruption as weapons in a conflict over the goals of the police department. In three of the cases, the other organizations were newspapers that had employees at various levels who took an interest in changing the organizational character and goals of the police department. In the fourth case, the organization was one of the victims of the "excessive" corruption of the police department's evil fringe. As a business enterprise, the victimized organization had a financial interest in changing the character of the police department, specifically in putting an end to police burglaries of the corporation's local branch.

While it may have been possible for individuals external to the corrupt departments to have generated conflict over the departments' organizational goals, it is more likely that only organizations had the necessary resources for winning such a conflict. The newspapers had the power to make public attacks on the character of the police departments. Sears, Roebuck and Company had the power to demand that the state police and a prosecutor's office allied with the police department undertake an investigation into police corruption. In other instances of police corruption scandals, federal law enforcement organizations have been the organizational actors generating conflict over the police department's goals. In an organizational society, it may well be that deviant organizations can be controlled externally only by other organizations.[6]

The final condition for the mobilization of punitive scandal against corrupt police departments is the manipulation of public appearances to reveal the departments as deviant organizations. In all four of the present cases, the labeling of the police departments as organizationally corrupt seems to have hinged on evidence of the departments' lack of interest in controlling the corrupt acts committed by their members. The failure of internal control of corruption was used to reveal the departments as being not what they had appeared to be (organizations committed to the goals of honest law enforcement), but rather as organizations committed to the goal of personal profit for their members (or for those in control of the departments). The unmasking of the organizations' false public identities made possible a collective public definition of the police departments as deviant. In order to impose a deviant identity on the departments, of course, the audience of the scandal must define the police corruption as deviant from the audience's own norms.

All three conditions seem to be necessary for the mobilization of a punitive scandal. Many corrupt police departments experience failures of information control, but if other organizations make no use of the information to generate conflict over the organizations' goals, punitive (or "big") scandals do not result. The little scandals that we have described, for example, all involved failures of other organizations to act on the revelations. Even if other organizations do participate in the generation of conflict over organizational police goals, they may fail to manipulate the appearance of the department's identity in a way that reveals it to be a deviant organization. Federal investigators, for example, often concentrate on proving specific acts of criminal conduct

6. Richard Lundman, "Police Misconduct as Organizational Deviance" (paper presented at the Annual Meeting of the American Sociological Association, Chicago, 1977).

by police officers (which is, after all, their legal mandate) and fail to generate or dramatize information regarding failures of the entire police department to control corruption internally.[7] Of course, if there is no failure of information control about corruption to begin with, then there is no information available to the other organizations that might try to mobilize scandal against the police departments.

Yet a punitive scandal alone does not seem to be a sufficient condition for lasting reform of a corrupt police department. A punitive scandal may have a short-term deterrent impact on police corruption, as appears to have been the case in Central City. But the evidence from the three cases of reform that lasted for more than a few years suggests that external control is not the only condition leading to lasting reform. A major change in the nature of internal control also seems to be necessary.

Internal Control

In the three cases of lasting reform, the organizational policies for control of corruption were changed substantially from what they had been prior to the scandal. The new policies created a deterrent to corruption, as well as reducing opportunities for corruption to occur. In order for policies to produce those results, three common conditions seem to be necessary. One is the creation of a new dominant coalition to control the organization. Another is the removal of environmental influences encouraging corruption, either through changing the environment or through insulating the department from its environment. The third condition

7. For a comparison of the implied objectives of federal prosecutors in a Chicago police corruption investigation and the staff of the Knapp Commission in New York, see Herbert Beigel and Allan Beigel, *Beneath the Badge: A Story of Police Corruption* (New York: Harper and Row, 1977); and John F. Kennedy School of Government, *The Knapp Commission and Patrick V. Murphy (B)* (Cambridge, Mass.: Harvard University, mimeo, 1977).

is that the control policies be premonitory in focus and capacity, attempting to prevent corruption or to detect it as it occurs.

The creation of a new dominant coalition may be the most difficult task required for reforming a corrupt police department. In order to create a new dominant coalition, the old dominant coalition must be located and its influence must be destroyed. It is often unclear how the old dominant coalition works, however, and which actors it includes on which issues. The process by which key decisions are made is not always evident to long-term members of large organizations, let alone to "outsiders" hired to reform a police department. And because the dominant coalition is a process rather than a concrete group, simply getting rid of certain people is not sufficient for changing it. The creation of a new dominant coalition requires a new process for making key decisions, a process that will exclude certain *types* of people (for example, corrupt politicians) who had participated in the old dominant coalition, and include or give greater influence to other types of people.

The dominant coalition in Oakland was changed by the creation of a new level of top management (deputy chiefs) and the exclusion of politicians from covert participation in police personnel and enforcement decisions. The dominant coalition in Newburgh was changed in a similar fashion by modifying the type of person who could be appointed to head the department, as well as by adding a new layer of top management and excluding politicians from decision-making. The dominant coalition in New York was replaced by revolutionizing the conditions under which the field commanders worked, using demotions and pressure for retirement if they failed to take action against corruption. Much greater real power was moved to the level of the police commissioner in New York than there had ever been before because the reform commissioner made unprecedented, extensive use of his formal powers. The dominant coalition in Central City was changed somewhat by the appointment of new people to top management positions, but the most important change was, again, the apparent exclusion of politicians from police personnel decisions.

The creation of a new dominant coalition often involves some aspects of the second condition for effective internal control policies: the change in or insulation from the police department's environment. By excluding certain outside actors from the department's dominant coalition, the department insulates itself from its environment. More effective in the long run, however, may be an effort by the police department's reform administration to change its environment, or at least those aspects of it that are conducive to corruption. Insulation mechanisms, no matter how strong, do not guarantee that corrupting outside influences will not penetrate the organization. Oakland, for example, had strict autonomy for the police department written into the city charter in 1931, but the de jure insulation only became de facto in 1955, when the reform administration implicitly threatened anyone who tried to influence the department in a corrupt way. A change in the environment, to the extent that it can last, removes the danger of corrupt penetration of the department and makes the effectiveness of insulation less important.

Central City's reform administration announced that political influence in the department was over, and excluded party officials from decision-making affecting personnel. However, the reform administration did not attempt to change the political environment in any way. When the city administration shifted to the control of the other party, there were reportedly strong pressures for a return to the old pre-scandal way of running the police, a system of political control that had been followed in the past by administrations of both parties. While insulation may have been effective in the short run, a change in the environment may have been more conducive to a lasting reform.

The reform administrations in Oakland and Newburgh adopted both strategies for dealing with their organizational environments. Each of those reform administrations began by seeking complete insulation from illegitimate political interference. Each then sought to change the political environment by changing the level of integrity in civic affairs generally. The Oakland chief let it be known that he had intelligence on possible corrupt activity by city officials and that he was not afraid to arrest them if warranted, a move that reportedly raised the integrity of city politics substantially. The Newburgh police commissioner mobilized a federal investigation of local politics that led to the destruction of a machine that had long ruled the county and city.

While corrupt political interference was not an apparent cause of police corruption in New York, the resources provided by the task environment were a major source of corruption. To a limited extent, the reform administration in New York sought to insulate the department from those resources by restricting police authority to exploit them (for example, limitations were placed on enforcing gambling and Sabbath law violations). But to a much greater extent than in any of the other cities, New York's reform executive tried to change the task environment of the department. The central strategy for change was the policy of bribery arrests of citizens, an attempt to deter the public from offering bribes. Oakland's reform executive also tried to eliminate task environmental resources for police corruption by eliminating gambling and, to a lesser extent, other vice activities in the city.

The efforts to deal with the organizational environment as a source of corruption were also an aspect of the third condition for effective internal control of police corruption: a premonitory focus and capacity for control policies. The premonitory focus is on the anticipation and prevention of corruption and the conditions facilitating corruption. The attempt to eliminate the environmental sources of police corruption reflects the premonitory focus. A capacity for premonitory detection of ongoing corruption, however, also seems to be required. Without such a capacity, the police executive may not be aware of any penetration of the department by corrupting environmental influences. The premonitory focus requires premonitory information, and only certain kinds of strategies for gathering information can yield premonitory information. The specific tactics used to implement those strategies, however, may be different for police departments of different sizes.

In a department of one hundred officers or less, the bulk of the actual tasks of internal control must be performed by the police executive and his immediate aides. A separate corruption control unit is hard to justify in such small departments, and seems to be unnecessary. If the personal contacts of the police executive are well developed, as they were in Newburgh, he can gather enough information on his own to initiate investigations and have suspected officers monitored closely. Investigations of tips and formal complaints can be done by deputies, or by investigators assigned to such cases on an as-needed basis. By spending frequent evenings on patrol, the executive can put most of his officers and any suspected corruption locations under his personal surveillance. The Newburgh executive even leased a new car every month to avoid detection by his officers during his surveillance.

Police departments of approximately one hundred to nine hundred officers retain a crucial characteristic of the small police department: everybody in the department generally knows everybody else, if only by face and reputation. This fact has important consequences for the flow of information about deviant activities among officers. The overlapping networks of personal relationships among work units allow information about deviant activities to flow between units. The Oakland police executive capitalized on this information flow with a few loyal informants. Even if there is not a loyal contact in every unit, a few well-placed sources can capture most of the information that does circulate. If an executive can instill loyalty in the large majority of his officers, then specific officers need not be cultivated as "spies" for the chief.

In order to discover corruption information that does

not circulate among police officers, the general criminal intelligence unit can pursue corruption covertly. One excellent means is to use that unit for follow-ups on vice enforcement activity, to see if raids really "closed the joints down" or if a report of no activity at a certain location is really true. If any corruption intelligence is developed, it can be turned over to the Internal Affairs Division for a full investigation.

Once the size of a police department exceeds nine hundred, it is often said that officers cease to know one another. Kansas City and Central City, both of which grew rapidly during the late 1960s, report this phenomenon. The consequences of impersonality for information flow and the consequences of size for the complexity of potential corruption patterns both seem to require a highly complex approach to corruption control. Both Central City and New York required such an approach for developing a premonitory detection and investigative capacity, but only New York adopted the approach.

The key difference in internal control policy between New York and Central City was the extent and nature of the sources of information on corruption activity. Central City relied for the most part on citizen complainants to provide information on corruption, and such information was almost always postmonitory. New York developed many other sources of information in addition to citizen complainants, particularly sources with access to information about ongoing or future acts of corruption. The difference in the control policies resulted in a great difference in the frequency of sanctions that the two departments meted out for corruption. Regardless of the frequency of sanctions, the threat of detection implied by the premonitory approach to internal control seemed to be far greater.

All three general conditions—a new dominant coalition, the removal of corrupting environment influences, and premonitory internal control policies—seem to be necessary for the lasting reform of a corrupt police department. A punitive scandal may result in a short-term decline in corruption, but the changes in internal control seem to be required to prevent a resurgence of corruption once the external "heat" is off. Unless a new dominant coalition is created, the old dominant coalition may impose deviant goals on the organization as soon as it is safe to do so. Meanwhile, the old dominant coalition may obstruct reform efforts to insulate the organization from the environment or to implement a premonitory internal control strategy. If the environment is not changed or blocked off, it may continue to provide pressures and resources for a resurgence of corruption after the scandal fades away. If a premonitory control strategy is not adopted, the reform administration will have neither a sufficient deterrent to corruption nor an early warning system about environmental penetration or a resurgence of corruption.

The case of the Chicago Police Department provides further evidence for the necessity of all the conditions of external and internal social control suggested here. A little scandal in 1957 failed to become a punitive scandal when no outside organization acted on a *Life* magazine exposé. A police burglary scandal in 1960 resulted from a failure of information control due to the excesses of an evil fringe group of police officers. A recently-elected prosecutor who was a bitter political enemy of the mayor used the information leakage to generate a conflict over the police department's organizational character. The published revelations eventually included evidence that the department had tried to cover up the police burglary ring's activities. The prosecutor's office (an organization) skillfully manipulated appearances so that the department was revealed as a deviant organization committed to corruption. The conditions of punitive scandal as a form of external control were all met, and they produced the predictable response of the appointment of a new police executive with a mandate to remove the stigma from the public identity of the department.[8]

8. See, generally, Ralph Lee Smith, *The Tarnished Badge* (New York: Thomas Y. Crowell, 1965), pp. 157–212; and Mike Royko,

The new police executive in Chicago gained a national reputation for the effectiveness of his reform administration. He instituted sweeping changes in many aspects of the organization, and there was such an improvement in the outward appearance of the department that it was often mentioned as one of the finest in the nation.[9] In addition, the reform executive created a premonitory control strategy for detecting police corruption, catching a number of police officers in the act. He adopted a policy of bribery arrests against the general public,[10] and was reputed to have insulated the department from corrupt political interference.[11] The reform executive retired in 1967. In 1971, there began a federal investigation of police corruption in Chicago that eventually sent over sixty police officers to prison. Most important, the investigation uncovered the existence of highly organized corruption activities occurring as far back as 1964, as well as indications of corrupt political interference during the reform police administration.[12]

The failure of police reform in Chicago can be explained by the absence of two conditions of effective internal control. One is that the police department was not insulated from corrupt political interference, despite the public appearance that it was. Moreover, the reform administration made no effort to change the political environment. The other, related factor was the apparent failure to create a new dominant coalition. The people occupying the highest positions of command were all changed during the reform administration, but the way in which key decisions were made and the types of people participating in making them were apparently not changed. Like the New York City Police

---

Boss: Richard J. Daley of Chicago (London: Paladin, 1972), pp. 102–119.

9. Smith, *The Tarnished Badge*, pp. 174–190.
10. Goldstein, *Policing a Free Society*, p. 214.
11. Smith, *The Tarnished Badge*, pp. 175–176.
12. Beigel and Beigel, *Beneath the Badge*.

Department, the Chicago Police Department (second only to New York's in size) is so large that the dominant coalition seems to have excluded the top executive of the organization, running the department from field commands. In contrast to New York, the dominant coalition of the Chicago Police Department included the strong influence of local political figures. Even though the scandal-and-reform process in Chicago included many of the conditions for a lasting reform of the department, the absence of these two conditions may have been responsible for the ultimate failure of reform.

The six conditions of successful reform identified here are to a certain extent ex post facto interpretations. As such, they are merely plausible rather than conclusive.[13] To the extent that they are consistent with all available evidence on the successful reform of corrupt police departments, they may well reflect general conditions of that process. And to the extent that they provide policy implications for controlling police corruption, they raise important issues about the potential costs of reforming corrupt police departments.

COSTS OF REFORM

The reform of a corrupt police department is a major social change. Like most major social changes, it is achieved at a certain cost. In order to achieve an organizationally honest police department, some unintended and undesirable consequences may often result. One of those consequences may be an increase in the frequency of individualized police corruption or other forms of police misconduct. Another consequence may be a sacrifice of certain principles of civil liberties, at least as they apply to police officers. Worst of all, however, may be the hindrance of the goal of police departments furthering the democratic values of a free society.

The consequences of scandal and reform that were

13. Robert K. Merton, *Social Theory and Social Structure*, enlarged edition (New York: Free Press, 1968), pp. 147–149.

measured in this study were the changes in the amount of organization in police corruption activities. In many instances, the observed decline in the amount of organization present in police corruption was calculated in terms of ratios between more and less organized forms of corruption. While corruption may have become generally less organized, there may well have been an increase in the frequency of individualized corruption events. Given the possible needs of corrupt police officers to maintain a certain level of income because of such things as mortgage commitments, it may well be that termination of their participation in cooperative corruption activities leaves them with no alternative but to engage in individualized corruption activities. Only the Central City data actually showed such an increase, and even that increase was statistically insignificant. But the indicators were not meant to measure absolute frequencies of corrupt acts; the potential biases in the frequency of reports from year to year are sufficiently great to discount any of the data as measuring the actual frequency of either individualized or cooperative corrupt acts.

The amount of organization in corruption is important from a public policy standpoint as well as from a theoretical one. Highly organized corruption makes possible greater immunity of certain criminals from the threat of arrest. It is only when police corruption is highly organized that the law can literally be put up for sale to the highest bidder. There is a strong case to be made that the public interest is better served by a police department in which corrupt acts are less organized, given a constant frequency of corrupt acts. Yet there is also a case to be made that the public interest is better served by a police department in which corruption is more organized.

Consider the types of corruption that are defined as more or less organized. The more organized types of corruption include protection of prostitution, gambling, and violations of the liquor laws. The less organized

types of corruption include burglary committed by
police officers, police thefts from arrested persons, and
the "fixing" of crimes as serious as murder. The types of
corruption committed by lone police officers may often
be more serious than those types committed by several
police officers in cooperation. While it may be a more
serious general community problem to have the law put
up for sale than to have individual police officers committing crimes, the specific crimes policemen initiate are
usually more serious than the crimes they are paid to
ignore.

The response to this argument is that any resultant
increase in the frequency of individualized corruption
may be short-lived. A decline in the amount of cooperation in police corruption can have important long-term
consequences for organizational socialization patterns
and peer group support of corrupt activities. More
officers may avoid passive participation in corruption,
and this may provide a basis for building work-group
norms opposed to corruption. Pride in the department
as an honest organization could eventually pose strong
opposition to officers persisting in individualized corrupt acts. In the long run, a decline in the level of cooperation in corruption might also produce a decline in
the frequency of all corrupt acts.

Even if individualized corruption does not become
more frequent, another possible unintended consequence of reforming a corrupt police department might
be an increase in noncorrupt forms of police misconduct. The process of scandal and reform can be severely
debilitating to police morale. While the relationship between police morale and behavior is largely unexplored,
there is a possibility that the morale problems caused by
scandal and reform could produce an increase in excessive use of force by police officers. The number of citizen complaints of police brutality, for example, went up
sharply in Central City, where the scandal was the most
protracted and morale may have suffered the most.
Further, the number of police shooting incidents in

Central City increased during the scandal year by 250 percent over the year before, from eight to twenty-eight.

While the apparent increase in noncorrupt police misconduct may have been a result of scandal and reform in Central City, evidence from the other cities suggests that an increase in police misconduct is not inevitable. In Oakland, for example, a radical local attorney reported that police brutality against blacks declined sharply under the reform administration. Since this attorney, then a member of the Communist Party, was the only lawyer in Oakland who would sue the police for unwarranted assaults on blacks, his law practice may have been a reliable indicator of police brutality incidents against blacks. He had received a regular supply of clients complaining of police brutality in the five years prior to the scandal and reform in Oakland, but the supply dwindled away after the reform administration took office.[14] In New York, the frequency of police brutality is much harder to measure, but the frequency of police shootings clearly declined under the reform administration—apparently as a result of policy changes specifically directed at decreasing the frequency of police shootings.[15]

Police morale was described as "lower than ever" in New York under the reform administration, but it is hard to point to any specific or measurable deleterious consequences of low morale there. If a police department has high morale as a corrupt organization and low morale as an honest one, then it may be in the best public interest to have a demoralized police department, so long as police performance does not deteriorate. Nonetheless, morale is often invoked as an excuse for not adopting premonitory internal control policies. The

14. Interview with Oakland attorney Robert Treuhaft, May 6, 1975.

15. James Fyfe, "Shots Fired: A Typological Examination of New York City Police Firearms Discharges, 1971–75" (Ph. D. dissertation, State University of New York at Albany, forthcoming).

reform police executive in Central City, for example, strongly disapproved of the concept of using "field associates" to spy on other police officers, a key element of the premonitory internal control policies in New York.

While morale may not be an appropriate reason to reject the use of premonitory internal control policies, there may be other reasons to question their use. Civil libertarians oppose the use of covert techniques for gathering information about anyone, from gangsters to corrupt police officers. They argue that the use of spying for any purpose—whether through wiretapping, surveillance, or informers—is antithetical to the democratic values of a free society. To legitimize such techniques for one purpose, no matter how vital it may seem, is to open the door to the use of the techniques against anyone opposed to those currently in power. The recent history of Presidential abuse of federal law enforcement powers provides substantial support for such an argument.[16]

Civil liberties groups also argue that covert techniques, particularly paid informers and wiretapping, are ineffective, or at least cost-inefficient, in the control of criminal activities.[17] As applied to the control of police corruption, that argument does not appear to be supported by this study. While Newburgh is one case of successful reform that was achieved without the use of covert techniques (if one excludes the Newburgh police executive's information sources as mere gossip), both Oakland and New York depended heavily on those techniques as part of their overall premonitory control strategies. The use of deceit and the betrayal of corrupt police officers by the colleagues they trusted not to

16. One civil liberties official, in criticizing the Knapp Commission, observed, "If you legitimize these procedures for Whitman Knapp, how do you de-legitimize them for Joe McCarthy? You must not be in the position where you have to depend on the good will of good men" (*New York Times*, October 30, 1971, p. 18).

17. See, e.g., Ramsey Clark, *Crime in America* (New York: Simon and Schuster, 1970), p. 81.

"blow the whistle" may appear from some perspectives to be objectionable. But from other perspectives, the "spying" officers were merely upholding their sworn duty to enforce the law. And in terms of effectiveness, the corruption they detected would not have been detected otherwise, and the deterrent effect they may have had on corruption would not have been created otherwise.

The use of covert techniques against corrupt police officers does reduce the target police officers' freedom, and therefore it reduces the total extent of freedom in our society. The argument might be made that since liberty depends so greatly on the conduct of law enforcement agents, it may be necessary for those agents to sacrifice some of their personal liberty in order to insure that they do not violate the liberty of the public. Yet this argument may have a fatal flaw. It may be a gross contradiction to expect police officers to uphold freedoms that they themselves are denied. If police officers feel that their own rights are violated by their superiors, then they may be less willing to protect the rights of the public they police.[18] The loss of freedom in society may be far greater from the police failure to serve democratic values than from the actual loss of freedom by police subjected to premonitory internal control policies. Yet a general police failure to serve democratic values could be exacerbated by the use of premonitory controls against police officers. The question is empirical, but probably not amenable to easy study.

Despite the cases cited in this study, there is no apparent trend towards the use of premonitory internal controls in American municipal police departments. The actual trend seems to be exactly the reverse. The growth of police unions has made steady inroads on the discretion of police executives to employ various techniques for controlling the conduct of their subordinates. The adoption of the "policeman's bill of rights" in state law

18. See Goldstein, *Policing a Free Society*, pp. 12–13.

and police union contracts grants police officers *more* rights in relation to criminal investigations than the "civilian" public, not less.[19] The major obstacle to the reform of corrupt police departments may no longer be a corrupting organizational environment, but rather the application of more-than-due process guarantees to police officers acting through unionized strength. Ironically, this emphasis on due process for police may be just as harmful to due process for the public as would be a reduction in police officers' freedom from being spied upon. A police officer shielded from punishment for misconduct may be more likely to engage in misconduct, but again the question is empirical. In any case, the effort to avoid a possible cost of reforming corrupt police departments could ultimately result in the prevention of reform itself.

PERSISTENCE OF REFORM

Reformed organizations, like reformed individuals, often revert to their past deviant behavior. Just as their friends sometimes wonder how long ex-alcoholics can stay away from alcohol, observers of reformed police departments wonder how long it will take before the departments again become corrupt. To be reformed at all implies a change in character of some permanence, at least for several years. Beyond the first few years, however, there is an important question about the conditions required for keeping a police department reformed for as long as possible.

Few cases of long-term police reform are available for answering the question of why reform persists. Los Angeles has not had an organizational police corruption scandal since 1950, Kansas City has been reformed since the early 1960s, and Oakland has been virtually corruption-free since 1956. But other examples of fifteen and twenty years of reform are hard to come by. Relapses from reform, however, are even harder to discover, since it is impossible to tell without systematic

19. See, e.g., Florida Statutes §112.532 (Supp. 1974).

inquiry whether a department was truly reformed to begin with. Nonetheless, the conditions of the persistence of reform appear to include, at the very least, the conditions of internal control required for achieving reform. Should these conditions fail to persist, then reform may turn into relapse.

Another condition for long-term reform may be the long-term incumbency of the reformer. The reform executives in Los Angeles and Kansas City both served well over ten years. The reform chief in Oakland only served five years, but the reform city manager who chose him and his successors stayed in Oakland well over ten years. The long-term incumbency of a reformer may provide the time required to institutionalize a new character for the organization, which may have a more lasting effect than the coercive imposition of new goals on the organization. One consequence of a long-term incumbency is that the reformer can outlast most of the major internal and external opponents of reform. More important than the elimination of opponents, however, may be the development of a broad base of rank-and-file supporters of the organizational goals to which the reform executive is committed. Rank-and-file support simplifies the task of maintaining the conditions of reform—namely, an honest dominant coalition, insulation from the corrupting aspects of the organizational environment, and premonitory control policies. A rank and file dedicated to honest policing would mobilize external control against any new dominant coalitions attempting to revert to corrupt goals, just as they would arrest citizens attempting to bribe the police, and mobilize internal control against any of their colleagues who might engage in corruption. Where these responses become institutionalized, a reformed police department may be more likely to stay that way.

Unfortunately, the persistence of reform may soon become a moot issue. Unless reform is successfully created in the first place, questions of persistence are irrelevant. The mobilization of external control required for reforming corrupt police departments will probably continue to occur with some frequency, given the current investigative orientation of news organizations. But the internal control required for reforming corrupt police departments may become impossible to achieve, given the continuing erosion of the authority of the police executive and the increasing power of police unions. Scandal is a mighty weapon, but it is not sufficient for reforming a deviant police organization. In the long run, successful reform also requires that police departments control themselves.

Index